A MILLION BROKEN WINDOWS

Makarand Waingankar is one of the most widely read cricket columnists, best known for blending meticulous research with his own experience of a life lived on the cricket fields of India. Journalist, columnist, researcher, talent spotter and administrator, he wears a multitude of hats, each of which fits snugly on his head. He launched the Talent Resource Development Wing (TRDW) on behalf of the BCCI (Board of Control for Cricket in India) in 2002 and the TRDW has since been responsible for taking many small-town players to the national stage, including former India captain Mahendra Singh Dhoni. In fact, seven such players were part of the 2011 World Cup-winning team. Waingankar has also been the CEO of Baroda Cricket Association and consultant to the Karnataka State Cricket Association's academy. His first book *Yuvi*, published by HarperCollins, was a best-seller.

A MILLION BROKEN WINDOWS

WINDOWS

The Magic and Mystique of
Bombay Cricket

MAKARAND WAINGANKAR

Harper
Sport

First published in India in 2015 by Harper Sport
An imprint of HarperCollins *Publishers*

Copyright © Makarand Waingankar 2015

P-ISBN: 978-93-5136-534-1
E-ISBN: 978-93-5136-535-8

2 4 6 8 10 9 7 5 3 1

Makarand Waingankar asserts the moral right
to be identified as the author of this work.

The views and opinions expressed in this book are the author's own
and the facts are as reported by him, and the publishers are
not in any way liable for the same.

HarperCollins *Publishers*
A-75, Sector 57, Noida, Uttar Pradesh 201301, India
1 London Bridge Street, London, SE1 9GF, United Kingdom
Hazelton Lanes, 55 Avenue Road, Suite 2900, Toronto, Ontario M5R
3L2 and 1995 Markham Road, Scarborough, Ontario M1B 5M8, Canada
25 Ryde Road, Pymble, Sydney, NSW 2073, Australia
195 Broadway, New York, NY 10007, USA

Typeset in 10.5/14.5 ElegantGarmnd BT by
R. Ajith Kumar

Printed and bound at
Thomson Press (India) Ltd.

To all those tireless groundsmen, coaches and club secretaries who never get even a column centimetre of coverage in the media. Their dedication must not go unrecognized in the ups and downs of Bombay cricket.

Also, to Vasu Paranjpe and Ramakant Achrekar, eternal mentors and master coaches whose contribution to Bombay cricket is immeasurable.

CONTENTS

INTRODUCTION

E veryone who follows the game of cricket knows of the exploits of Bombay teams. While not everyone may be able to recall the precise numbers, connoisseurs of the sport cannot miss the contribution of Bombay to the cricketing traditions of India.

Bombay has won the Ranji Trophy forty times. Their closest competitors, Karnataka, come in at a grand total of seven. One-third of all of India's international runs have been scored by batsmen who have come through the ranks of Bombay cricket. While these numbers may amaze the readers they may not be entirely unexpected, for the legends of Bombay cricket are part of the oral tradition of cricket followers not only from the city but across the country.

Following and reporting on Bombay cricket for nearly forty-five years now, I am impelled to share with the readers the narratives underlying the numbers. It is the story of a cricketing culture that is infused with the spirit of the city – a city, whose 'way of living' defined its 'way of playing' so completely that its narratives are inextricably intertwined. Its way of playing eventually set the benchmark for the sport in the country and one that the rest would take decades to catch up with.

Hence the book begins by chasing the obvious question. What distinguishes Bombay cricket from the rest of India?

The underlying answers are anything but obvious. While the emerging picture maybe a telling narrative regarding the spirit of the game of cricket and cricketers, one will also find that the spirit of the players may not be distinguished from their individual characters. We will know that the city of Bombay inspired, challenged and hardened these players to not only achieve their individual best but also formed them to fight as a unit.

Telling the story of Bombay cricket invariably tells the tale of the city and the daily bother of living in the city – experiences that shape the Bombaikar and in the process form a tenacious cricketer. It is the story of many young men whose grit and discipline opened new frontiers in the game, which today is one of the handful of elements that bind the country that is as vast and diverse as India.

Tales of individuals overcoming personal tragedies and challenges to participate in this grand tradition of Bombay cricket are abundant. What is significant is that the tradition of the sport in the city offered enough inspiration for these individuals to make such a journey. It is the camaraderie and ethos in the cricketing universe of Bombay that not only inspired individuals but also provided them solace.

Complementing these narratives are fascinating stories of how Bombay cricket managed to develop the right fundamentals. Their dedicated and planned practice sessions, their organized fielding practice, the vibrant and highly competitive club cricket, all these together developed an intense yet disciplined passion for the sport that was part of the cricketing air of the city; air that would nourish every young cricketer to come through its ranks.

Perhaps the Kanga League is the most demonstrative piece of evidence of this spirit of Bombay cricket. Once played only during the monsoon, the league was founded to counter the temperamental weather of England, which the players in the early part of the twentieth century had to endure. The rains of Bombay provided the perfect simulation with added benefits. The club structure of Bombay not only ensured fierce competition as players like Sunil Gavaskar, in their prime, hopped off airplanes on their way back from tours to head straight for the grounds, but on days the conditions proved truly unplayable, brought together the eclectic mix of retired, national and young players to exchange anecdotes. Cricket truly proved to be a way of life under the umbrella of the Kanga League in the rains of Bombay. It would not be incorrect to say the league was one of the mediums for sustaining the philosophy of Bombay cricket across generations.

While seasoning the narrative of Bombay cricket with narratives of the life in the city and the stories of individuals, as it is essential to understand the legacy of Bombay cricket, the book also takes a hard look at the on-field aspects of the sport, in chapters such as 'The Batting Gharana of Bombay' and 'The Best Bombay XI'.

As already mentioned, Bombay's batsmen have been the pillar of Indian cricket for decades. While theories regarding the success of Bombay batsmen are abundant, the chapter 'Conversations on Cricket' attempts to extract the insiders' view regarding batting techniques and mindsets. After all, it is the city that has produced international-quality cricketers right from

the early days of Vijay Merchant and Polly Umrigar, all the way
to Sunil Gavaskar and Sachin Tendulkar. The book attempts
to bring forth not only how such quality was achieved, with
Bombay being the hub for the most technically sound batsmen,
but also how that philosophy of playing was sustained for over
half a century.

All these facts and stories together lead to an obvious question:
what is the ultimate or the best Bombay XI? With players from
across generations upstaging each other on the national and
international stages, selecting the best Bombay XI is a truly
difficult task. It is never enough to look at the numbers when one
is grappling with a legacy. Each player faced different challenges,
so it is not only the players' individual styles that need to be
pitted against each other but the environment in which those
styles proved to be successful. This is a near-impossible task but
the chapter 'The Best Bombay XI' attempts do exactly this. This
would never satisfy every connoisseur but hopefully will provide
a window to the readers to participate in recalling the collective
greatness of Bombay cricket as the best of the best from across
eras are juxtaposed and discussed together.

However, the story of Bombay cricket is not intended to provoke
internal debates. It is the tale of a ruthless competitive spirit that
is complemented by an ethos that inspired camaraderie. All these
elements together frame the story of Bombay cricket. The numbers
come at the end – as a result of these stories of human bonding.

Lastly, the book discusses some of the challenges Bombay
cricket is currently facing, and the possible solutions for the same,
with former players joining the discussion. It is this cricketing
tale, which I have not only witnessed and reported on over the
years but also cherished, that I would like to share.

1

KHADDOOS

What is it with Bombay? This entire book is a modest attempt to answer this question. How has Bombay managed to capture the imagination of Indians for all these years? Why does every dream story begin with Bombay and end with Bombay? 'The city of dreams' they call it. But life is anything but easy here. Every moment here is characterized by struggle and strife. Roads are congested, trains are crowded and houses are small. Why then is Bombay called the city of dreams? This face of Bombay is not unknown, yet the city has not lost its tag.

Every day, hordes of people land on the platforms of Bombay's two main railway stations to live the Bombay life. Film stars, cricketers, engineers, labourers and beggars – Bombay is the dream destination for all of them. It is the place where dreams come true. Everyone wants to make it big; and make it big in Bombay. Everyone wants to transform their reality into the reality of their dreams. Everyone comes here, to this life of crowded trains, only in the hope of escaping it someday and making it to a life of luxury. Some do, many don't.

But the heart of Bombay is not made by the few stalwarts who make it big. The heart of Bombay is made by the thousands who don't, and the thousands of others who strive towards it every day. I would say that Bombay's speciality is not that people achieve their dreams here; it is that people never stop dreaming. Bombay's special air is not due to its status as the city of dreams but as the city that makes the journey to dreamlands possible.

Like a crowded train journey, what matters in the end is not that we reached our destination early or late, it is the fact that we travelled. It is the travelling that makes a Bombaikar; the journey of living in Bombay every day. It is in the everyday life that the dream of Bombay lies. What makes Bombay so full of life? How is it so invigorating? 'What is it with Bombay?' The question keeps presenting itself time and again.

What is most surprising is the bond between Bombay and cricket. It has been there for decades and continues to daunt the Indian cricketing world. What is it with Bombay, really, that it has continued to be the heart of cricket for years together? If one thinks about it, Bombay and cricket are poles apart in their essence. Much have been written and talked about Bombay's fast-paced life. Bombay, 'the city that never sleeps', never has time to stop. It is always on the go, just as its trains and the people on its trains. To live in Bombay is to live life on the move. To live in Bombay is to live to the fullest. Every moment is packed with excitement and action, with life bubbling at its seams. How in the world, we might wonder, have people of this never-stopping city taken a fancy to the delectable game called cricket, which can only be enjoyed slowly? Bombay and cricket are opposites, like fire and ice. And yet they make the perfect cocktail.

Why is it that Bombay keeps winning the national championship with religious regularity, as if it was its birthright? The rest of the teams put together don't even make for half of what Bombay alone has won. Bombay, its excellent cricketers and its passionate cricket lovers make the perfect love triangle. Together, all three make Bombay unbeatable in cricket, outclassing everyone in both playing the sport and loving it. The houses of legends of cricket have become tourist spots of Bombay. To see the gate of the house of Sachin Tendulkar is like taking aashirwad (blessings) from the God of cricket himself.

My mind rushes to an incident that will always be written in golden letters in the pages of Bombay's cricketing history. It was the 1968-69 finals of the Ranji Trophy against Bengal at the Brabourne stadium. For once, Bombay was in a terrible position and its esteemed crown, the trophy, was in jeopardy. They had only themselves to blame for the state of their team, having spilled dozens of sitters. After spinners Eknath Solkar and Milind Rege sent Bengal's top order back to the pavilion, Bengal skipper Chuni Goswami, the former India football team captain, had two big partnerships with Debu Mitra and Gopal Bose to add 262 runs. When Bengal got out for 387, the diehard Bombay fans were confident that Bombay's batting line up would get past that total without any fuss. Years of brilliance had moulded their thinking so. Defeat was not only unacceptable to Bombay cricket and Bombay city but inconceivable. And it was the true testament of Bombay cricket that no Bombay player or fan ever thought of defeat even in challenging or dire circumstances

But this was not the real story of that game. The real story of this game was actually happening off the field. When Bombay was preparing hard for the final with only a few days remaining for the big day, all-rounder Eknath Solkar was spending sleepless nights at the G.T. hospital. Solkar at twenty years of age was young and talented. He was the son of a Hindu Gymkhana grounds man Dhondu Solkar. Dhondu had himself served Bombay cricket all his life. On the fateful day of 9 February 1969, Dhondu had slipped and tumbled down the stairs to the ground floor. He was rushed to the hospital. The fall had immediately rendered him unconscious. Days passed but Dhondu remained in a coma, hardly responding to the treatment.

The date of the Ranji final was approaching and Bombay needed Eknath's expertise, but how could he take his mind off his ailing father? Hardly anyone in the Bombay team or the cricket association knew what Eknath was going through. 'For more than a week, I hadn't slept. The Ranji final was approaching and I didn't know what to do. Hemant Mafatlal (cousin of Arvind Mafatlal of Mafatlal Industries and one who had been an invaluable mentor to Eknath) told me to be tough. I decided to play the match but never mentioned to anyone about my father's condition,' Eknath recounted.

The day of the grand final came and Eknath decided to play. His team carried the legacy and burden of a decade of wins. To lose was not an option. And yet, Bengal had reduced them to a situation of crisis this time. On day four, when two youngsters Eknath Solkar and Milind Rege, the two overnight batsmen, returned to the pavilion at the end of play, they did not even have double digits against their names in the scorecard. The Bombay camp was tense. There was fear and unrest and most daunting of all, there was the fear of losing, something that Bombay had never known. In the middle of this, came the news that Dhondu Solkar had passed away. Eknath had just come out of the field; his mind was absorbed in his team's crisis. The news of his father's death shook him out of his senses. With tears rolling down his young cheeks, he performed his father's last rites like a loving son. He lit the funeral pyre and said bye to the father who had made him the person and the player that he was. One would think that his father's loss would have made him forget Bombay's plight. How could one think of a match after losing one's dear father? But it was in fact the opposite for Eknath. It was his father's loss that made him more determined to take Bombay out of the crisis. In a later interview, he said that the two crises remained together in his mind. Thinking of one automatically made him think of the other crisis.

The entire Solkar family was absorbed in mourning the death of the head of the family. They were shattered. The young Eknath turned to his mother and said that his team needed him. The next morning he was there on the field, more determined than ever before. The tears had dried up from his face but the memory hadn't. Solkar and Rege faced the lethal barrage from the duo, Ramesh Bhatia and Subroto Guha; and they did so with tremendous courage. Their fight had paid off, managing to get the first inning lead; and on the virtue of that lead, Bombay won the Ranji Trophy.

Eknath Solkar had lost his beloved father but he won the hearts of Bombay's cricketing fraternity for his spirit. He continued to give everything he had to the game for years to follow. One of the greatest close-in fielders ever, Eknath Solkar used to take blinders at forward short leg. He had much to do in making the spin quartet of Bedi, Prasanna, Chandrashekar, and Venkataraghavan look invincible. He kept contributing to

Bombay cricket year after year, until he breathed his last. Solkar passed away in 2005.

Solkar's story can wrench the hardest of hearts. But call it Bombay's greatness or that of its lovers, the legend of Bombay cricket is filled with stories of such heartening cricketers. Wasim Jaffer was another person who rose above personal tragedy to help his team. It was the elite Ranji Trophy match in Bombay. The match was against Himachal Pradesh at Wankhede and Jaffer was fielding on the fourth day when he received a message that his mother was no more. She had suffered a mild heart attack a few days earlier, but had recovered well and was said to be out of danger.

Wasim had talked to her only the previous evening. He had little idea that as he gave his blood and sweat for the victory of his team, his mother was taking her last breaths. The four Jaffer brothers had struggled hard to make ends meet. Their father worked as a bus driver in the public transport company, Bombay Electric Supply and Transport Undertaking (BEST), and Wasim's mother had always been the pillar of strength for the family. The family was shocked beyond measure when she had to be hospitalized. She rarely fell ill, always having been the one who had remained firm and strong. Now she was no more.

Wasim was fielding in the slips. It was right there that he was told that his mother had passed away. Dazed, he began walking back towards the pavilion. 'I was too dazed to take a decision but coach Chandu Pandit said that even if I went home then, the funeral would be in the evening.' Bombay needed two more wickets to wrap up Himachal Pradesh's innings which had still to chase more than eighty-odd runs. In the same daze, Wasim went back to the field and continued his duty as a cricketer.

Wasim knew that as an opener he had to get the runs without losing a wicket to get the bonus point for his team. As he walked out to the field to open the innings, he looked heavenward and prayed for his mother. But he was determined to get those runs without losing a wicket. And he did. Bombay won with their opening partnership intact thus earning a bonus point.

Jaffer says, 'Though my mother's loss can't be compared to anything else, my team too needed me to get those runs for the bonus point. That's the way I played my cricket.'

Bombay's cricketers have given it all to the team. Their obsession with the team has given birth to a great collection of stories which can be told and retold without either the teller or the listener ever tiring. These stories of a romance between a city and a sport are for the ages. There was yet another devoted Bombaikar. His sacrifice can hardly be compared to Jaffer's loss of his mother and the brave face that he wore even after the tragedy. However, the anecdote is worth recounting because it manages to highlight the passion and the strength of Bombay cricket and the type of devotion that the jersey with the lion crest inspired.

Sudhakar Adhikari's tale is light and heartening. His decisions on the day of his wedding may not be the most popular for any bride and groom and yet the incident makes for the most amusing anecdote. Sudhakar Adhikari must consider himself lucky that his wife did not apply for a divorce the very day they were wedded. The story of this unbelievable day has to start with a trivia. This is the state of Bombay cricket in the 1960s, an atmosphere which was horribly competitive and cut-throat. There were many in the queue for the prestige of being in the team. The degree of competitiveness was so fierce in the 1960s that the established opener Sudhakar Adhikari didn't want to take the risk of not playing the league match against Maharashtra on the day he was to wed his fiancé. There was always the risk that he would not be able to recover the place in the line-up if he left.

The muhurt (an auspicious time) for the wedding was at 9.03 in the morning. It was to take place at Matunga, a central suburb which is about an hour's travel from the Brabourne stadium, the venue of the match. The captain of the Bombay team, Polly Umrigar, was surprised when Adhikari told him that he would be a little late for the match that day. The match was to start at 10.30, but the toss and other formalities and warm-up began much earlier. Adhikari requested to be excused from attending formalities for that one day and informed his captain that he would reach by 10.15 a.m.

Umrigar remembers, 'Here was a cricketer getting married an hour before the Ranji match and yet wanted to play because the competition for each slot in the Bombay team was immense. He was worried that if he didn't play, he might lose his place in case his replacement managed a big score or a fine performance. He then would have had to wait till his replacement failed. And even then the candidates for that single slot in Bombay would have only increased. I told him that if he has to play he has to be in the dressing room when I leave for the toss, and as luck would have it, just as I was leaving for the toss, he emerged from nowhere.' Adhikari managed to attend his marriage and then run to the match venue to save his place in the team. In the end, he could manage both.

Solkar, Jaffer and Adhikari – each in his own indomitable way – represent the spirit of millions of lovers of Bombay cricket. The legend of Bombay cricket is replete with tales of players who have overcome great personal crises to honour their commitment to the team.

The history of Bombay cricket goes far back and with it, its players, accomplishments and stories also present a diverse array. The Triangular, the Quadrangular and the Pentangular were the tournaments of Bombay cricket. These tournaments started attracting players from all over India. The competitiveness with which those matches were played was a learning curve, a trial by fire that imbued toughness into Bombay cricket.

Soon the idea of a national championship emerged: the Ranji Trophy. The Ranji Trophy was named after the great Ranjitsinhji. Little would people have realized that the Ranji Trophy was to become instrumental for the development of Indian cricket a few years down the line. The Ranji Trophy came and it was finally a stage where Bombay could display its game in front of the entire world. And it lived up to every bit of the promise.

Till date, Bombay has won the coveted Ranji Trophy forty times. It exemplifies a rare resolve and strength of character, something that every cricketer in Bombay is nurtured with. The records run into pages. But the only question that the consistently startling achievements of Bombay cricket raise is 'How?' How is it that Bombay has won the Ranji Trophy forty times? While Delhi and Karnataka have won it only seven times each, Hyderabad and Tamil Nadu have won it twice each. The disparity in the level of wins is unbridgeable. It cannot be coincidence or luck. There is something in Bombay that makes it happen always. What is it?

I know many whose answer to this question will undoubtedly be 'Bombay's Khaddoos attitude', a 'never say die' attitude. It is Bombay's unique Khaddoos-ness that is at the heart of its success. But what is this Khaddoos attitude? The lion on Bombay's crest is not just a hollow symbol. It is the epitome of Bombay's spirit and attitude. In the Indian cricketing fraternity, it is said that a team will have some chance of winning the Ranji Trophy if it somehow gets past the lion when it is asleep. But once you provoke the lion, trouble is unleashed upon you in full measure. In my long career of following Bombay cricket and covering more than 300 games, there have been very few brave hearts to pose a challenge to this lion. Many opposition teams sense victory too early and become complacent when they achieve a commanding position. They forget that it is Bombay that they are facing. Their overconfidence only shakes the sleeping lion from its slumber, inviting its wrath; and eventually they lose their winning position.

Wearing the crest of Bombay itself does something to a player. Dilip Sardesai once said that when a player wears the lion crest of Bombay on his person, he will have to play like a lion on the prowl and not like a pussycat. The Khaddoos attitude of Bombaikars is their never-say-die spirit – the attitude of never accepting defeat in advance, of struggling to the end. This attitude is an intrinsic part of Bombaikar's life. It is something that every citizen of Bombay grows up with.

Why would, after all, a cricketer brave the extremely crowded and congested train for hours, asked former Test player Nilesh Kulkarni who used to travel four hours to and fro Dombivali by train every day, if he did not wish to play the game well? The challenges of life in Bombay act as a sieve that separates the weak-hearted from the 'lion'-hearted. There are hordes of players who travel every day from far-flung places like Virar and Kalyan to central or south Bombay to practise and play matches. Therein lies the spirit of the Bombay cricketer. This spirit has endured for decades now, to form a legacy in the annals of Indian cricket history. The spirit of Nilesh Kulkarni can be seen even today in many bright youngsters who have devoted themselves to cricket at a young age.

Fifteen-year-old Prithvi Shaw lost his mother when he was only four. At the age of ten, he used to wake up at 4.30 every morning. He had to catch the 6.09 train from Virar, where his home used to be – which is also the last station of the Western Railway line – so that he could make it for the school practice sessions at Bandra or play a match at Churchgate. Young Prithvi used to return in the evenings in the same overflowing trains. At fifteen now, he is a batsman of class and has a unique presence in the Bombay junior team. In 2013, he scored 546 in only one innings, batting for two whole days. He now leads the A Division team. He has already scored over 4,000 runs in school cricket. They say he is the next Tendulkar. But 'Tendulkars' are not just born, they are made. And it is Bombay's life which is making the boy the cricketer he is.

Anyone familiar with the local trains of Bombay would know that it is like a survival game in itself. To board the train in record time, push yourself through the crowds to make just 20 cm of space, to be able to extend your hands enough to grab the handlebars, every moment of the travel is truly a struggle. To get enough room to be able to plant your feet and not get pushed out with the flow is a skill in itself. And this young boy Prithvi is experiencing it every day. Every day it makes him grow into a more determined player.

It is this kind of life that makes a Bombay cricketer mentally tough. Once above twelve years, a boy is considered a major by the railway rules and he cannot travel in the ladies compartment.

Every day he has to make way for himself and his huge kitbag amidst older and robust men. This is how boys become tough here. A Bombaikar fights for his life every second. Nothing comes easy to him. But a Bombaikar also loves challenges. There would be no other way to do it. Look at one brilliant example in the form of the Kanga League.

Bombay cricket is a microcosmic manifestation of the city and the city's spirit in many ways. This statement is true even though cricket is inherently a slow sport. Bombay is the city of dreams, the city which never sleeps; and the same can be said of its cricket and cricketers. There cannot be a greater testament to this than the Kanga League. Cricket is inherently a weather-sensitive game, with rains being the most frequent spoilsport. Bombay, a coastal city in the tropical region, suffers from this predicament enough. However, only in Bombay could this scenario have been turned into an opportunity. The Kanga League of Bombay is one and perhaps the only tournament in the world that is actually played only during the monsoon season.

Deeply loved by Bombaikars, the Kanga League is definitely one of the most unique tournaments in the world. Who could imagine that the elitist, gentlemanly and sophisticated game of cricket could be converted into a rain carnival! Cricket is a game of nuances. Every little thing is fussed about. Things as minuscule as half an inch of grass on the pitch can cause a world of difference. A crack or footmark on the pitch, the slightest wetness of the ball, the direction of wind on the ground; pundits find these factors indispensable to any match of cricket. But the

Kanga League innovatively reduced this list of factors as mere accomplices of cricket and shifted the entire focus of the game to the spirit of cricket! The spirit that Kanga League evokes is unparalleled. Some may call it cricket in a distorted form. But perhaps it can be called cricket in its most pure form, because it captures its essence like nothing else does.

This one tournament is immensely responsible for teaching a Bombay cricketer to survive. It has made him realize that pitches, umpires and weather are all unpredictable and a part and parcel of life. It has taught the cricketer that the tree of nepotism might grow but when a Bombay cricketer wears the lion crest, nothing matters but cricket and if he is honestly playing for his team, he will always find passionate supporters backing him with all they have.

It has to be said that the Kanga League was Vijay Merchant's brainchild. He was the one to recommend a monsoon league and made sure it got implemented by the authorities in the year 1948. But even he would not have imagined the effect that the league was to have over the years. It almost became the centre of Bombay cricket. It became the foundation of the psyche of the cricketers of Bombay.

To play in the league, many cricketers would start early in the morning from far-off places like Dahanu, Boisar or Kalyan. The day would be filled with bright sunshine when they left in the morning, but the afternoons would be pouring heavily. Train services would often be disrupted because of the rain and it would be a feat to get back home. But never did this result in lack of motivation for any player. It strangely motivated them to participate each day, to play with all their heart and live life like every moment was important. Whoever has ever been involved in the Kanga League can never take the energy of the league out of their selves. They talk about the league passionately years after having played.

All these factors are helping us understand the psyche of the Bombay cricketer and the spirit of Bombay cricket. I am not saying that the never-say-die attitude is something Bombaikars are born with. No, an inheritance would be too simple an explanation and a story not worth telling. No one can become a good player by relying on inheritance. The players are inculcated with the spirit, and so thoroughly, that it becomes ingrained in them like their genes. One example of the never-say-die attitude that immediately comes to my mind is the Ranji semi-final against Bengal at the Eden Gardens in 1976. On the first day, leg-spinner Rakesh Tandon's ball hit the bails but went on to hit wicket keeper Hazare in the face. Hazare started spitting blood then and there and for the next three days he was kept on a liquid diet. He was feeling weak, but Captain Ashok Mankad wanted him to play because he knew the importance of Hazare's wicketkeeping to their team. The injured and unwell Hazare did not only manage to keep wickets for the entire game but also came to rescue with his bat when Bombay collapsed while chasing Bengal's total. (More of it in the chapter 'Interesting Matches of Bombay').

All this is not to say that Bombay is special because it always wins. It is not because they win in the end that they are called Khaddoos. It is because of the way they play – the process of striving every minute of the match. Take another example. The lobby of the Cricket Club of India (CCI) has a replica of the Ranji Trophy. Rajsingh Dungarpur, who played for Rajasthan, is famous for having played in all the seven Ranji finals in which Rajasthan came up against Bombay. And yet he couldn't be part of the winning team even once. Bombay always defeated Rajasthan. Dungarpur was frustrated, he was trying his best to defeat Bombay, but he couldn't; and nor could his entire team. Once in fact, he went to the extent of employing superstition in his efforts to defeat Bombay. He invited a person who was considered inauspicious and the Rajasthan team posted him next to the Bombay dressing room. All hopes were placed on this man. What no one could do for years was supposed to happen by divine intervention or at least by the presence of this one man. However, Bombay again came out victorious. Rajsingh would love narrating this story whenever the slightest scope of telling it occurred. His angst of not winning against Bombay was masked by respect for the perseverance of the Bombay team. He respected the team for their brilliance.

Respect is the word that often comes up when talking about Bombay cricket. They might not have been liked by their opponents but were certainly respected. However, all this success does not happen merely by virtue of the players living in a city. Attitude is one thing, but hard work is never dispensable to success. Bombay cricketers might be inherently Khaddoos, but is it enough of an explanation for its success? Is it their attitude or their meticulous planning that allowed them to win the Ranji Trophy time and again? It has to be said that it is a combination of both.

The never-say-die attitude is not only ingrained in the cricketers of Bombay by living in the city, but also by working hard every day towards perfection. The Bombay team has also been known for its meticulous planning. It can be said that they are Khaddoos with their planning as well. They do not get satisfied with a plan easily, and strive towards excellence. Attitude is a very important ingredient of the Bombay cricketing culture. The slightest display of the lack of the right attitude can finish a player's career before it starts. Unlike players of other state teams, no Bombay team would ever pay heed to provocation. Bombay players do not get affected when sledged and teased; they do not lose their plan of action like players from many other teams. In fact, history is a witness to the fact that additional pressure makes them even more boisterous and determined to win.

In the Ranji finals of 1971, Bombay team was missing half a dozen star players who were playing for India's national side on the West Indies tour. The opposition was the star-studded Maharashtra team. And yet, Sudhir Naik surprised everyone by shrewdly leading the Bombay team to victory again. But more than the victory, the way Bombay got the victory has to be told and retold in cricketing history. On the eve of the final day, the Maharashtra team led by Chandu Borde needed sixty-two runs to win. They had a whole day to make that meagre number of runs with five wickets in hand. Victory seemed to be in their fists. Anticipating the victory on the eve of the final day, the administrators of the Maharashtra Cricket Association started preparing for celebrations for the next evening. After all, it was to be a huge feat. Defeating Bombay was the dream of every cricket team in India. They had to make sure that when it happened, they celebrated it with the fanfare it deserved. The Maharashtra association booked a big room in one of the city's five-star hotels and esteemed supporters were hastily invited. Champagne bottles were stacked up, amidst other paraphernalia of celebration. On the morning of the final day, the invited supporters had already reached Bombay from Poona. They were all set to celebrate victory. Only the formality of the day was to be done with and then Maharashtra could celebrate the rarest of rare moments.

However, what happened on the field that day was to transform the anticipated party into an evening of shock and disbelief. It was Milind Rege's beautiful catch that started the proceedings. He took a blinder in the gully to get rid of Borde. And voila! The rest of the Maharashtra batsmen collapsed like a house of cards. Bombay snatched victory from the jagged jaws of defeat. But perhaps the most surprising part of this story is yet to be told. It so happened that the hero of the win, the man who changed an imminent loss into a win – Sudhir Naik – was seen carrying drinks the following year itself. Blame it on the intense competition in the Bombay team or the ruthless selection politics, the greatest have found it difficult to survive within the Bombay team. No great player could take his position for granted. Bombay cricket has no scope for those who get complacent. Take a breather and you are gone for good. Bombay team has been full of cricketers who never take a moment to relax. Perhaps this is why they make such a formidable team.

The former Test player Brijesh Patel who played for Mafatlals rightly assesses the Bombay cricket team in the following words: 'Give them a slight opening and they are all over you. Don't open the game, because they know how to close it. When they are on top, they close the game.'

The stories are far too many and far too recurrent about the Bombay team and in all those stories these elements – a Khaddoos, ruthless team that more often than not won – is never missing. They say that it had a life of its own, a life that is much larger than the sum of its individual players. In the 1972 Ranji Trophy final between Madras and Bombay at Chepauk, the pitch was tailor-made for Venkataraghavan and V.V. Kumar. That it was prepared for both these great spinners to take advantage was apparent to the Bombay team. But no one talked about it in the dressing room. There was no cry of despair, no scream of panic. Neither was there any discussion about it in the team nor any nervousness on the face of Bombay players. No one worried about how to negotiate the subtle varieties of those two spinners at the last minute. They knew they can get through it because they had prepared amply.

Bombay scored 151 and Madras appeared to be taking a good lead when they were at sixty-two for two. Michael Dalvi and Abdul Jabbar had applied themselves well with a partnership of fifty-six runs. That evening, Dalvi and a few of the players of the Madras team felt a lead of 200 was good enough to crush Bombay. They made the same mistake as Maharashtra made just a year before in getting complacent against Bombay. The next day, Kalyanasundaram was to bat last and was sitting with ease in coloured trousers. The moment the first ball of Shivalkar's turned at right angles, his colleague V.V. Kumar told him 'Kali, change into whites. Both of us will be batting within an hour.'

It was almost prophetic. What Kumar told turned out to be true in the end. Shivalkar hit his length early in the spell and before anyone could register the reality of what was happening, Madras lost the next eight wickets for eighteen runs. Shivalkar had figures of eight for sixteen in the first innings and five for eighteen in the second! The unbelievable, deadly bowling by Shivalkar was coupled with a typical Khaddoos batting by Sudhir

Naik in both the innings. Bombay had again won the Ranji final, and again won it from a point where the opposition thought that it had the match in its bag. Moreover, Bombay won the match in merely in two days time! (Only one ball was bowled on the third day.)

Time and again, Bombay has emerged out of nowhere and won games. It is perhaps impossible to describe the glory of Bombay to today's generation. The glory of Bombay had to be felt in the days when it was considered easier to get into the national team than the Bombay Ranji team. Many people in the country would proudly say some decades ago: 'What Bombay cricket thinks today, Indian cricket thinks tomorrow.'

What has happened to the glory of Bombay? We can hardly say that it has faded away. Bombay remains a strong team and continues to provide the nation with great cricketers year after year. Paradoxically, a close look at the statistics reveals that though the percentage of runs scored by the Bombay batsmen for the country is really high, the percentage of failed cricketers is also equally high. Why is it that many Bombay cricketers couldn't capitalize on their tremendous domestic performances at the national level? The number of international cricketers Bombay has been producing of late is certainly on the lower side when compared to the years gone by.

Bombay boasts of eighty tournaments played by over 25,000 registered cricketers. Add to this the fact that 250 schools take part in under-fourteen and under-sixteen tournaments. The century-old inter-school tournaments are played on 100 turf grounds.

But though it is always good to have multiplicity and a range of options, one risk that so many matches pose is the promotion of mediocrity. Bombay's legacy is huge and quality control should be a must in every tournament. Bombay is the team that once used to have nine players from its side in the Indian national team. We still have teenagers Prithvi Shaw and Arman Jaffer playing in the maidans of Bombay and there is every hope and reason that they will contribute vastly to the glorious history of Bombay cricket.

What cricket means to Bombay and what Bombay means to cricket are questions that none of us can answer. Their relationship is sublime. It has spanned for decades together, over many matches, millions of balls, thousands of sixes, gallons of sweat and an immeasurable amount of spirit and life. Bombay continues to give to cricket what it has received from it: recognition, respect and reverence. At the end of a long and brooding attempt at answering a question that troubles the cricketing world, I again ask, 'What is it with Bombay cricket?' The answers, as we saw, are many. There are too many reasons that seem to make sense. Bombay makes cricketers tough, Bombay teaches to never give up, Bombay cricketers practise very hard.

The bond between Bombay and cricket is too complex to be defined in exact terms. But what can be said with an absolute assertion of faith is that the two share a very close relationship. Cricket is etched in Bombay's heart and it can never disassociate itself from Bombay. There is a deep connection between cricket and the trains, the lifeline of Bombay. The trains are what have made cricketing culture even possible in this vast city where aspiring youngsters always know that they can reach the farthest of places if they really want to. It is full of sacrifices and difficulties; travelling on the trains of Bombay is often one of the most difficult tasks. But what we have to understand is that there would be no cricket if there were no trains! The courage to play cricket in the rainy season, to leave home at the break of dawn, to return home late after a hard day of practice – this confidence, this ability to give one's soul to cricket has been granted by the Bombay trains whose spirit echoes the heartbeat of the people of Bombay.

In a way, all things add up to make Bombay the city of cricket that it is. In the subsequent chapters, I explore this question with greater depth and follow Bombay's glorious cricketing journey with a microscopic eye, an admiring mind and a passionate heart.

2

THE BATTING GHARANA OF BOMBAY

We know what goes into the making of a great team: great players in a good combination. But what is a glorious cricketing legacy made of? A legacy is not as simple as a team. It is a team extended over years and years and made of people who have not necessarily played together or shared the same space and yet are part of a shared legacy that binds that group across time and space. Bombay has been the team it is because of its players. But what distinguishes a team from a bunch of individuals is a feeling of togetherness. The legacy of Bombay is not just made by a lot of legends stacked together. It is made by there being a clear commonality in all of them, a deep sense of connection. Bombay players form a whole – individuals who have gelled together as a team and teams across decades together form the legacy of Bombay cricket. They are united in spirit and not just by the name of the team. Bombay players have a common attitude, the attitude of not giving up.

But how do all the Bombay players develop the same attitude?

Where did they learn it from? The answer is simple: they learnt it from the legacy of great players who have preceded them, great players who one after another have adorned the galleries of Bombay cricket. Bombay players need no special coaching, the process of playing itself means being a witness to the greatest of the greats. And greats as they might be, they are never inaccessible to aspiring Bombay players. They continue to be a source of inspiration and help. In fact, one would not be wrong in saying that this intermingling of young and old, experienced and inexperienced, international, club and state players in various competitions is what defined, raised and sustained the standard of Bombay cricket for so long.

The galleries of Bombay cricket are not just full of legends, they are full of lakhs of young and experienced players who throng to more than eighty official tournaments to try their luck. Bombay is not the place where legends are born; it is the place where legends are made. They are all nurtured into the grand gharana of Bombay which is full of passion and rigour. It is the process that makes them legends.

We have already touched on the spirit of everyday life in Bombay that moulds these cricketing warriors. However, is there a magic formula that Bombay coaches pass on to their trainees? There must be some reason for the fact that Bombay had remained the unchallenged champion of domestic cricket for years. The wisdom must certainly have come from the good old men of Indian cricket. What is the formula then? Well, actually it is called 'stay at the wicket and runs will come'. That is all. Once in a while, a bright but restless teenager gets confused at hearing this maxim and asks the crucial question: 'How?' True, how do you even manage to stay at the wicket for so long? But again, there is a stereotypical 'magic' reply to this as well: 'Keep watching the ball with concentration and you will stay at the wicket and when you stay at the wicket, the runs will flow.'

It will take the teenager many matches and an experience of real-life playing to realize the truth of this simple maxim. It is as difficult to implement as it is simple to understand. But Bombay has managed to practise this motto for years, for decades together. One morning Vijay Merchant, well past his best and coming close to the administrative retirement age of the state government, was invited to the L.R. Teresy nets at the Hindu Gymkhana by coach Vinoo Mankad. A documentary film-maker wanted to make a film. Vijay bhai, as he was respectfully addressed, put on the pads as he was instructed. The film-maker wanted Merchant to bat against young fast bowler Kailash Gattani. Now Gattani was young but no rookie. He was a prodigy picked by the Rajasthan Ranji team when he was a schoolboy.

The bowlers were strictly instructed: 'Bowl outside the off stump.' In fact, it was the art of leaving the ball that was to be filmed. The bowlers obliged and Vijay bhai kept leaving the ball. Gattani thought of impressing Merchant and his coach Mankad. He bowled an inswinger and the next second, the congregation witnessed Vijay bhai effortlessly put his back leg around the off stump. The bat intercepted the ball and the famous late cut was executed. Gattani was spellbound but not as much as the rest of the young boys.

Merchant was the idol of idols in that era. He was technique personified. Always seen immaculately attired, batting was like a business to him. He had a simple principle for batting. 'In business, you invest energy and time discretely to be successful. In batting too you prepare yourself against all odds to spend more time at the crease to score more runs.' And Merchant practised his words as much as he preached them. More often than not, he succeeded.

Be it any match, tournament or series, Merchant would prepare meticulously. Before the England tour, he ensured that the practice pitches at the Hindu Gymkhana were adequately wet. He wanted to be completely ready for the moisture and wetness of the English pitches. It can be said that an entire generation of Bombay cricketers grew up watching this one legend. There were Polly Umrigar, Nari Contractor, Vijay Manjrekar, Madhav Apte, Manohar Hardikar and many collegians who grew up watching Merchant with awe and got motivated to play for the star-studded Bombay team.

The tall and well-built Umrigar was a stroke player and had the reputation of being a palm tree hitter. The openers Contractor and Madhav Apte idolized Merchant so much that they tried to emulate his technique. 'If you have to be a good opening batsman, you must be careful about which one to play,' Merchant kept saying and they stuck to it as their Bible.

Merchant sowed the seeds of Bombay's long-lasting success in the form of a whole generation of Bombay cricketers. For players like Contractor, Madhav Apte and others, Merchant's mantra worked. They assumed the role of wearing the bowler down. On the other hand, there was Umrigar who, though equally inspired by Merchant, made a unique niche for himself. He not only played shots but would often use soft hands to place the ball short of the inner circle fielder and dash off for a quick single. Jokingly he would say, 'Play the bowler from the non-striker's end.'

Vijay Manjrekar was the best of the lot. The more time he

spent at the crease, the more formidable he looked. Technically he was the closest to Merchant, but Manjrekar had even more strokes in his repertoire and it was a treat to watch him execute the strokes. He would place the cut shot to a nicety and play the hook shot with aplomb. When he got going against a left-arm spinner, he would time his flicks off the back foot through midwicket. He could do this with poise even on a turner, which Dhiraj Parsana learnt the hard way. It was a shot that his nephew applauded from the non-striker end only to be told 'Don't try. It requires a class'.

His mantra was to 'wear the bowler down' and while youngsters watched it more and more, they subconsciously grasped his technique and imbibed it. The technique could not be learnt by some dry piece of theory or through a string of words. The technique had to be watched, experienced, relished and absorbed. Youngsters in Bombay grow absorbing many techniques of great players in the same way. They watch and watch, till they think it is a part of them. Like all great batsmen, Merchant's footwork was said to be precise. The batting gharana of Bombay was formed on the solid ground of the Merchant school of batsmanship. It is the base, the essence and the spirit of Bombay batsmanship all at once.

Bombay owes Merchant much more than the technique and rigour that he instilled into the team, due to which those batsmen to follow him for years after him will idolize him and continue bringing laurels to Bombay. Merchant was also a visionary. It was he who mooted the idea of playing matches in the monsoon. He felt that it would help batsmen when they toured England. And yes, the monsoon league helped immensely in making the batsmen more Khaddoos. Most of the time, the pitching of every delivery will lead to spurts of mud flying off the ground, and a team score of seventy was considered a winning score.

The next major era in Bombay cricket was in the 1960s when the group of Dilip Sardesai and Ajit Wadekar emerged. They were part of the team that won the national championship for fifteen consecutive years. Sardesai was from Goa and no sooner did he come to Bombay, he was spotted by his Wilson College coach 'Manya' Naik who had a good eye for talent.

Sardesai's footwork was as soothing as cool water sprayed on tired eyes. He did not do anything in half measures – either forward or back. If you flight the ball, he would step out and drive, just like another batsman, Ramnath Kenny. Coach 'Manya' Naik felt that Sardesai made one crucial error in his career – of opting to open the innings. When he didn't succeed, he went back to playing in the middle order but his return to his original position of fame wasn't to be smooth and seamless. He failed miserably after the famous tour of West Indies in 1971.

Watching Sardesai face the new ball, the connoisseurs of the game would smile self-satisfyingly thinking to themselves that India has found a genuine opening batsman. It has to be remembered that this was at a time when India was truly struggling to get a good international opening batsman because Pankaj Roy had just retired.

Nari Contractor was the captain on the West Indies tour and he was deeply impressed with Sardesai's approach to the new ball. Sardesai was seriously being marked as the permanent future opener for India. However, fate had different things in store for

Sardesai and he soon started to fail as an opener. To get back in the middle order was going to be a mighty difficult task and Sardesai couldn't make it big again.

Ajit Wadekar was Sardesai's contemporary. A stylish left-handed batsman from Shivaji Park, Wadekar had never even played school cricket. For such a person to enter mainstream cricket is exceptional because there was tremendous competition at the school level itself.

Wadekar had joined the prestigious Elphinstone College which had a strong cricket team. One day he met his Shivaji Park friend Baloo Gupte who went on to play for India as a leg-spinner. Gupte had an offer for Wadekar. He said that if Wadekar becomes the twelfth man for the college matches, he could get Rs 3 as lunch allowance. Wadekar was tempted and agreed. Wadekar had never thought or dreamt of playing cricket. He was a student of science and was devoted to his studies.

Soon, however, Wadekar happened to switch over to Ruia College. The coach 'Joe' Kamath at the college was well known for making good choices when it came to talent. He saw Wadekar and selected him for the college team. No sooner did he get selected, Wadekar began to exhibit his talent. Everything about Wadekar's play was stylish – his walk from the pavilion to the middle, his drives, pulls and cuts, everything had his own brand stamped on it. Moreover, Wadekar was an extremely alert slip fielder with sharp reflexes.

He always managed to amaze everyone with his ability to attack the opposition with consistency. In his dictionary, the nightwatchman slot never existed. Even if there were two balls to go before close of play, he would himself go out to the middle. 'Why sacrifice a player who is not good enough to bat when you are playing as a batsman?' he would say. The confidence he showed along with responsible batsmanship is commendable. His famous Ranji Trophy knock of 323 against the likes of Prasanna and Chandrasekhar at the Brabourne stadium exhibited his range of shots. One of the big question marks in the fat book of Bombay history is: why did Wadekar not succeed as a batsman at the international level?

The 1971 tour of West Indies made Sardesai known as the renaissance man of Indian cricket. But a young twenty-one-year-old Sunil Gavaskar was just around the corner. Fresh from inter-university cricket, the future Little Master of Indian cricket was just about to be discovered. Gavaskar had an aura about him which could be felt by every fan of Bombay cricket.

Cricket ran in Gavaskar's blood. He was the nephew of former India stumper Madhav Mantri. Since an early age, Gavaskar came to be known in school-cricketing circles as someone who is able to score centuries at will. A man who was short in stature but hardly in the effect he caused, Gavaskar continued to consistently score in three digits. Be it at the inter-university level or the inter-zonal Vizzy Trophy, Gavaskar would get mounds of runs.

Gavaskar was among the typical Bombay kids who grew up on the staple diet of the maxim of 'stay at the wicket and runs will flow'. However, though Gavaskar's batting was initially based on fine technique of defence, he had his shots in the right places. Once he settled down, he would play shots with grace and poise. There were very few shots that Gavaskar couldn't produce with elan. When he came to open the innings, the team felt a strength that is indescribable in words.

Genius that he was, Gavaskar never ever took batting for

granted. Since his teenage days, he was very particular and fastidious about every single tenet of technique. When he practised as a young boy, he would try hard to locate the area where he went wrong, and once identified, he would almost obsessively shadow-practise till he was absolutely confident that he had got the technique right.

Gavaskar happened to be the key figure for India to play a horde of drawn games. It has to be understood that a draw at those times was as difficult to achieve as a win today. India's batting used to struggle and Gavaskar became the sheet anchor to hold things together. Though Viv Richards came to be widely known as the batsman who dared to play without wearing a helmet, Gavaskar too didn't wear a helmet. However, there was one point in his career when he started sporting a skull cap. Whether it was for technical reasons or fashionable ones, only Gavaskar can tell us.

Gavaskar was a genius but his genius was not his own. He was the product of a series of legends of Bombay cricket. Gavaskar was a product of Merchant, Manjrekar and Sardesai and many other great cricketers of Bombay who had bequeathed the legacy, the conditions, for Gavaskar to come and play. Later, Gavaskar too became an inspiration for many other cricketers from Bombay – a story that is well known too. Can there be a finer example of legacy?

In the shadow of the compact Gavaskar grew a tall player who became famous as Dilip Vengsarkar. The skinny teenager from the bylanes of the Hindu Colony in Dadar was notorious for troubling bowlers much elder to him. He would blast their deliveries to all corners of the ground. Vengsarkar pursued his passion and talent and soon joined the famous Dadar Union club where Gavaskar used to open with the aggressive Ramnath Parkar.

With an upright stance, Vengsarkar preferred to play the ball on the up. However, he loved aerial shots while playing spinners. If the bowler made the mistake of tossing up a delivery even marginally, Vengsarkar would be seen out of the crease in a flash and in the next moment one would see the ball sailing over the boundary.

Vengsarkar was noted as a special player from early on. He did exceedingly well in inter-university matches and got to make his first-class debut soon. However, on his debut match, he got out for a blob. Since the middle order was jammed with competition, there were high chances that his failure on debut would mean the end of his career. The competition in Bombay was so tough that even a player like Gavaskar was dropped after his failure in the Irani Cup of 1968. In fact, Gavaskar had to wait for another two years to get his voice heard.

Fortunately, immediately after his return to the Bombay team, he accompanied the Bombay team to play the Irani Cup at Nagpur. Chasing a modest score of 210 versus the Rest of India team, Bombay lost three wickets, that of Gavaskar, Ramnath Parkar and Sudhir Naik. It was in such a situation that Vengsarkar walked in to join Ashok Mankad.

One over before the tea break, Vengsarkar found himself on a slow turner. And facing him was the worst thing a batsman could expect: the combination of Bedi and Erappalli Prasanna. For them, Vengsarkar was just one more batsman whose wicket they had to bag. They just had to capture his wicket and increase their goody bag. However, when Vengsarkar walked out of the pavilion after tea, no one had an inkling as to what the world-class spinners were going to be put through. Vengsarkar had the time of his life that day. Time and again, he danced down the wicket to clear the ground with towering sixes.

His mastery was his control over the willow in his hand and while his ground shots pierced the field like lightning, his lofted shots defied wind direction. That day, Nagpurkars were reminded of Col. C.K. Nayudu. It was the day of the arrival of a new star who would go on to play 116 Tests for the country and continue to serve the game over years and years to come.

Ashok Mankad was senior to both Gavaskar and Vengsarkar. Ashok Mankad became known as a prolific run-scorer on the domestic circuit. He put a high price on his wicket and created a reputation of being a run machine. He could analyse situations astutely and almost immediately, and then handle them with wisdom. More than the technicality of batting, Mankad was known as the Mike Brearley of Bombay. 'Give him ten donkeys and he would win you a game,' people would say. He was the go-getter. He made sure things are done. However, like Sardesai, he too succumbed to the temptation of opening the innings. It is from that point that his downfall started. It was only after the downfall that he would realize the huge difference between first-class cricket within India and the game at the international level.

Mankad had the spark of a true leader. Had he succeeded at the international level, he would have surely led the country. Robust at strategy, he would always be on the prowl to overpower the opposition. No sooner did he notice a small chink in the technique or the mental state of the opposition batsman, he would instil his bowlers with confidence and venom.

Just as Gavaskar was bidding goodbye to international cricket, a new set of geniuses had arrived on the horizons of Bombay cricket. Three youngsters – Sanjay Manjrekar, Sachin Tendulkar and Vinod Kambli – had hijacked the sports pages of newspapers with some impact knocks. Tendulkar was in a different league but when Kambli and he got going together, they made a partnership of such stature that bowling to them seemed purely a waste of time. Their humungous partnership has got the celebration it deserves, but it was not the big totals that made Tendulkar. It was the struggle.

Sanjay Manjrekar like his father believed in the old approach. His father ensured that Sanjay didn't thoughtlessly aim at just accelerating the score, an approach that was becoming fashionable in that era. Defence became an obsession for junior Manjrekar, to the extent that he forgot his shots. He showed only a few glimpses of it in the West Indies and later in Pakistan.

Vinod Kambli was a huge talent that got washed away because he just couldn't handle fame. The tremendous ball sense that he possessed made bowlers look like buffoons. But perhaps Kambli was an exception to the Bombay gharana of batsmanship.

Kapil Dev feels that Bombay batsmen were the best at handling pressure. He says, 'They could handle it better than anybody else because they played with a free mind. When you have depth in your team you can always play better. They played tough cricket and that is what allowed them to handle pressure better. Ability to handle pressure and attitude are tested when your team is struggling and when making twenty runs looks bigger than scoring a century under different conditions. Sunil Gavaskar was one player who could build an innings under pressure. Sachin wasn't known for finishing. But in fact if you see his performance, he hasn't done too badly while handling pressure. Vengsarkar thrived on pressure which got the best out of him.'

Sandeep Patil was a contemporary of Dilip Vengsarkar. He began his first-class career as a medium pacer who batted lower down. In one of the local matches against Mafatlal, captain Ashok Mankad saw potential in this aggressive batsman. He was literally toying with quality Mafatlal bowling. Next thing that Mankad did was in the quarter-final match against Uttar Pradesh: Patil was promoted to number five in the Bombay team. Patil failed miserably but Mankad had so much faith in his ability that he asked him to bat at the same number in the next match against Delhi and when Bombay lost three quick wickets, Patil strode out and scored 139 with some breathtaking shots.

Though personal problems cut short his international career, he played some unforgettable knocks in Test cricket against England and Australia. After being hit on the head by Len Pascoe at Adelaide in the 1980 series, he returned to the crease after receiving treatment and hit Aussie fast bowlers out of the attack while scoring a gutsy 174.

At Old Trafford he similarly hit Bob Willis and others to score a brilliant 129. He was an entertainer and would have relished the T20 format. As Vengsarkar and Patil were going out of the game, there emerged the lot of Amol Muzumdar and Wasim Jaffer.

Tall and elegant, Wasim Jaffer is an artist. As a teenager he didn't have to manufacture any shots. He could judge the line and length of deliveries early and employ perfectly balanced shots between two fielders. As he matured, he became more consistent especially at picking deliveries which he could dispatch to the boundary. In his very second Ranji match, he scored a triple hundred against Saurashtra.

A back-foot player who could murder any type of bowling on surfaces conducive to top-class fast bowling, he had no problems negotiating pace and bounce. He scored two double hundreds in international cricket but was dropped when in one series he was sorted out on the front foot. The fast bowlers kept pitching up and the great driver of the ball was found wanting against the wobbling ball.

Perhaps the national selectors were looking for an opener who could block one end up as Sehwag from the other end would inevitably and unfailingly play an attacking game. One can understand that the selectors didn't want both openers to attack, although the example of Gordon Greenidge and Desmond Haynes, who were both attacking batsman and yet forged one of the best opening partnerships in world cricket, comes to mind.

Amol Muzumdar was a prodigy. On first-class debut, while scoring 260, he showed class and maturity. He loved occupying the crease and like Kambli played big. Batting at number four for Bombay, this technically sound batsman rarely failed in the season. In succeeding seasons he would diligently pile on the scores but was most unfortunate not to earn an India cap. With Dravid, Tendulkar, Ganguly and Laxman showing consistency in scoring runs, there was no place for Muzumdar.

Almost after a decade, when he finally had a poor season, Muzumdar was axed by the Bombay selection committee. Recounting the season, he wrote an emotional piece in *Wisden Asia* in 2004:

4, 28, 7, 12, 33, 17, 14, 38, 5... the scores read, 'Amol is Finished' was the call from all corners. In Mumbai, if a batsman has such scores there is no mercy shown to him and so it should be! But was it really the end for me??..... was I really finished???...by the end of the season, thoughts like these began to crowd my mind.

During the 10 years of cricket that I have played for Mumbai, I have averaged over 55. It is not easy to keep motivating yourself year after year without getting the desired results. The season of 2002-03 really shook me; the only satisfying moment was that we had regained the prestigious Ranji Trophy.

He went on to recount the fact that in 2001-02 he was the highest run getter for Bombay and how he failed to play any big knock in 2002-03. But he was determined to make a comeback. He left for England in May 2004 to represent the Bishop Auckland club in Durham. Following coach Ramakant Achrekar's dictum that 'batting is nothing but just concentration', he started training with rigorous workout and strict discipline – long hours of batting sessions and hard fielding practice. He also took seriously this author's suggestion that he should practise batting in the front 'V'. The programme proved effective and gradually he started accumulating runs.

But to his disappointment, Amol did not find a place in the Bombay squad to play the Irani Cup matches in 2004. But that did not diminish one bit his determination to get back into the Bombay team. His excellent performance in the Times Shield tournament, with the highest personal score of 175 not out, ensured that finally he was back in the Bombay team for the

Ranji Trophy. In the match against Andhra Pradesh, he scored 115 runs. Though he had narrowly missed scoring tons on three consecutive occasions, he entered the finals with an air of confidence and scored 146 runs.

Muzumdar ended his long article saying:

Each one of you will have to find your own success formulae. You have to keep strictly following and implementing it. My success formula has been, physical training + playing in the 'V' zone + hanging ball + meditation + visualization. Visualize your dream and your body follows it...

It is indeed a very touching piece of writing. Eventually, when he was dropped for the Ranji final in 2009, he went over to Assam and later to Andhra and emerged as the leading scorer of the Ranji Trophy.

From Vijay Merchant to Sachin Tendulkar, how many players has Bombay seen come and go? But these are such players who never truly go, in a sense. Once they have arrived, they can only go leaving their footprints behind. But footprints only indicate where this team has been. What about the future of this great batting gharana? Let us try to understand where the batting of Bombay is headed and the pros and cons of the changes we are witnessing. Who will represent this future and what are the changes they will bring to the game?

Well, one sees a lot of promise manifested in the form of batsmen like Ajinkya Rahane and Rohit Sharma. These are a new breed of Bombay batsmen. Owing to the rise of different formats of cricket and the frequency with which the formats change in a given season these batsmen have a different game from the classicists of the gharana – the likes of Vijay Manjrekar, Sunil Gavaskar and others. They are prone to attacking the bowlers at times and play shots whenever the opportunity arises. These are also batsmen who graft shots even of good balls. With that preliminary description, one is compelled to say that these young batsmen are not inheritors of the legacy of the Bombay gharana. Then could it be that Bombay is at the end of its great batting legacy? Is it the end of the batting gharana of Bombay?

The emergence of the T20 format, Indian Premier League (IPL) and increased frequency of One Day International (ODI) matches necessitate that batsmen of the modern era add more arrows to their quiver. The traditional ideas regarding batting in Bombay need to be updated. With the need to score quickly in the shorter formats, batsmen can no longer employ the same strategies as was done by the greats of the game in the past.

Bombay batsmen relied on skill and technique to win matches. With their airtight defence they would grind bowlers down. Once the bowlers were tired, it was time to capitalize and pile up runs. The phrase 'pile up runs' is not an exaggeration here. It was the strategy of Bombay often to bat the opposition out of the match. This meant batting cautiously in the beginning and scoring runs once the bowlers were tired.

The modern game does not necessarily allow the luxury of time to the batsmen. The shorter formats compel them to develop a fluid or attacking style of play. This style of play at times is at the cost of technique and safety. Hence the approach of the young guns such as Rohit Sharma and Ajinkya Rahane is not entirely their fault, or even a fault at all in the modern game.

However, such shuffling between different formats affects the technique and game plans of batsmen. Organizing an innings in different formats requires adaptation. This has become one of the measures of the modern-day batsmen. The shuffling between the formats is also a challenge for them. It is here that a slight difference emerges between the two batsmen. Rohit Sharma's batting is easy on the eyes. He has time to play his shots and they always flow from his bat. However, it seems that this is mostly true on good batting wickets. On seaming pitches in an aggressive batting style he thrusts his front leg down the wicket which encourages bowlers to bowl in the corridor of uncertainty. His Bombay colleague on the other hand is a predominantly back-foot player who covers the movement of the seaming delivery well. Both are attacking batsmen – Ajinkya Rahane too can change gears when required, but what sets them apart slightly, comes down to adaptation. In this matter Rahane scores over Rohit Sharma.

This is not a challenge exclusive to Bombay batsmen but all modern-day players. One can say that the most demanding aspect of professional sport in the twenty-first century is the calendar. Many, if not all, struggle to adapt perfectly. While we see some shot making in Test cricket, we also witness the defence of many batsmen not being as tight as we are used to seeing in Test cricket of the past. But the formats necessitate this change in approach, albeit the new approach does not represent the tenets of the Bombay gharana of batting.

However, to simply say that is not enough: we all know the troubles a team can run into in a Test match or series if batsmen are short on technique. Five days can seem very long. Perhaps the last in the line of the gharana is Wasim Jaffer. A technician who uses his wrists and has the ability to place the ball in the gaps on either side of the wicket, always opens his innings by looking to play straight. Having settled at the crease he unrolls his scoring shots off the back foot. It is this ability to drop anchor at the crease in the beginning of the innings and then play scoring shots that makes a successful batsman. It is possible mostly because of the technique. It allows the batsmen to be in the most optimum position for a shot, thereby drawing the best results from a shot. This is true of Wasim Jaffer too.

While it is true that when we talk about the Bombay batting gharana we are mostly referring to the past, it might not be all that futile to look at some examples of the past for relevant lessons for the modern-day batsmen. The likes of Wadekar and Vengsarkar come to mind. Both of them could score freely and play an attacking innings. But they would set up the foundation of such an innings on their defence early in the innings, and eventually go on to pile up runs. While it is true that these batsmen did not have to hop from format to format in their time like Rahane or Sharma have to these days, it does not make the lesson any less relevant. Like any metaphor or analogy, there will always be some aspects that remain exclusive to each domain or part of the aspects being compared. This is true when juxtaposing two eras too. However, we must focus on the parts that do intersect or overlap and that is the issue of technique as a prerequisite even to build an attacking innings.

While we may be sympathetic to the changes made by the

generation of Rohit Sharma and Ajinkya Rahane, one does not want to see the spirit of the Bombay cricketer slip away – the 'Khaddoos' who finds a way to win regardless of the challenge at hand. As important as it is to have technique as an international batsman, to obsess over it can only take one so far.

Connoisseurs and classicists cherish technicians for their ability as well as the aesthetics they bring to the game. A technically correct batsman is a handsome batsman to watch. He is pleasing to the eye. Sanjay Manjrekar comes to mind in this regard. He was a technically sound batsman. After proving himself against the formidable bowling attacks of the West Indies and Pakistan of that era, Sanjay Manjrekar slowly came to a halt. His obsession with technique drove him to defend the entire time and drop anchor at the crease so much so that even against ordinary domestic bowling attacks he missed opportunities to score. Perhaps that's the way he was brought up by his technically sound father Vijay. But one mustn't forget that during the period from the 1950s to the 1970s, when Vijay played, cricket was based on sound technique. And Vijay Manjrekar was one of the best batsmen around then. As Mansur Ali Khan Pataudi once said, the width of the bat looked much wider when Vijay batted: so perfect was he in batting. Keeping apart the aggressive players like Sharma and Rahane, we can contrast Sanjay Majrekar's play to other technicians such Vengsarkar who never missed an opportunity to score or put the bad ball away.

However, technique alone is not what competitive sports are about. It is only one of the building blocks to achieve the target – victory. The other important building block is temperament. It is in this regard that we may look back and look at a player like Manohar Hardikar. He was never pleasing to watch but

had a very good temperament, and found ways to score in
difficult conditions. Sure enough, when the conditions were
alien or tough Hardikar would perform well. This was due to
the temperament of Hardikar. The determination and the desire
to do well and to succeed is what helped the performances of
Hardikar. This stomach to put up a fight is just as important in
competitive sport as technique. Different players have the two
in different proportions but it is a mix of the two that leads to the
success of a player in professional sport.

It is in this context that Ajinkya Rahane and Rohit Sharma
have to sort out their respective techniques and find the strengths
in their game to score runs. As long as they do not let the
Khaddoos spirit leave them, they will continue to be batsmen
of the Bombay gharana.

The memories and contributions of the greats leave a mark
not only on the scorecards in golden letters but on every young
heart that happens to come in touch with them. Bombay
youngsters are literally bred on watching such geniuses. It is this
legacy that is at the foundation of players like Rohit Sharma and
Ajinkya Rahane and many other Bombay youngsters practising
today on the maidans of Bombay. It is almost as much a part of
their growing up as a glass of milk in the morning.

Bombay youngsters have the opportunity to walk the fields
that the greatest of greats have, and the field offers them many,
many lessons to learn. The field itself is burdened with the
amount of history it holds. It can't help but pass it on to others.
Bombay is not about a team, about eleven or fifteen great players.
If that was the case, it wouldn't have won the Ranji Trophy again
and again for years together with a multitude of players. Bombay
cricket is a gharana, a training school where knowledge is passed

as if it was the lesson of life. Cricketing techniques are taught as if they will come in handy in saving life one day.

Bombay cricket is a big family, a family which is replete with people who are happy to pass on their genius to others. This is precisely why the talent bed of Bombay never gets barren. Greats retire but there are always new players waiting in the wings. We feel bad when greats go, we think that replacement for them is out of the question, and yet often new players take the team – and our imaginations – by storm. This only makes us realize that life goes on, and that we have to keep learning and, most importantly passing on what we have learnt.

In Bombay, we see players who are as unique as players can be. They all have a distinct style of their own, be it their characteristic swagger or elegance with which they play, or their very own dialect to the language of cricket. But it is this very unique language of Bombay cricket, where the training in the grammar of the language is compulsory and unfailing, that binds these dialects together. Players are bags full of charm. But the cord of hard work and determination strings them all together into one gharana of Bombay cricket. Bombay cricket is as incomplete without them as they are without the shelter of Bombay cricket. Together, they form one of the most productive and successful communities in world cricket.

3

THE SUCCESS MANTRA OF BOMBAY CRICKET

The success of Bombay cricket is as overwhelming to the present-day supporters of the sport as it was to their opponents during Bombay cricket's golden years, rather decades. We have spoken about the batting legacy of Bombay cricket and decades of talent that Bombay produced. To this, add the statistics of eighty Ranji finals, forty of which ended with victories for Bombay – fifteen of them in a row. Moreover, their closest rivals in the Ranji finals, Rajasthan, who faced off against Bombay in the finals for seven times were defeated every single time. So there is no need to explain the success of Bombay cricket against other teams.

The point of briefly reiterating the astonishing feats of Bombay cricket is to acknowledge the fact that for historians, archivists, connoisseurs and lovers of the game alike, this scenario may be hard to comprehend and the task of trying to repaint this picture from the viewpoint of the present is, no doubt, harder. The task leaves so much to the imagination that the achievements of Bombay cricket through those decades seem unbelievable. However, the numbers, statistics, mentioned above testify to this success. While we may concede the numbers, it is still difficult to comprehend such domination. Statistics will be at the end. It is precisely this aspect of the narrative that makes the story worth telling. But let me hasten to clarify that as magical as the results appear to be, the means with which they were achieved were very real.

As with any magical story, one never wants to explain away all of the effects, for it is this mystery that allows us to be inspired and for more such accomplishments to be conceived, as well achieved. However, it is equally wrong to not acknowledge the labour, the sweat and the brilliance that went into the foundation of such a regal cricketing castle.

In this chapter this is precisely what we will try to accomplish.

Cricket is hardly about statistics. Those are there just to point to the real game. The wins are, in fact, the symptoms of something else. Shouldn't there be a deeper truth explaining Bombay's run at the Ranji Trophy? Shouldn't there be some reason that explains why after all it was Bombay that won year after year after year? Shouldn't there be a success mantra, a magical formula that has made this miracle possible? India is a country of mantras after all. There must be a mantra. What do the connoisseurs have to say about this?

Dilip Sardesai was one person who was part of the team that won the trophy for fifteen years on the trot. He attributed Bombay's famous run to captain Polly Umrigar. Sardesai said: 'He had a simple answer to every question about his leadership: "Why play the game if you are not keen to win?" Umrigar believed in winning matches. All his strategy, planning, selection of players, batting slots, bowling changes had one common motivation and that is to win the game. He was a shrewd captain and pretty tough off the field too. When on top, he believed in crushing the opposition. He didn't let his players relax even for a second. He was very methodical – he urged his players to execute the plans and one must say his plans were realistic. Let there be a club or office or first-class match, Polly was tough.'

There is more to the mantra than what Sardesai had said. Umrigar commanded immediate respect because of his performances, and personality. He did not care about who the opposition were, and utilized his resources discretely. It is another thing that Umrigar was lucky to be the captain of a team with strong players. But it wasn't just about luck; there was good captaincy underneath it. As he put it: 'I had told my players that when they play for Bombay they must take pride in their performances.'

It was Umrigar who inculcated the winning culture in Bombay. But call it modesty or legacy, Umrigar attributes the credit to Madhav Mantri, his senior. Mantri, uncle of Sunil Gavaskar, was very disciplined. He read the game well and he excelled in strategy. It was he who began team meetings. His discipline showed through in his captaincy too. He directed the players on the field, getting them to play according to his plans. This disciplined approach would go on inculcating the winning ways in the Bombay team. 'That approach helped us perform better,' says Sardesai who played under Mantri for the Associated Cement Companies.

'No quarter asked, no quarter given' was Bombay's policy. To the outsider, it seemed that Bombay was always on the prowl. It would seem that Bombay is waiting to snatch opportunities like a hungry tiger. Bombay's strength was in pouncing on the opposition whenever they saw the slightest of scope. But the truth is that, spontaneous as it might have seemed, strategies would have already been planned meticulously in the practice sessions. Mantri's practice sessions were like rehearsals of a match. What he planned for a match, he would get his players to practise. He said, 'When we prepare for an examination, don't we study as per the plan. We don't prepare on the morning of the paper. Cricket is similar.' He was the perfect example of a man who did not leave the smallest of margins for error.

Umrigar imbibed the qualities of his guru well. He absorbed all the discipline and knew how to handle a team. Whether it was a weak team like Saurashtra or a stronger team like Rajasthan, the regime of perfect practice under Umrigar was a lovely sight. The practice was more planned than a match can be! There was never noise or useless laughter. The players would seriously prepare for the match and the confidence could be seen shining on their faces on match days.

Bombay was the toughest of the tough teams. But its reign did not go unchallenged. If any team offered a competition to Bombay at any time it was Rajasthan, especially in the Ranji finals. Rajasthan did everything in their might to win. They tried all the tricks of the trade but one by one, and seven times in all, the contest ended with Bombay ruthlessly crushing their opponent. What is the reason for this? Biased critics say that Bombay bowlers bowled a negative line, that they are happy winning on first innings' lead alone. This I think is being unfair to the Bombay team. Sure, they can be very dogged, with their backs to the wall, but the truth is that the thought of being negative never enters their mind. That is just not the way Bombay players are bred. They are raised with a dose of optimism.

Ashok Mankad was another shrewd captain in Bombay's long list of smart men. He explains their sound strategy: 'We all learnt from Polly kaka to assess situations and act accordingly. Retreat and attack are the two aspects of any strategy. Now, if retreating to thwart the opposition is termed as negative I don't know my cricket. During the time I played for Bombay, we attacked even when we were three down for nothing because we just didn't let the opposition to come back.' Once Bombay lost three quick wickets immediately after the 1976 Ranji final started against Delhi at Ferozshah Kotla but Ashok Mankad and Rakesh Tandon didn't defend. They transferred the pressure on the opposition by keeping the scoreboard ticking.

However, any talk of the implementation of strategy will be incomplete without mentioning Ashok's father, Vinoobhai. One match makes for the best of stories. It was against the star-studded Hyderabad team with Jaisimha, Pataudi, Abbas Ali Baig and Abid Ali. Bombay had conceded a lead of sixty-odd runs and in the four-day knockout match Hyderabad was leading by a few runs at the end of the second day.

Ashok remembers that evening after he came back from the match: 'I sat to remove my shoes. But before I could remove them Vinoobhai asked me the score.

'I said "Vinoobhai, we have lost on first innings".

'He stared at me. "What's your plan?" he asked.

'"What can anyone plan in a match when the opposition is leading by sixty runs and they have all big players?" I replied.'

Within half an hour, Vinoobhai called out to Ashok in the shower. 'Come Ashok, I have a plan: attack from the first ball; convert ones in twos and twos into threes; put them under pressure and declare after getting 150–160 runs lead.'

Ashok was not brave enough to counter his father. He nodded.

The next day when he conveyed Vinoobhai's plan to his deputy Sudhir Naik, he didn't agree. 'Such a strong team and you are going to get them out in 150 runs. No way,' Naik said. When Vinoo Mankad came to watch the game after lunch, he was shocked to see Bombay still batting. Language gets the most creative in situations of distress. And that day Vinoo's language gave jitters to the team. Ashok was forced to declare and soon enough Bombay won the match outright.

Vinoobhai had the uncanny knack of reading the game even without having to watch it. Once, a young Mafatlal team was playing against a strong ACC team. The Mafatlals were bundled out for less than 150 which was evidently gettable for the ACC which had Umrigar, Nadkarni, Sardesai and others. It was a one-and-a-half day game. That evening again, when Ashok came home, Vinoobhai asked him about the score and the plan. Ashok replied in the best way he could, but Vinoobhai had his own theory:

'Look, Ashok, when Polly comes to bat, he will ask for a runner because he is getting old. Don't give it to him. Once you give him a runner, he will ensure he is there till the target.' Ashok was in a quandary because Polly was like a family member. Polly was adored. How could Ashok say no to Polly kaka? At the fall of the first wicket Umrigar came to bat. The moment he arrived at the crease, he asked Ashok for runner. Vinoobhai was right; he had read Umrigar correctly.

Now, Ashok faced a huge dilemma in front of him. If he defied Vinoobhai by agreeing to give a runner to Umrigar, and if ACC won the game, Vinoobhai would come down hard on him. At the same time, if he denied a runner to one of the seniormost Test players of the country, Ashok would be severely criticized. Eventually, Ashok mustered enough courage to decline a runner to Umrigar who was shocked and obviously angry. Umrigar had an insistent habit of wanting to score off the first ball he faced. Vinoobhai had told Ashok to refuse a runner and get all the fielders in the circle so that a run of the first ball wasn't possible. Under pressure, Polly ran for a non-existent single and was run out at the other end. Mafatlal won the match.

As Ashok remembers, 'This was nothing but a mind game which I wasn't aware of as a youngster. By refusing a runner, I hurt the ego of Umrigar who was a great player. Secondly, the time spent by both of us in arguing upset him more. Third, seeing so many players in the circle got to his nerves. One could sense his anger and in that frame of mind, he ran for a single and he was run out. From that incident I learnt to play within the rules and not bother about the reputation of the opposition player.'

That Bombay reigns as the undisputed champion of domestic cricket, having won the Ranji Trophy forty times is surprising when we account for the victories of the others. Karnataka have won the trophy seven times, Delhi six times and Hyderabad and Tamil Nadu two times each. These teams have also had some great international players. In fact, these teams have been abysmal against Bombay. No good team would take a match lightly. It is obvious these teams would have to give their best to try and beat Bombay, but they have failed to effect it. One wonders what the opposition was thinking all along in the glorious days of Bombay cricket. It is but natural that a certain battle of egos would emerge once in a while.

It is true that many of the grand comebacks of Bombay have been because of the fault of the opposition. They have often offered the space to Bombay to bounce back. Bombay had lost five wickets without scoring a single run in the second innings of the Ranji semi-final against Baroda once. And yet, Bombay was let off eventually! Jacob Martins proved to be absolutely unimaginative. Here were the pacers, Irfan Pathan and Rakesh Patel, performing magic with the ball and Martins removed them and instead introduced spinners. And Bombay, champions of comebacks that they are, scored rapidly and Baroda was under pressure.

This really can't be said of other states. For starters, no one can remotely compete with the number of tournaments Bombay has. At a given instance in a year, around 25,000 registered cricketers play 100-odd tournaments. Thus, in a year, 3,100 matches are played on ninety-eight different grounds in Bombay. Out of eighty tournaments, at least twelve are of the most supreme quality.

The captain has always been an anchoring figure in the fate of Bombay's various teams. The captain debates with his players and selectors but in the end takes a strong call by himself. Many a time, captains take major decisions on the basis of sheer gut feeling. It does fail at times, but as the famous proverb goes, fortune favours the brave. Sometimes, captains have become lifetime celebrities because of one major decision they took based on their instinct. It happened in the case of Dilip Sardesai and he became a hero.

A simple decision of a captain has determined the fates of many a life. Captain Ajit Wadekar was given the choice between Sardesai and Chandu Borde for the 1971 tour of West Indies. Vijay Merchant was the head of the selection committee then. Now, Wadekar was faced with a dilemma. Both Sardesai and Borde had been to West Indies in 1962 and they were both experienced. In the end, Wadekar opted for Sardesai and the media went berserk. Their allegation was that Wadekar chose Sardesai because he was from Bombay.

As it turned out, the same Sardesai was the one responsible for India's unbelievable win in the series. No wonder he began to be called the renaissance man of Indian cricket. After the hullabaloo settled down, Wadekar broke his silence on the issue and criticism. 'I had played with Dilip from the university days and his game perfectly fit in my strategy because not only was he in form at that time of selection, but had the experience of West Indian pitches.'

This is the thought process of a Bombay captain. It is not individuals who are chosen. It is not each player's individual capacities and talents that are considered. What is chosen is an individual's contribution to the team. The team is the focus, not the individual. While choosing the team, they decide whether a player is capable of fulfilling his role in the team. 'Role play' in Bombay cricket is very important. In the end, it is the entire team that has to win the match.

Former Bombay captain Milind Rege presents a different

perspective about why Bombay players don't succumb to pressure against even the toughest opposition. He says: 'The single largest contributing factor to the success of Bombay winning the Ranji Trophy on forty occasions is the Times of India tournament. This is the heartbeat of Bombay cricket. Over the years the Tatas, ACC, State Bank, Mafatlal, Nirlon, Indian Oil and Air India have been singularly responsible for players getting jobs and thereby relieving the players of any tension regarding their futures. The Bombay cricketer has always been confident of displaying his skills as he was pitted against the best.

'Never was he ever daunted by reputations. And why should he? He played with giants like Umrigar, Wadekar, Gavaskar, Vengsarkar, Patil, Nadkarni, Sardesai, Mankad, Shivalkar, Gupte, Manjrekar and Tendulkar to name a few and against Pataudi, Salim Durrani, Budhi Kunderan, Hanumant Singh, Brijesh Patel, Abid Ali, G. Vishwanath, Syed Kirmani and many more. Competition was at its stiffest and no quarter was either given or asked for. So when he faced a situation he was never daunted by reputation. That made the Bombay cricketer a tough nut to crack.

'"Khaddoos" is the famous term that he coined for himself. To add to it all, the opportunities that he got were far too few; you failed once and never got a look in again. He therefore had to hang on to that chance and make the most of it. Gavaskar failed in his first attempt and had to wait for two years to get that break. Rubbing shoulders with and against the best made him a strong cricketer ready to face the toughest of challenges. To crown it all, the senior Bombay cricketer always had time for youngsters – he watched, guided and, more often than not, scolded one for "throwing it away".'

Coach Chandrakant Pandit, a former Bombay captain, says:

'Forming a strategy and implementing it meticulously is part of the Bombay cricket culture. It has something to do with Bombay's fast life. A drive for success can be seen even in maidan cricket. Even the club matches of Bombay form strategies a day before the game. When I played for the first time under Ashok Mankad, I saw him dish out move after move. All I had to do was observe these moves to learn. Ashok gave us, the youngsters in the team, the comfort of having confidence in us but when we let him down, he wouldn't spare us.'

With Ashok's guidance, Pandit developed a coaching model of his own. 'Like Ashok, I too would look out for the weaknesses of opposition players and our strengths. Temperament of opposition players was a very important factor for us at that time. Technical issues were discussed threadbare and then the attack would be ready with full force.'

Pandit was famous for the discipline he imposed both on and off the field. He does not just start to train a player's skill. Unless a player is first seen to be totally focused, no gyan can be given to him. Strategy can't be implemented without discipline. Pandit seems to echo Polly Umrigar. Umrigar too used to treat nets with the seriousness of a match. Whatever was expected to be implemented in the match had to be practised thoroughly in the net sessions.

Balvinder Singh Sandhu is definitely one of the best coaches in the country. But the department in which he is the best of the best is tactics. In the two seasons that he was the coach of the Bombay team, it won seven out of eight titles. Sandhu too was groomed by his seniors. Ashok Mankad and Sunil Gavaskar, two of his captains, were both tough captains who expected nothing less than 100 per cent from each player.

'Players would be picked on performance and temperament and once they are picked, they were expected to perform. And we were expected to bat and bowl strictly according to the team's strategies. Sanjay Manjrekar was the captain when I became the coach of the Bombay team. In the first team meeting I asked them if our team can field better than the Indian team. Everyone loudly said "Yessss". I firmly said, "This is not a joke. To be best in the country you will have to work hard." At the end of the season the entire team put together had dropped only two catches,' says Sandhu. It was not only about planning; it was about planning with passion.

That Bombay's USP lies in its formulation of strategies is something we have constantly been hearing. But how exactly are tactics formulated? What is the process of chalking out the defeat of the opposition? How does it work? Sandhu gives an example: 'In a match between Bombay and Australia, we were unable to stop the ball within the circle, and many of them would go all the way to the boundaries. Captain Sachin was very upset during the interval and told me to speak to the boys. I told them that since there is no limitation here about the number of players that can stand outside the thirty-yard circle; they should stand a little behind the mark. They were standing too close and were letting shots go through as they could not cut them off. Once they started to stand a little behind, they were in a position to anticipate the ball and stop it.'

Kapil Dev played a lot of matches with Bombay players. He puts our analysis of Bombay in a nutshell. 'Bombay players were always more professional than others. The professionalism was in terms of how to build an innings and how to play at the right time. Since they had dominated domestic cricket for almost

30–40 years they knew how to finish the game. They had a lot of talent and confidence and that is why they produced such great cricketers. Bombay cricketers were always ready to grab an opportunity unlike players from other parts of India. They had class and ability. They also had the advantage of former players who encouraged younger players.'

Ravi Shastri is a true product of Bombay's legacy of tough cricket. He takes us down the memory lane of his formation as a player. This is, in fact, the story of every Bombay player. 'When I played, one took pride in performing for Bombay. The work ethic was such that one worked extremely hard and then played to win. Hard cricket was the order of the day and the fact that Bombay had a great track record for winning was a huge incentive. A Bombay player plays a lot of cricket and at a young age struggles at the competition in club cricket. Whether it is inter-company or inter-club, we were all taught to win. Obviously, we had to tackle many situations. So having mastered the art of staying at the wicket and not giving anything away, we could handle the pressure situations in international cricket better.'

He recounts one incident that throws light on his analysis in a better way: 'In one innings on the tour of the West Indies, I had bowled twenty-eight long overs and taken four wickets. In the next innings, we lost a wicket on the first ball itself. The bowler was Marshall. At that time, I had barely changed my shirt. I was tired, having bowled those twenty-eight overs, and my feet just refused to move while batting. In front of me were four West Indies quickies: Marshall, Bishop, Ambrose and Walsh. However, I was determined to stay at the wicket that day, refusing to throw in the towel. And I survived with India reeling at sixty for six. The next day, with my mind alert and feet fresh, I went on to get a hundred.' However, what is most heartening in the story is that it is not his century that Shastri prizes most but the struggle on the day when he was completely exhausted. 'The real hard work was done the previous day itself.'

Mansur Ali Khan Pataudi has studied the cricket culture of Bombay. He played corporate and club cricket for a few years in Bombay. He has been on the receiving end of Bombay often. 'That a player could play for India but not for Bombay just shows the sort of standards we were talking about. They had the batting certainly and they would out-bat anybody. The bowling may not be there but if you are chasing 600 it wasn't that easy against Bombay. Gradually other teams caught up – Tamil Nadu, Karnataka... despite that Bombay still continued to win.... We have to go back to their strength for an answer, and Bombay's strength was its clubs and the system ... which was more professional than even southern cricketers.'

Well, the success mantra does exist and it is more real than we think it is. Bombay's stupendous record is not a mystical event that we cannot make sense of. There is no magic acting here, there is an actual adhesive holding the team together and it's real. The fact is that each and every one of the Bombay players knew their roles. The combination of specialized roles results in brilliant execution of strategy. In fact, the selectors rarely picked a novice. There have been many unfortunate players but the selectors believed in getting the combination right. The pattern of inter-club and inter-office tournaments was quite tough. In fact, it was said that if there was a Ranji match happening at the Brabourne stadium and a Tata vs ACC match at the nearby Parsi Gymkhana, the crowd would, in fact, be stuck to the Tata vs. ACC match. The level and spirit of competition was intense.

Those who performed consistently in the Times of India shield and inter-club matches could hope to get picked for the Bombay Ranji team. There was no compromise on skills in the case of batting or bowling or fielding. Even someone like Gavaskar did not get it easy in this Bombay team. He played his first class match in 1968 against Rest of India in the Irani Cup and failed in both the innings.

Also, to play for Bombay meant that there were no permanent batting numbers. One had to be prepared to bat at any number. The culture of winning had spread so deep in Bombay cricket that the players struggled hard to fit into the team. They fought till the last. Since getting into the team itself was so difficult, players valued their spots when they did get a look in. There were many occasions when the Test stars were away and newcomers had to replace them against strong Ranji states. But each time it was Bombay who won the Ranji Trophy because even the youngest were completely prepared. There was something in being a part of the Bombay team that made a player quite different.

The option of not performing didn't exist. In his debut match against a weak Gujarat team, a seventeen-year-old Vengsarkar got out without scoring a run. He had been picked for Bombay because of the commanding manner in which he scored. But now realizing that he had let go of his first and perhaps only opportunity, Vengsarkar wept bitterly in the makeshift tent of Bulsar. Spectators were surprised to see a player weeping.

However, scavengers of temperament as they are, the selectors seemed to not want to let go of Vengsarkar now that they had found that temperament. He was included in the Irani Cup at Nagpur a few days later. It was in this orange city that Vengsarkar hit a century that included seven towering sixes against the likes of Erappalli Prasanna and Bishan Singh Bedi. He didn't let the failure of the first match bother him and played scintillating strokes to well-flighted deliveries by dancing down the wicket. Bombay was three wickets down and the pitch was assisting spin.

And what is also true is that Vengsarkar never let go of the temperament he showed in his first match. Be it facing the blunt attack of Holding or any other ferocious fast bowler, he never flinched. Vengsarkar had gained a lot watching the batting of Gavaskar from the other end. When he opened for Dadar Union club his partner was Sunil Gavaskar. On the other hand, Sanjay Manjrekar grew as a batsman while watching Vengsarkar bat. This was the cycle of Bombay cricket, the cycle of partnerships, of togetherness. Partnerships sowed the seeds of Bombay cricket culture.

Cricket is not only about the national or the Ranji team for Bombay. The passion is not for celebrities and fanfare but at grass-roots level. Each club or a top office team had a cricketing culture. When senior players like Ashok Mankad, Parthsarathy Sharma, Eknath Solkar and Brijesh Patel were slowing down in their career, they made it a point to mould Lalchand Rajput, Chandrakant Pandit and Raju Kulkarni for the future. Also, there were many who benefited from playing with Sachin Tendulkar. Bombay survived and thrived on the experience of senior international players whose presence would rub off on the younger players.

The glory of Bombay reached its pinnacle when in 1998 Bombay beat world champions Australia comprehensively.

Vinod Kambli, Amol Muzumdar and others were all striving hard to declare that they were champions of the highest quality. When the Dadar Union product, Sanjay Manjrekar, became the Bombay captain, he made winning a habit. There was never room for a loss. Perhaps it is this confidence of Bombay that makes it so distinguishable and special. Certainly, this confidence borders the line of overconfidence and often plunges over as well. Bombay has paid the price for such indulgences. But at the end of the day, they save matches like no one else can. The unwillingness to give up comes from the excessive training, from the fact that an average Bombay player plays around fifty matches during the season from July to May itself. Rough conditions and hard work have prepared players for every challenge in a match; after all their real lives are strewn with bigger challenges which they gracefully combat every day.

The more people we hear, the more voices we will hear. If there is one thing that all these legends of the game agree on, it is the fact that Bombay is a really special team. But at the same time, it is not accidentally special but has developed itself consistently through the years to reach that stature. Bombay is what it is because of the love and heart of its players, coaches and well-wishers, which have moulded it into a team of geniuses over many, many years.

Bombay cricket is not about glamour, it is about hard work. The success mantra of Bombay, the magical wand of the team, is clear: 'There is no substitute to hard work'. And this precisely is the point I wanted to make in this chapter. Bombay has built castles in the history of Indian Cricket and the reason they have stood for so long and continue to stand is that none was built in the clouds. Bombay teams were the leaders, be it in the planning of their practice sessions or the matches, or be it in their work ethic or passion for the game. All of these factors combined with that unpredictable and elusive magical factor – tying together intelligent and talented players, and the tough city life with their hard work – to write a fairy tale in the annals of Indian sporting history. Need there be any other success mantra?

4

THE CONUNDRUM THAT IS BOMBAY BOWLING

The story and glory of Bombay cricket so far has revolved mostly around batsmen. That must be clear to every reader so far. From Vijay Merchant and Vijay Manjrekar to Sunil Gavaskar, from Dilip Vengsarkar to Sachin Tendulkar, Bombay has produced batsmen – batsmen who are not only competitive at the national level but are also truly world class. All this begs the question: where are the bowlers? The question perhaps is addressed too late in the book but is a fair one.

Even while discussing Bombay's triumphs while defending totals the emphasis has been on the 'Khaddoos-ness' of Bombay, the cricketing culture and attitude of the team, rather than the skill and guile of its bowlers. We speak of the pressure the team was able to create with tight bowling, chit-chat and good fielding rather than how the bowlers won Bombay the game. This is not a deliberate attempt at undermining the contribution of the bowlers to the success of Bombay cricket. Bombay had been blessed with many all-rounders who afforded the team balance and contributed to the victories. The likes of Vinoo Mankad, Dattu Phadkar, Polly Umrigar, G.S. Ramchand and Bapu Nadkarni come to mind. Amongst these, Mankad and Umrigar were also leaders whose acumen for the game brought out the best from their teams. However, the fact remains that they were players who would comfortably be categorized as all-rounders.

None of this is to ignore or undermine the role of bowlers. The likes of Padmakar Shivalkar, Ramakant Desai and Subhash Gupte come to mind immediately. However, the important distinction between the story of bowlers and batsmen of Bombay cricket is the representation at the international level. While generation after generation of Bombay batsmen have been considered in debates that accounted for the best in the world by experts and enthusiasts alike, we struggle to do the same with Bombay bowlers. This even the cricket fans know. It may not be true of those who witnessed and followed Bombay through those years, but it is true of most of us.

We first have to accept the fact that Bombay did not produce many bowlers who went on to thrive in the national team. The more difficult task is to explore the reasons or contexts that explain why that was the case, and continues to be the case. This is what I attempt to do in this chapter.

However, before we dive off at the deep end, let us also recognize that the problem of producing international-quality bowlers is not unique to Bombay; it has been the history of Indian cricket. The problem accentuates in overseas conditions. It is necessary to clarify that the purpose of this chapter is not to point an accusing finger at Bombay cricket specifically but discuss the context in which this problem is rooted.

While we agree that it is a good question to ask of Indian cricket as a whole including Bombay, let us consider if this question contains any unique significance with respect to Bombay cricket. There is no need to splatter the statistics that sing praise of the success of Bombay cricket here again. That has been well established. However, we all recognize cricket to be a team sport with three disciplines. If what we have considered so far is true, it goes that Bombay won the Ranji Trophy forty times and dominated national cricket for decades on the strength of only two disciplines, with functional contributions from the third. Every cricket lover and enthusiast knows that this can explain a team's victory in one match or even over a short period, but is it possible to reign at the top of the pyramid that is national cricket, for decades, with disproportionate contribution from the bowling department?

Or is it that simple an explanation – that Bombay batsmen set up the foundation of the team and batted the opposition out of the match leaving the bowlers little to do but keep it tight and be miserly? While it may be perplexing, the answer may even be that simple. So, was this the case? The obvious answer to this question is: no, it is not possible. The same answer applies to the question in the previous paragraph too.

This however, is the common-sense and instinctive response to the questions. With the above considerations in mind, let us begin at the basics by considering common-sense views. Bowling, particularly fast bowling, is laborious. The best bowlers today and in the past have all been very good athletes – sportspersons who know the capabilities and limits of their own bodies and have managed to use that knowledge to keep themselves fit. We must here acknowledge the fact that very few of our cricketers are interested in any physical activities or alternative sports other than cricket. This very fact inhibits the overall conditioning of the body, making one prone to injuries. The rate of risk of Indian bowlers sustaining injuries rises above the general wear and tear that every fast bowler experiences.

Interestingly, Bombay, the city of dreams, the city that never sleeps, with all the hustle and bustle of its local trains and the mad rush for daily survival – has embraced cricket as its beloved sport, and a particular brand of cricket at that. Bombay has embraced cricket as a sport of batsmen. This sentence may sound harsh but that is the way it appears at first glance. Bombay has embraced the slow-grinding innings of technically correct batsmen who tire the opposition into submission while batting them out of the game. For a city that never stops moving, that never stops working, its cricket seems to lack the one component – the only organic aggression that the aristocratic sport of cricket has to offer, i.e., bowling, especially fast bowling. At least at first glance it is a peculiar absence considering the Khaddoos attitude with which Bombay played its cricket.

So, where do we start? There is no dearth of theories. Some seem logical and some weird. But what all of them do agree on is that in contrast to the many top-quality batsmen of Bombay, most of the great bowlers who played for Bombay were imports. Bombay does not 'produce' bowlers; bowlers are not grown in Bombay. It is only because of the good reputation of Bombay cricket by virtue of their batsmen that bowlers from other states have come to Bombay and settled here. In fact, internationals

Ramakant Desai and Subhash Gupte were the only exceptions to
this; they were born and brought up in Bombay. Vinoo Mankad,
Bapu Nadkarni, Karsan Ghavri, Rakesh Tandon, Rajendra Jadeja,
Salil Ankola and Zaheer Khan were all imports who spent much
of their young life growing up in other states. Some of them came
down to Bombay in search of better job opportunities and others
were simply poached. Many of them were all-rounders and fitted
perfectly in the strong Bombay team.

It has to be said here that Bombay selectors were shrewd.
They did not create a ruckus based on the origins of players or
which state they really belonged to. They did not care about
such petty concerns. Whoever impressed them while playing
against Bombay was later drafted into the team. The selectors
wanted the best players and that is all. Also, whoever came from
other sides became as much a part of Bombay as anyone who
was born in Bombay. Outsiders they were, but only by birth,
not in spirit. The passion in the Bombay team ran so high that
it encapsulated a new player in no time. Often the dedication to
Bombay by players from other states was much more than that
of those from Bombay.

But this situation does reveal another misfortune: the fact
that Bombay cricketing mechanism is indeed not producing
good-quality bowlers. That a team of such quality and legacy
needs to rely on good players from other states – having to come
to the decision to leave their own states and come to Bombay –
must be worrisome to the players, administrators and fans alike.
Is it a case of not spotting the talent that exists or is it that there
is, and has been, a dearth of talent in the bowling department?
One common reason often cited is that the Indian cricketing
system itself is biased towards batsmen. Tiger Pataudi feels that

small boundaries in several maidans don't encourage spinners to flight their deliveries. 'They are mentally tuned to bowl flat around the off stump and are happy bowling a containing line. When they play on big grounds against good-quality batsmen, they are sorted out. Not that they were bad bowlers but they weren't able to handle the playing conditions, especially the flat pitches,' Pataudi says.

Pataudi is not alone in thinking so. Many old-timers agree with Pataudi's analysis. The grounds at the Kennedy Sea Face, for example, have really short boundaries on the side; all that a batsman needs to do is beat the infield and he gets a boundary. The bowlers are pushed into a perpetual dilemma. If they set an attacking field, they come under immense pressure because the slightest of errors can result in boundaries. In the end, they prefer to take the safer option and bowl with a field that will have four out of nine fielders on the fence. This defensive approach is inculcated in their very psyche.

It is not that this approach never works. One might win some matches with such a strategy at the local level. But it gets difficult as one goes higher up. Having had these ideas so deeply ingrained in the style of their bowling, one finds it difficult to adapt to different conditions and grounds. This weakness at the very foundational level gets magnified as these bowlers play higher classes of cricket. The strategy is 'one size fits all' and is easily exposed to be a very inefficient method indeed.

Umrigar said that this could not work at the first-class level. Instead, Umrigar has another theory for the lack of quality bowlers. 'Bombay pitches may have bounce but by and large they are absolutely flat. They turn slowly. Ramakant Desai was great initially, but later he was made to bowl too much in every match he played. Bowling twenty-five overs per innings totally burnt him out in a couple of seasons.'

So, is the basic infrastructure itself to be blamed? Flat pitches drain all energy and hope out of bowlers. Is it then, that such pitches slowly infuse defensive bowling into the game of bowlers at very young age, making it harder for them adapt as they progress? However, one can understand why Ramakant Desai was used as much as he was. At a time when there were hardly any fast bowlers of quality, Ramakant Desai was every captain's delight. He would often intimidate the batsmen with his sharp bouncers. His captains at club, company and state teams, in their awe of him, didn't realize that they were pushing him a bit too hard. Desai's body was not ready to take that kind of load and it soon succumbed to the pressure. But herein is the puzzle: it is necessary to utilize the current talent to win matches ensuring that the long-term prospects of the team are not compromised. After all, that is what competitive sport comes down to. The predicament is to sustain and nurture this talent for an entire generation and put in place systems to build a pool of players for the future based on that talent. However, before we continue the analysis on the general state of bowling in Bombay, let us briefly pause here and focus on the case of Desai. We might learn some insights that help with the broader discussion.

Nari Contractor puts the rise and fall of Desai in perspective. He played Desai in inter-college matches. 'Playing for St. Xavier's, I faced Ramakant who was playing for Ruparel College. He was very quick, and very accurate for that pace. His frequency of getting wickets impressed the CCI which was to play against a strong West Indies team soon. After picking five wickets in that match, he was picked in Tests. This was the rise.'

However, Desai's wicket spree came to an end a bit too soon. Contractor says: 'He was over-bowled in all the matches that he played. Thus he could be a good quick bowler only for two or three seasons. Every captain was tempted to over-bowl him because he got quick wickets in the shortest possible time. In 1962 he was a medium pacer, but by the time he went to Australia in 1967 he had lost his pace.' Bedi who was on that Australia tour says that he felt Desai was bowling leg breaks in the nets.

It is sad that one of India's finest fast bowlers had come to this fate. Bedi's comment on Desai's bowling transformation reflects more on the systems that underlie Indian cricket and the milieu in which a bowler like Desai attains the status of a rare commodity. The allusion here is, of course, to spin bowling. This is clear once we know about Desai's partner in crime in that era. The main reason behind the downfall of Desai was that till the 1970s, there was no quota of overs for bowlers in a fifty-over match. Ramakant Desai and spinner Shivalkar together would share fifty overs in almost every match. Match after match, season after season, they would keep on bowling. The atrocious conditions of maidans affected the pacer Desai much more than it affected the spinner Shivalkar. But Desai never complained and bowled constantly without a sigh. While a spinner may have survived such heavy workload, especially on Indian pitches that regularly assisted them, it wore out the fast bowler.

In a way the story of Desai is the story of many bowlers of India. How many promising bowlers have we seen in the last decade itself? Every season there is at least one talented bowler who presents himself from nowhere. When we see him, the entire country thinks: 'Finally we have found a fast bowler.' This has become a ritual. The next stage of the ritual is exhaustion of the bowler and the subsequent loss of spark. The fast bowler who once looked dangerous now looks playable at will.

There are other bowlers who dealt with the exhaustion better. Shivalkar survived the burnout better than Desai. But he was made to suffer in other aspects. One of the finest spin bowlers ever, Padmakar Shivalkar was spotted by the great exponent of spin bowling, Vinoo Mankad, himself. Shivalkar could bowl not just to the wicket but he could bowl out a batsman's mind. A Bombay batsman dreams of a century even before he brushes his teeth in the morning. Shivalkar would always be thinking of a five-wicket haul. Whatever the state of the wicket, he kept bowling from the same spot of the crease, varying his line and length very subtly. Bowling was a passion that could only be fulfilled by more and more bowling. He would practise bowling thousands of balls for hours. Shivalkar had more than mere ambition for the game; his was a love affair with sport.

As often happens with every love affair, this too contained some heartbreak for Shivalkar. Two questions often emerge with regard to Shivalkar. One is, was he better than Bedi? The debate remains inconclusive till date. The second question is, why wasn't Shivalkar selected after Bedi was dropped in 1979? Bedi got the right opportunities, grabbed it with both hands and went on to play sixty-seven Tests with distinction. Shivalkar didn't.

Shivalkar debuted for Bombay in the 1965 Ranji Trophy. He was an understudy to Bapu Nadkarni who had already played Test cricket. To add to the pressure on Shivaklar, Nadkarni was an all-rounder. The competition in the Indian team was threefold; all-rounders Nadkarni and Durrani were pitted against a genuine left-arm spinner. By taking wickets against Sobers's side before the Calcutta Test in 1967, Bedi impressed everyone.

Much of Shivalkar's fate was decided by Nadkarni perhaps. Many former Bombaikars feel that if Bapu Nadkarni had not shifted to Bombay from the Maharashtra team, Shivalkar would have done more with his opportunities.

We again find ourselves facing the same question – who is better of the two – Bedi or Shivalkar? Chandu Borde puts an end to the comparison with simple cricketing logic: 'Since he played with the strong Bombay batting line-up, Shivalkar rarely had to defend a small total of, say, 200 runs. Bombay would often bat out the opposition by scoring more than 450 which would release pressure on Shivalkar. To top this, he got a lot of extra support – Wadekar in the slips, Solkar at forward short leg, Ramnath Parkar at silly point. Bedi on the other hand played for Delhi, North Zone and India. He never had that kind of luxury. He rarely got 450 to defend.'

'Pataudi agrees with Borde. But what does Bedi himself have to say about the comparison? Ask him, and the magnanimous Sardar says: 'Paddy was a damn good bowler.' Now we come to the second question. Should Shivalkar have replaced Bedi in 1979? The answer from the cricket lovers is known. They felt Shivalkar ought to have been picked ahead of Dilip Doshi since the then captain Gavaskar knew the ability of Shivalkar. However, perhaps people forgot that Shivalkar was thirty-seven and Doshi only thirty-one. In the end, the prestigious cap of India eluded Shivalkar. This is one saga that Shivalkar often explains in the form of Hindi songs. Perhaps the heartbreak is also shared by the cricketing universe as we missed out on watching a highly skilled exponent of spin bowling on the grandest stage of the sport – and due to no fault of the tweaker himself.

Now let us come to the one aspect of bowling that India has been fairly good at, especially compared to fast bowling. And this is the spin department. Unlike pace bowling, which often looks like an imposition on Indian tastes, spin is something that seems to suit Indian nerves. We seem to be comfortable with it, we seem to be able to handle it as batsmen, and be pioneers as bowlers. Bombay had two great spinners in the form of the Gupte brothers: Subhash and Baloo. Both were good leg-spinners but Subhash had an extra edge to him. He was slightly cunning, had a lovely loop and a very good variation – things that his younger brother Baloo fell behind on. Chandu Patankar kept wickets for both the brothers. He says: 'Baloo was a little quicker in the air like Kumble and had a better googly than Subhash. However, once Subhash spotted the weakness of a batsman, he would be at him all the time. He was one leg spinner who would be very comfortable bowling to left handers.'

Polly Umrigar echoes Patankar's opinion. Umrigar is, in fact, one person who got to watch these talents develop from close quarters. He was in the slips when Gupte rattled the mighty West Indians with his nine-wicket haul in the Kanpur Test. 'Subhash mesmerized the batsmen and they, rendered clueless, had no option but to surrender. They had no clue about the subtle variations that he was employing.'

Baloo would exploit the turner very efficiently but unlike Subhash, he wasn't comfortable bowling to left-handers.

Subhash would have no problem shifting the line when a left–right pair was in the middle. The comparison between them is unfortunate but inevitable. But on the whole the two Gupte brothers contributed equally immensely to Bombay cricket.

Complementing Subhash Gupte was a crafty left-arm spinner, Vinoo Mankad, who had left his hometown to play for Bombay. Lacking education which would provide him employment, Mankad left for Bombay after completing his apprenticeship. Vinoobhai, as he was respectfully called, was a three dimensional player. He batted at all numbers and bowled to top batsmen like Sir Don Bradman, Sir Len Hutton, Dennis Compton and many others. His bowling style was unique; he could release the ball from different positions.

Madhav Mantri who kept wickets for him says: 'The release of each ball was different when bowled from a different angle. This would confuse the batsmen even on a placid pitch. He was a great fielder, and especially when he bowled he was sharp in anticipating a caught and bowled.'

Mankad grew up to become the wise old man of Bombay cricket. Having an intrinsic eye for talent, he picked and groomed Shivalkar, Solkar and many others. Much more than technique, his aim would be to drill the essence of performing in a match. Comparison between him and Bedi never ceased. The argument often touted was that Mankad got wickets of top batsmen, whereas during the Packer 'circus' Bedi bowled to batsmen of much lesser calibre.

It is almost impossible to compare two players who belong to different eras. Times change so much and so do variables for judgement on performance. Nonetheless, the beauty of comparison is that it is one of the few things that make the life at the maidans and clubs run day by day.

Bapu Nadkarni was often called a defensive bowler and the man himself hated the title. 'If I am being labelled as a defensive bowler because of my accuracy that no batsman could master, then blame the batsmen and not my bowling. In my career I got many bowled and leg before wickets, and that proves that I was an attacking bowler,' Nadkarni retorts angrily.

Born in Nasik, Bapu Nadkarni moved to Poona and played for Maharashtra. However, he soon realized he was wasting his time playing in a team that had no big players. He then joined the Associated Cement Companies (ACC) that had Mantri, Umrigar, Modi, Sardesai and Desai. There, he fitted perfectly in the role of an all-rounder.

Nadkarni had a simple mantra. Practise for half a day! It required no debate, no discussion. Practising was his only solution for perfecting the art of spin bowling. When he was in Poona, he would request former India wicketkeeper Nana Joshi to keep wickets in the nets while he would bowl for four hours. The duo would break for lunch and return in the afternoon for another four hours of practice.

Nadkarni wasn't a big spinner of the ball and he has no qualms in accepting it. However, he knows that he made up for it with accuracy. In the Chepauk Test against England he bowled twenty-one maidens in a row and returned with figures of 32-27-5-0. In the 1959 Test at the Brabourne stadium against the Australians, when Norman O'Neill and Neil Harvey were dancing down the wicket to Subhash Gupte, Nadkarni claimed six wickets for 105 runs.

Does Nadkarni have an answer to why Bombay hasn't

produced many international class bowlers? He replies by narrating an incident: 'In 1968 there was a seminar at the Khar Gymkhana about the bowling problems of Bombay. I suggested that we were playing too many tournaments and bowlers didn't get time to rectify their faults. Bowling in match after match with the same faults served no purpose. The bowler got thrashed and his confidence loosened. However, nobody in the meet bothered about my insight.'

Another bowler who should have got a chance in the Indian team was the offie, Sharad Diwadkar. People compared him to the English off-spinner Jim Laker and he was nicknamed 'Jimmy' because of the varieties he could churn. However, the strong Bombay team became a problem for him. Weaker oppositions and very good Bombay attack meant that Diwadkar was under-bowled. He had everything that an offie should have but like Shivalkar he too missed the bus. Perhaps Shivalkar and Diwadkar were just born at the wrong time when bigwigs had already settled their foot in the sands of the Indian team. Prasanna and Venkataraghavan were the darlings of the team at Diwadkar's time and he had little chance to make it big.

The next player in line is the charismatic Ravi Shastri. Can we try putting all-rounder Ravi Shastri in the galaxy of spin-bowling all-rounders? In 1979, the lanky seventeen-year-old reported for an open under-twenty-two selection trial at the Wankhede stadium. The selection trials were flooding with over 500 hopefuls with dreams in their eyes. Now, where there are so many dreams, there will be chaos, and, yes, the administration was in an expected mess. There were clear implications that the selection parameters had already been fixed. The trials hadn't begun but selections were well on their way. While some players got ten balls each to bat and bowl, the rest got only a single ball to display their skill! The logic was somewhere else, but it was certainly not within cricket.

Ravi Shastri was not one with prior 'settlements'. The selectors thought that Ravi Shastri had no cricketing background. He hardly got any deliveries to perform. 'You want us to pick players from a school that encourages only football,' someone overheard one of the selectors say. The gentleman did not realize that the 1967 Indian Schoolboys team to England was led by Ajit Naik, who also came from a school that wasn't a part of the inter-school tournaments of Bombay.

Shastri's genius would have been swept away if it wasn't for the interruption of one selector, Jimmy Diwadkar, who thought that Shastri deserved a look-in and he went to Sunil Gavaskar. Diwadkar would have hardly anticipated what was to happen next and would consequently change the history of Indian cricket. Gavaskar insisted that Ravi Shastri should be included in the Bombay Ranji team for the quarter-final against Bihar.

The same set of selectors that had rejected Shastri were instructed by the India captain Sunil Gavaskar to include Shastri in the Bombay team for quarter-finals game against Bihar. In that match, Shastri picked up three wickets and batted well. Shastri was in the Indian team.

Starting modestly as a lower order-batsman, he slowly gathered himself on the international stage improving as a batsman. He noticed his limitations and worked on them and eventually went on to open the innings for India. Ravi Shastri stands as a testimony to the fact that if you are mentally strong and have the knack to adapt, there is no limit to success.

The stories of Bombay bowlers range from the emphatic

tale of Shastri's rise to the sad account of Shivalkar's bad luck. But even with all the potential, it must be said at this point that Bombay bowlers could never really create magic. Bishan Singh Bedi who played against Bombay on several occasions says, 'I may be wrong but I always carried the impression that Bombay bowlers weren't willing to work hard. Bowling is bloody hard work. Also, another reason could be that since Bombay produced such top-quality international batsmen, everyone wanted to bat. Apart from Shivalkar, and Zaheer Khan – who isn't a Bombaikar – I never came across a bowler of international class since I started playing against Bombay. I am not talking about Vinoo Mankad and Gupte brothers. I never got to watch them.'

Funnily enough, one reason that is always stated to account for Bombay's weak bowling is their strong batting! How would we ever think that something fortunate can turn into a curse when looked at from the other side? Says Bedi: 'Since their batting was strong they would pile up scores of over 500 and put pressure on opposition batsmen via Shivalkar. Once they got the lead they would sit on the first-innings lead. If the approach had been to go for an outright win, they would have produced more bowlers.'

But this is Bedi's perspective. It must be remembered that he is an outsider to the team. This is not to say that his view is any less relevant. In fact, he is most likely to inject a refreshing dose of frankness to the debate. However, the point is that Bedi's perspective is but one perspective and we have different accounts.

Take the case of insider Sunil Gavaskar. According to him, it is not a question of Bombay's batting at all and the problem is technical instead. He says that the outfields in maidans were not properly maintained but pitches were conducive to batting. This could be the reason why Bombay didn't produce quality bowlers.

'Since Bombay is the city of dreams for so many people, it is a competitive world in its own and one learns early in Bombay that there will be no favours done and you have to stand up on your own feet. So there's a survival instinct that comes naturally to Bombaikars and that's why Bombay has produced more international batsmen than bowlers.'

Perhaps, Sandeep Patil can give us a better view as he is a living example of a player who, from being a decent medium pacer, shifted completely to batting. He is another good example of a player who thrives in the liminal space between the insider and outsider in the universe of Bombay cricket. But his analysis is with respect to the inside and outside of shifting from being a bowler and a batsman at different times. He says, 'I loved bowling but as I went on playing, the pressure of a being an all-rounder was a bit too much. I had a long run-up. I noticed the pitches were placid. Eventually, I cut down my run-up and began to bowl cutters.'

'Let's face the facts,' pronounces Ravi Shastri. 'Boys in the cities are unwilling to work hard. There are far too many distractions for the boys. Bowling is hard work. Another reason could be that we have too many one-day tournaments. When you have to bowl ten overs in an ODI, and four overs in a T20, how will you announce your skills? I used to bowl a lot because it wasn't that easy to get in the Indian team only based on your batting. I get the feeling that Bombay boys love batting, but again, how many have played for India in the past decade and how many have cemented their place?'

The venom that is the new method of playing cricket, seems to be a common motif amongst the legends of the game. Take Wadekar, for example. He remembers how 'one-day matches

had a funny rule. There was no limit on the number of overs
an individual bowler could bowl. Thus Ramakant Desai and
Shivalkar would end up bowling twenty-five overs each; or V.S.
Patil and Urmikant Mody would share the fifty overs. And there
would be more scope for batsmen to play in the team.'

However, after Bombay won the Ranji final in 1984, beating
Delhi in a pulsating match, Bombay's supremacy could be
evidently seen as diminishing. In one particular match against
Maharashtra, Bombay's score of over 500 runs was easily
surpassed. The situation worsened and in 1988, a forty-eight-
year-old Shivalkar was coaxed into staging a comeback against
Karnataka.

Chandu Borde, former India captain, played for Maharashtra,
and since Maharashtra and Bombay were in the same zone,
he played against Bombay more often than players from other
parts of the country. He says: 'My observation is that Bombay
bowlers were bowling in too many matches. Apart from Ramakant
Desai who was a medium pacer, Gupte brothers, Shivalkar and
Diwadkar were very good spinners. Bowling continuously on
the maidans of Bombay may have affected the bowlers. But let
me tell you that though Bombay batsmen stuck to their style,
some of the Bombay bowlers were trying to be too technical.
The moment they would stop getting wickets, they would get
into technicalities and that would not work.'

Pataudi's view is a little different. And with his view, for
the first time we witness a break in what by now seems to be
the popular opinion. In fact, he puts a question mark over our
major hypothesis itself. He does not completely agree with the
hypothesis that Bombay hasn't produced great bowlers. He
opines: 'Subhash Gupte was probably the best leg-spinner I have

seen apart from Shane Warne. There was Ramakant Desai. There was Shivalkar. They all stand as examples. Shivalkar... I thought, he was a very good bowler but then Bedi was there and Shivalkar couldn't get in. It was very difficult for Shivalkar to get in as long as Bedi was there. I agree that they should have produced more bowlers but perhaps we are saying this only because of the wickets. The wickets in Bombay were superlative for batsmen, both at Ranji level and club level. It was a bit disheartening for bowlers. That's why I think most of them stuck to batting. Probably, bowlers found it tough to bowl to high-quality batsmen on good batting tracks. In fact, I got the impression that Bombay bowlers hated to bowl to their batsmen. That could be the reason why youngsters opted to take up batting.'

These commentaries have to be deeply valued, as the thoughts of these esteemed gentlemen have added to refining our understanding of the issue. However, these answers individually fall short of providing a satisfying answer to the questions with which we began this discussion. Especially in the context in which those questions were placed – the long-term success of Bombay cricket. Hence, let us ponder a little more on the reasons for the vast disparity between the quality of batting and bowling in Bombay.

I undertook a socio-economic survey with cricket as the focus, which revealed that in the earlier decades, cricket in Bombay spanned across south to central Bombay. However, after 1980, middle-class families residing in small rooms began to shift to far-off eastern and western suburbs. But the cricketing facilities remained in the south and central area. The findings of the survey indicated that there was a need to unearth bowlers in the suburbs and that is how the Bombay Cricket Association (BCA, now MCA) – came to launch the Mafatlal scheme for bowlers in October 1990.

The scheme began with a programme that invited pace and spin bowlers for selection trials at various centres. After screening, the selected players were coached by one of the most experienced coaches in the world, Frank Tyson. The products of this scheme, Salil Ankola, Abey Kurvilla, Paras Mhambrey, spinners Nilesh Kulkarni, Sairaj Bahutule and many others helped Bombay demolish opposition after opposition for a decade starting from 1992.

But the situation of bowlers in the city today makes this feel like a distant dream. A fact one finds hard to reconcile with is that success was only over a decade ago. Coaching standards have dropped considerably. Every other day, a new coaching centre mushrooms in some nook of the city. Coaching is a major source of income for these institutions. Within the BCA–Mafatlal bowling scheme two decades ago, young bowlers were not only selected after a lot of scrutiny, they were also subjected to a rigorous system in place which monitored the progress of the twenty-odd trainees. Further, it must be noted that this was at a time when information technology wasn't available. And yet, the training was systematic and it helped nurture bowlers of quality who went on to serve Bombay for more than a decade.

Nari Contractor remembers: 'During my time, no other place had three-day matches except Bombay. If you play a match for three days, a player learns to develop skills and learns to handle situations. That's possibly the reason Bombay players could handle pressure better, but now every team is competing with Bombay's skill levels. Players from the other teams too have learnt the art of handling pressure.'

Prasanna's analysis of the situation is from a more tactical angle: 'Apart from Paddy Shivalkar, who was an attacking bowler, the rest of the bowlers would usually bowl to a 7–2 off-side field and they kept bowling outside the off stump. They tested the patience of batsmen. It worked in domestic cricket, but in international cricket, unless you attack the batsmen you can't succeed.'

The reasons are rooted in the fundamentals and opinions differ. The only thing that can be said with certainty is that bowlers have missed out in this great city of cricket. Whether the reason is something as natural as the Bombay way of life or as mundane as the inefficiency of the administration over the years, we can hardly choose. All these reasons have come together to create hurdles for bowlers. Perhaps, given the batting craze, genuine and natural bowlers are opting to become batsmen. The bowling standards of Bombay have to be resurrected. How this will happen is no mean question. After all, we are talking about Bombay, the greatest of great teams in Indian cricket. It took Bombay years to build a batting line-up of invincible repute. Funnily, while batting was at its peak, bowling suffered. Now that more and more teams around the country are becoming competitive, Bombay can't be complacent by continuing to rely only on its batting in the future. Bombay needs a good bowing unit and should be ready to work for it.

This will not happen overnight. Like Bombay's batting legacy stretches back half a century, there is no doubt that building a bowling legacy will take time too. But that is the talk of legacies.

Building a bowling unit which is formidable and competitive need not take that long. The Mafatlal scheme proves that. Ramakant Desai could have been the inspiration to young pace bowlers, like Gavaskar or Merchant was to aspiring batsmen. Role models help in building legacies but there needs to be a system in place that protects such talent. While some of Bombay's spinning talent may have had the misfortune of playing at the wrong time, it is clear that pace bowlers and spinners alike need better systems. The likes of Zaheer Khan and Abey Kurvilla can stand as examples to future talents. But all this needs planning and takes time, but action is necessary and fruits of such labour will definitely be sweet. Till then, Bombay needs to steadily chip away at this task so that Bombay bowling becomes as formidable as its batting.

5

KANGA LEAGUE

In the first chapter we have already discussed how the trinity of Bombay city, cricket and cricket lovers have mutually nourished each other and in the process sustained a romance for the better part of the last century. In this process, Bombay dominated Indian cricket and contributed to eventually raising the standard of the sport in the country as a whole. How did this happen? It certainly is not an overnight phenomenon. The success of Bombay cricket validates the grand saying: 'Rome was not built in a day.' In this chapter we discuss one of the driving forces behind that success.

The sport of aristocratic birth and pace found its home in the fast-paced city that never sleeps. Then it must go without saying that the city and its people were to give something back to the game; something that was born out of the spirit of Bombay. Give the game played in flannel whites a dash of Khaddoos. It is here that we must mention the birth of the Kanga League – the only one in the world that is played in the monsoon. That is right! For the first time, white flannels would be dirty and the spongy uncovered pitches would get a new limit.

But we are getting ahead of ourselves. Let us rewind to why and how this league was born.

Cricket is a gentlemen's game or at least it was considered to be so for a long time. That is how the connoisseurs would like to remember it too. By birth at least, cricket was a gentlemen's game; played in England, mostly by the aristocrats. People played in whites and even at the end of an entire day's play the whites managed to retain much of their pristine form and colour. But cricket has reached far and wide, to many corners of the world. When a game travels, it becomes open to being reinterpreted by other cultures. Although cricket initially 'colonized' India, today the game has been passionately adopted. The way cricket is played in this country certainly gives every impression that it is our very own sport. Perhaps, after more than a century of playing the game and falling madly in love with it – a torrid and passionate affair that has managed to sustain all this while – it is *our* sport also.

Today, we may say that regardless of the way the game came to India it has been truly ingrained in the imagination of this country and weaved into its fabric. It does not carry the weight of its colonial legacy any longer. Instead, it is one of the few things that truly spells nationalism. In this process of adopting and engaging with the sport, India perhaps has managed to produce some unique versions of the sport. Although not all of them can technically become official events or formats, they present evidence of how the sport has captured the imagination of the country and in turn how the country has strived to fit it in the different settings and landscapes that is present here. We have brought cricket to every street, every gully, every backyard and every garage. Playing cricket does not need stumps; playing cricket does not need helmets, or even a bat. We have plastic bats, we have cardboard slabs, we have sheets of paper from our notebooks which we roll into balls and play cricket in classes.

Cricket is not in its rules, or its paraphernalia, it is in the charm of three simple things that make its essence: batting, bowling and fielding. India keeps it simple, sees what is available and plays the game with these simple facets of the sport. We even play cricket with no grounds, bats or balls; book cricket, which only relies on page numbers, is often the pastime of students inside classrooms as they endure drudging lessons. The point here is that even a backbench pastime activity that risks punishment if caught is couched in the metaphor of this great game. The aristocratic game has evolved to become a democratic sport within this country because of the place it has in our imaginations. It is perhaps one of the few activities that brings together an otherwise irreducibly diverse country.

However, for a sport loved so deeply, one of the big challenges was not playing cricket in India but for Indian players to play cricket in overseas conditions. This was especially true in England. A nice warm day could be interrupted by showers, thereby changing the nature of the pitch and in turn the position of the game itself. And even without interruptions, Indian teams always found it daunting to play on wet wickets and in cold conditions. It is in this context that the Kanga League, an idea of Vijay Merchant, was born. Kanga League is easily the most fascinating cricket tournament in the world. The Kanga League challenges the biggest fear of cricket: rains! That is right. The summer and spring sport of cricket takes the covers off the pitch even in the tropical 'drizzles' of Bombay, as it can be done only in Bombay.

Rains have been the spoilsport of many historic matches. Rains have changed destinies of crucial matches and chases. It has twisted the careers of cricketers and captains. Rain is indeed cricket's biggest nemesis. It has also taken the sting out of competition and reduced the sweetness of victories by taking away the possibility of competition. But Kanga League does not hide from the rains; it faces the showers with enthusiasm. The sight of seeing cricketers travelling by public transport with an umbrella in one hand and cricket gear in the other is unique to Bombay. Nowhere can we get to watch cricket matches being played in a drizzle. Nowhere can we find puddles of water in the middle of the run-up of a bowler, or tall grass being the villain by stopping a genuinely powerful stroke. Only the monsoon of Bombay, coupled with the enthusiasm of cricketers, can bring this bliss that is otherwise unheard of, anywhere else in the cricketing world.

Enthusiasm is perhaps the only way to understand and explain the Kanga League. A day before the match, players start obsessively looking at the sky for signs of the kind of rainy day it is going to be. Very few weather forecasters will be as interested in the sky as players are on those days. Be it a veteran or a debutant, the excitement, the nervousness is the same. The strategy of the playing eleven is determined by the colour of the sky. Often the hot and sultry weather of a Saturday breaks into a heavy downpour on Sunday morning. While the city rejoices, players feel dejected. The Kanga League is a bagful of surprises. It has kept players on their toes and their hopes on the edge for more than half a century now. This is perhaps living truly at the mercy of nature. Braving a tournament right in the middle of the monsoon says something – something about Bombay and its cricketers.

Bombay has often been called the heart of cricket in India. It has produced a series of legends, dozens of international cricketers and has been at the forefront of domestic cricket in the country. But interestingly, this heart has another heart at its core – the Kanga League. It is this monsoon league that makes Bombay cricket what it is.

Kanga League is an example of the pure spirit of Bombay cricket. Having begun in 1948, it has captured the heart and soul of every Bombaikar. The birth of the Kanga League was the result of the astuteness and perhaps Khaddoos-ness of one Bombay player, Vijay Merchant. He toured England with the Indian team in 1936 and 1946 and realized the need to play on uncovered pitches. It was he who mooted the idea of launching the monsoon league. He came back and proposed the idea and voila, it actually became a reality. The actualization of the idea is underlined with a stroke of surprise and excitement, because the idea may have been deemed as absurd anywhere else in the world, but not in Bombay. Bombay took it in its stride, and it became the rage in the city; at least within the cricketing world of Bombay.

We consider England, Australia, New Zealand and South Africa as extremely difficult in playing conditions. But the Kanga League manages to create the most difficult playing conditions in the middle of Bombay. Mud would be flying thick and fast and bowlers would be jumping over small puddles on their run-ups as if they are avoiding landmines. Fielders pretend to search for the ball in the tall grass when it is already hidden in their hand. The batsmen, confused and suspicious, scurry across the pitch like children, inevitably inviting a run-out.

The conditions are ideal for producing such remarkable

and amusing scenes on the cricket field. However, the very same conditions also make the game highly unpredictable and slightly dangerous. After all, imagine the batting paradises of Bombay maidans that spoil their batsmen and grind down their bowlers turning dangerous under the grey clouds as demons surface in every inch of the pitch. Kanga League produces challenges that demand and bring out the Khaddoosness in every player – a quality that defined the champion cricketing culture that won the Ranji Trophy forty times. This is what the Kanga League does, it combines frolic in the rains with serious cricketing business.

It might seem like a lot of fun, and it is, but its intensity can be matched by very few tournaments. Former India opener and Bombay captain Madhav Apte played the Kanga League for fifty-five years till he was seventy-one! He says: 'What one learnt was how to adapt. There were different conditions every time you played. I joined Fort Vijay club mainly because I wanted to open with Vijay Merchant and watch him tackle situations. The morning would see sunshine and batsmen would play freely. And suddenly a sharp shower would come which would change the nature of the uncovered pitch. The bowlers would then get on top. It got very difficult to survive then. Kanga League really taught you to negotiate bowlers. I remember few lines that the great cricket writer Sir Neville Cardus once wrote about Sir Jack Hobbs. Cardus wrote, "There could be an error of judgement in gauging the length and line of the ball but there could never be an error of grammar (technique) on his part." The Kanga League was one of those few occasions in the world where the grammar of batsmen would be corrected.'

Even the great Sunil Gavaskar hardly missed a Kanga League

game; and this was the case even when he was at his prime in international cricket. The 1979 Test series against England showcased to the world Gavaskar's class. He scored 221 in the last Test against England in that series. But as soon as he got back to India, he rushed to play the Kanga League match for Dadar Union. This was a time when pitches in international cricket weren't covered either.

This small example provides a good picture of the Bombay cricket world in those times. Firstly, the point is that the Kanga League matches were played during the monsoon with all the challenges that came with it. Secondly, as challenging as it seems this could have very easily descended into an entertaining pastime or a community event if that is all it had been. The league in its inception was designed to help Indian players play in conditions that were alien to them. Hence retired cricketers of India and Bombay, current players of both state and country, club cricketers and enthusiasts and connoisseurs of the game all rubbed shoulders with each other. Club and local players played in these challenging conditions with national and international players. These two aspects of the tournament were important in building the strength and depth of the different Bombay squads over the years. This is also the reason why the Kanga League was mentioned as being the heart of Bombay cricket in the beginning of the chapter.

Madhav Apte was posted for fifteen years in Kuala Lumpur. Whenever he happened to travel to India, this enthusiastic man, now eighty-two, would call the captain of Jolly Cricketers on Friday or Saturday evening to request that he be included in the team for the Sunday match. He would fly from Kuala Lumpur, often welcomed by heavy showers at the airport, to play in the league. More often than not, he would be the first to reach the ground.

It is this unique mixture of players and the idea of the monsoon league that produced an atmosphere in Bombay cricket unlike anywhere else in India at the time. This mixture elevated the spectacle of the Kanga League to a training field for battles.

An example of this monsoon league's ability to produce, and testify, talent is perhaps best found in the accounts of Hemant Kenkare. He was the captain of the Cricket Club of India (CCI) when Sachin Tendulkar made his debut in the A Division of the Kanga League tournament and captained Tendulkar in other matches too. 'When he made his A Division debut against Karnataka Sporting Association at Cross Maidan, the cricketing populace of Bombay was keen to see how this young tyro – who had phenomenal scores in school and age-group cricket – would perform. Would he be able to pit his skills with senior cricketers? Would he be able to raise his game on questionable pitches and in difficult circumstances? Would runs flow from his bat the way they did in Giles and Harris Shield matches?' These doubts could not have been uncommon in the minds of many, regardless of the level of talent displayed by a batsman. Maturity and application are often not associated with youth, and while those who witnessed Tendulkar believed in his talent, everyone waited for the prophecy to be fulfilled.

Kenkare continues: 'A sharp shower before we were about to begin our innings meant that the pitch would worsen. To compound our (CCI) troubles we were playing with a depleted batting line-up. Our regular star players including Sandeep Patil (the captain for the season), Alan Sippy and Shishir Hattangadi were away playing club cricket in Kenya and England. The message passed on to our second string batsmen were to stick it out and play for a draw.

'When Tendulkar walked in, it was two wickets down for almost nothing. The pitch had become a minefield. The bowler, Sharad Rao – a former Bombay and Karnataka seamer – was known to be a wily customer and was regarded as a major threat on Kanga League pitches. Being the non-striker, I did my duty of warning the young debutant of the kind of stuff he would receive from the experienced bowler and retreated to the safety of the non-striker's end. The first ball bowled by Rao was short of good length, the type that causes a furrow on a batsman's forehead. Without being flustered, the young Tendulkar promptly dispatched the ball straight above the middle stump of the non-striker's end.' The bowler, umpire and Kenkare watched the ball soar into the drab sky for a perfect sixer. It was a perfect cricket shot played in the most atrocious conditions, that too against a bowler of repute. Before anything else, it was the Kanga League of 1988 that gave Bombaikars a taste of what they were to savour over the next twenty-six years.

Tendulkar managed to shock Kenkare again and again. He recounts another match that took place only a few matches after the earlier one. 'We were pitted against a strong New Hind CC side at the Brabourne stadium. Our team, as was the norm in the first half of the Kanga League, was depleted with most reputed players being away playing club cricket abroad. The incessant rain had ruined the normally placid pitch and we were on the defensive before the first ball was bowled. Having been put into bat after losing the toss, we lost two wickets in the first hour of play.'

When Tendulkar walked in, Kenkare was at the non-striker's end once again. Kenkare says, 'I remember telling him how important it was to stay on the wicket and spend as much time as possible so that we can save the match. Till lunch was declared, both Tendulkar and I pottered around and managed to see through the first session without any damage, with the score reading thirty-odd for two. As we walked out to face the second session, Tendulkar asked me if he could play his natural game and go after the bowling. I issued a feeble "yes" and what I saw next, from the non-striker's end was simply unbelievable. Over the next five eight-ball overs, I witnessed the finest batting that I have seen in the Kanga League. Copybook shots were displayed by Tendulkar scoring to all corners of the ground. Inside-out lofted drives, hard pulls and ferocious square cuts all were on display and the ball singed over the tall grass and suddenly the New Hind skipper was sent running. He was posting his field as if it was the end of a tall-scoring fifty-over match.'

Sachin's sheer genius made the dicey wicket look flat. What was more, it motivated other batsmen to match his brilliance. The team was being automatically steered to a winning position. Tendulkar got a horrible decision and was adjudged caught behind. 'A wrong decision was probably the only way he could have been dismissed that day. Needless to say, CCI won the match with plenty to spare,' says Kenkare.

As it was in the case of Tendulkar, former India captain Nari Contractor sees Kanga League as a great preparatory course: 'It is a tournament that prepares you mentally and technically before the start of the season. Not only do you play in all sorts of different conditions, but you have to adapt to perform, and that helps you during the season.'

Mehil Irani, a former Bombay player who played in the 1950s, played Kanga League for fifty years in a row till the age of sixty-eight. He recollects: 'Kanga League taught me discipline. Once, Parsi Cyclists was playing Dadar Union. Dadar Union captain Madhav Mantri dropped Ramnath Kenny because he was late by five minutes. The point to be noted is that Kenny was a Test player. Many are under the impression that Kanga League was just fun, but to us it was serious business.'

The importance of that story cannot be comprehended until it is mentioned that Mehil Irani played for the Parsi Cyclists team. The Parsi Cyclists team had an army of national players in its team: Contractor, Polly Umrigar, Rusi Surti, Salim Durrani, Abbas Ali Baig and Farokh Engineer. These players were indispensable to the Parsi Cyclists team as they were to the national team of the time. It was indeed a strict and brave decision for the captain of the opponents of that Parsi Cyclists team to drop a Test player from their line-up.

These statements go to show the degree of competition in the league and what the competition meant to these players. Is it then any wonder that the players that Bombay produced were such great players and Bombay managed to churn them out for all those decades?

It is difficult to capture what the Kanga League meant to players and fans alike. After all, how can we ever express what it meant to willingly get drenched in mud and to struggle for hours in the rainy season to reach the field, often only to be told that the match stood cancelled due to heavy rains and yet do it week after week? Statistics and numbers are irrelevant in explaining what Kanga League meant to the players. It is only memories that survive as a testimony of the great times of Bombay cricket that coincided, not surprisingly, with the heights of Kanga League. They all present a different story, each unique in its own, each showing us a different Kanga League. And yet, there is something common in all of these and that is what holds Bombay cricket together – it is the spirit of Kanga League. Let us ask ourselves what else might have brought back these international players, many, many passionate players and supporters to the league year after year. The secret has to be in its spirit.

We cannot understand this elusive reference to 'spirit' that many people make about the Kanga League during the golden decades of Bombay cricket until we pay heed to some of the following testimonials. Old-timers unanimously feel that the camaraderie that the Kanga League matches build is crucial in the task of character building. It taught one to be loyal to the game and to play for the team. It unearths the real beauty of cricket and sporting spirit. Nowadays, matches are played on Sundays for convenience of players who come from long distances. But often on Saturday evenings, MCA leaves an announcement on its answering machine: 'Due to unplayable conditions tomorrow's matches are cancelled.' Contractor is peeved about the announcement of cancellation of matches: 'During our time there was no announcements in the newspapers, even on the morning of the match if it was cancelled. When it rained, we would all meet at the ground with an umbrella in one hand and the kit in the other, have a chat over a cup of tea and biscuits and if the match was called off, go to a hotel to have lunch together before going home.'

There is some charm exclusive to the Kanga League. No one can dispute the intensity or the seriousness of the league. Kanga

League exuded an enthusiasm that was unprecedented and unmatched. Players would travel from the border of Gujarat to play the league. The Iranis of Dahanu, for example, would start early in the morning in bright sunshine to travel for at least three hours to Bombay, only to find heavy rains at Azad Maidan. 'Oh, no!,' they would exclaim, before starting to hurl curses making everyone laugh. Rain acquired the status of a god during the league. One single shower could ruin a team's hopes. At times it rained in one part of Bombay while the other part was dry. While one match in south Bombay would be washed out because of the heavy rains, another match in a different part of Bombay was played to its entire length.

The outfield during Kanga League matches is a piece of art. It looks like a paddy field with water shining like a mirror. The tall grass would compel the batsmen to hit good ground shots. When the batsmen play forward trying to get to the pitch of the ball, the muck from the field would splatter on their face because of the ball's watery thud on the pudgy pitch. Bats are treated like gods by superstitious cricketers today. However, they were used in the Kanga League as a gardener's shovel to level the spots! The game is never played merely to win. And there is something about this fact that made the wins sweeter.

However, with all its challenges the Kanga League has remained a favourite with old Bombay cricket lovers. It evokes nostalgia about the glory of Bombay cricket when it was at its peak. Sunil Gavaskar had donated two trophies for the A Division teams. One is the M.L. Apte trophy for the the best batsman and the other is the V.S. Patil trophy for best bowler. These two men have been absolute legends of the game. Apte, the former India opener, has the highest career aggregate with 5,046 runs for CCI and Jolly Cricketers. Patil has been the highest wicket taker, claiming a whopping 759 sticks for Dadar Union – an indication of club loyalty. Moreover, it has to be remembered that Kanga League wasn't avoided by stars the way they do now because of their international commitments. There were many peaks that remained to be scaled and yet the league was as emotionally fulfilling as it could get.

Nowadays franchises pay bags of money to players to buy their loyalty, their dedication to the team. But Kanga League had little money to offer players. All it had was the sheer pleasure of playing the sport.

With so many cricketers muddying their clothes in the Kanga League over the years and constantly looking up to it as a source of comfort, the Kanga League stands as the backbone of Bombay cricket. If Bombay's batsmen have scored 31 per cent of India's runs, the Kanga League is responsible for it to a great extent.

Madhav Apte recounts an incident from the late 1960s when Jolly Cricketers were playing the last round match of the tournament against the New Hind team. The venue was the latter's ground at Matunga. At the very same time, another match was being played between CCI and Shivaji Park which was hardly 10 km away at the Shivaji Park Gymkhana (SPG) in Marine Drive.

'Both Jolly Cricketers and New Hind were at twenty-nine points in the tournament and needed a first-innings win to reach thirty-two. Both CCI and Shivaji Park were behind at twenty-eight points. A first-innings' lead would have taken either of the teams in the SPG ground to thirty-one points and Jolly Cricketers would have still won the championship. Both the teams had stalwarts. Manjrekar was leading SPG while Rajsingh

Dungarpur was leading CCI. Both the captains mutually agreed to declare their first innings after playing one over each and go for an outright win in the second innings which would have meant earning five points, thereby giving both teams a crack at beating Jolly Club.'

There were no mobiles and yet news could travel fast and with much enthusiasm – perhaps because of the lack of the ease that technology now affords. At lunchtime, Apte's team was comfortably placed in the first innings and was on its way to winning the championship. 'But just as we headed back to our tents at lunch, Vinoo Mankad described the proceedings of the match at the Hindu Gymkhana. After hearing what was happening in the other match, the New Hind sportingly agreed to play the second innings and Jolly Cricketers won the game outright and also the championship,' said Apte.

Shishir Hattangadi, former Bombay captain calls the Kanga League 'the spirited curtain raiser of Bombay cricket'. 'It was tough and intense,' he says, 'but had its light moments that kept it going.

'The uncovered monsoon pitches make batting an experience, and bowling a luxury. Playing for Karnataka Sporting Association in my first year in the B Division, I encountered colourful characters that had a lasting impression on me. There were professionals from other walks of life who played the league just to enjoy the game. On a damp monsoon day, which was truncated with rain, Karnataka struggled to make 100-odd runs, batting first. Opponents Elphinstone's key bowler Dr Saraiya (a Bombay Gymkhana member) had bowled from one end without a break. The long spell had to culminate in a relaxing shower in the elite dressing rooms of the colonial club.

'There must have been an hour left before tea break when the doctor picked up his muddy spikes, lit his cigar and wishing luck to his opening batsmen, walked away from the Sassanian pitch towards the Bombay Gymkhana. Exactly an hour later, the cigar smoking doctor returned to the tarpaulin tent to find the openers going out to bat post-teatime. He was delighted with the obstinate performance of his boys and applauded them as a good captain should.

'However, a sudden realization dawned on the doctor right after he had completed his round of applauses. 'The openers of his team had been dismissed for a paltry twenty-five-odd runs in the first innings and he had been timed out due to his unavailability. How the mood of a cricket match can turn on its head within the span of a mere moment – it turned from the sublime to the ridiculous. The least funny of all things was when players from the opposition "empathized" with the doctor for being timed out.'

But perhaps winning wasn't the point of Kanga League at all. For Hattangadi, Kanga League exceeds the trivial concerns of wins and losses. 'The charm of club cricket is a niche of its own; the mix of players, the passion to give it all.' And more important than anything, as Hattangadi puts it, is that 'the constant creation of unforgettable events give it a life of its own'.

Kenkare corroborates Hattangadi's understanding of the league: 'The most charming aspect of Kanga League was the camaraderie on display. In leaky tents in Azad, Cross and Shivaji Park maidans, players bonded. It did not matter if the players were Test or first-class cricketers or simply enthusiasts who played the sport. Kanga League was a great leveller in that sense and was a great example of the spirit of cricket and that of Bombay:

Whoever you may be off the field, once you don the flannels you are a cricketer and an equal to all the others.'

For former Bombay captain Milind Rege, Kanga League was about being made to persevere with wit. Rege remembers his captain Vasu Paranjpe as the wittiest cricketer one could have known. 'Our captain at the Dadar Union, he was ever ready with his repartee. After a long spell on one such steamy afternoon, I bitterly complained to captain Paranjpe. "It is too humid," I said. At once he stopped the game and told our twelfth man to bring an umbrella. The player did, Paranjpe promptly handed it over to me and said, "Go on son, hold on to it with one hand and continue with your spell." The entire team was in splits. We loved Vasu Paranjpe, he made us laugh and if ever one enjoyed the game it was under his leadership. And I actually bowled one ball that way! The stiff team of Dadar Union that we were, we did have our fun moments.'

Urmikant Modi was one of the deadly bowlers in Kanga League. He took over 400 wickets. He remembers one match against Shivaji Park Gymkhana when he was bowling, and facing him was the great batsman Vijay Manjrekar.

'I was bowling round the wicket and the ball hit his right pad, (in my opinion he was plumb lbw), and I appealed for an lbw, which umpire Mr Gothoskar declined. The second delivery hit him on the pads and I appealed again, and Vijay bhai used foul language to mock me about my appealing. Since he used foul language, I could not stand it and I told him, "A player of your calibre knows when you are out lbw; you aren't going hence I have every reason to appeal."

'This was a time when I was the baby of the team. Mr Madhav Mantri who was my captain was in first slip and shouted at me:

"Urmi, go back and bowl, no arguments". I had to go back to my end to bowl. On the next day, Manjrekar was at the Shivaji Park bus stand and I was riding my scooter to go to office. I saw him and offered him a ride to his office.'

The bottom line that Modi wants to emphasize is that even if there was great tension on the ground, it was traditional rivalry and off the fields, the friendships forged during the games were carried, not the tiffs.

These entire set of match statistics and anecdotes are not to emphasize the numbers, but to demonstrate how the spirit that the league cultivated came about. Playing in tough conditions meant, inevitably, that the players had to deeply rely on each other and enjoy the challenges posed by the conditions. Consider the following incident that stand in contrast to the example of captaincy offered by Rege.

The second incident that Modi remembers dearly was a match played between Dadar Union and Shivaji Park in Matunga Gymkhana in an invitation tournament. 'Ajit Wadekar was dropped at mid-on by Vijay Tulpule. The next delivery I bowled was a change of pace and Ajit smacked it for a four. Naren Tamhane was our captain as well as wicketkeeper, and he shouted at me "Do you know to whom you are bowling?" I felt a little sad, but in the next two deliveries, I first got Ajit out and then in the very next ball I got Hardikar out. From the non-striker's end, former Test wicket keeper Chandu Patankar made a comment, "Is this the effect of the scolding that you got from your captain?".'

While the comment may appear to have put the bowler, quite harshly, 'in his place', it also becomes an environment of playing high-standard cricket. As Modi did, one identifies the players who have set the bar and that provides a goal for the rest to strive towards. The method paid off as Modi was able to get two wickets in successive deliveries.

Another incident that stays with Modi is the Dadar Union vs CCI match, at Brabourne stadium. 'We were all out for sixty-two runs and we had to win the game, to be an A Division champion. Our captain, Vasu Paranjpe, gave the ball to me and said "Urmi, whatever you have done throughout the season means *nothing*, if we do not win this game today".

'Dilip Sardesai played a ball towards deep third man and while taking the first run, he called the non-striker for the third run. Amar Vaidya, picked up the ball and Dilip was run out.

'During lunch, Dilip was telling his wife that he will be there at the race course by 3 p.m., as they had to score only sixty-three to win. They were all out for forty-two runs and it took them three hours to score that. We won the division championship too. Those were some great days of Bombay Cricket.'

Hemant Kenkare was a former CCI captain. He went on to religiously play Kanga League for twenty-five years. Talk about the effect of Kanga League on shaping Bombay cricket, and this is what Kenkare, who as we know was a witness to the debut of none other than Sachin Tendulkar, has to say. The Kanga League, he says, has fascinated him from his adolescence. As a pre-teen, he would tag along with his elder cousin, Sunil Gavaskar, to the many maidans of Bombay to watch the tournament that was played bang in the middle of the torrid south-west monsoon. 'From Azad Maidan to Shivaji Park and Matunga I saw many a Bombay greats play. From Manohar Hardikar, Ajit Wadekar and Ramakant Desai to Dilip Sardesai, Budhi Kunderan, Eknath Solkar, Sharad Diwadkar and Bapu Nadkarni, I have seen all of them display their wares on rain-affected wickets.'

Madhav Mantri and the late Naren Tamhane played the Kanga League for Dadar Parsee Zoroastrians (DPZ) much after their retirement. In fact, they played till the late1970s. DPZ used to play in the lower divisions and had a lot of youngsters in their team. Kenkare recounts an incident in 1977 when he was leading Sassanian CC in the C Division, against Dadar Parsee Zorastrians. The Sassanians had been told by Mr R.V. Achrekar to report to the ground at 8.45 a.m. for a 10.30 a.m. start. 'All the young boys were told to come with shoes blancoed (the white shoe shine) as Mr Mantri was a strict disciplinarian. Mr Mantri and Mr Tamhane walked into the Sassanian tent at Azad Maidan sharp at 9.15 a.m. and were amazed to see all the opposition players in neat cricket clothes with the shoes shining and bats sandpapered clean, etc.'

The experience of playing in Kanga League made a person feel like a serious cricketer at one instance but let him transform into a crazy fan in the next moment. Says Kenkare, 'For us youngsters playing for the Sassanians, it was a treat to see the formidable Parsi Cyclists as their wicket was bang next to ours. We learnt a lot watching Polly kaka (who played an occasional game). Hoshie Amroliwalla, Mehil Irani and Anthony Fernandes (Baroda seamers) played there too. And if we were lucky to be playing a home game and if Parsi Cyclists were hosting Shivaji Park Gymkhana or Hindu Gymkhana or Dadar Union, we could see all our heroes up front. There they were within touching distance! Sunil Gavaskar, Ashok Mankad, Karsan Ghavri all playing at close quarters from us.'

This mixture of fun and the seriousness with which the league was played has built a cricketing culture of winning, but the way in which this has been accomplished is the most notable. It is the combination of all elements that we find noble in sports and cherish. As we have seen, the seriousness and rigour on the pitch was accompanied by camaraderie off the pitch. The Kanga League is also sustained by the numerous amusing anecdotes that surround it. Fortunately, the close community that this league helped produce along with quality cricketers ensures that these stories remain alive within the 'oral traditions' of the community of players, administrators and fans.

One such incident happened on the debut of Tendulkar in the A Division of the league. We already know of the performance of young Tendulkar in that match. What we do not know is why we have to miss out on a photograph of his batting prowess in that match. Kenkare recounts the hilarious story of the late Sharad Kotnis, a reputed cricket journalist and former managing committee member of the Bombay Cricket Association (BCA) who had sent his senior photographer to get a picture of young Tendulkar playing his first A Division match. 'The sullen gentleman – whose Sunday (the only holiday media persons have) was ruined – was not in the best of moods and wanted to leave for home after filing his picture with the press which was located close to the ground, as soon as he could.

'I happened to be the CCI captain and having lost the toss, we were asked to field first. I distinctly remember the photographer saying, "I'll take a picture of him walking out to field and leave." Undoubtedly, he would have been asked by his editor to click a picture of Tendulkar while batting. Our photographer friend was not willing to wait for the second innings and forsake the Sunday festivities with his family. He got one click of Tendulkar walking out with his CCI teammates, and the photographer was on his way. The rest as they say is history. Too bad for the photographer, he had just missed the picture of his lifetime!'

Yajuvendra Singh is one of the former India players whose association with the Kanga League has survived many years now. He has given the league his best since the mid-1970s. He played his last match in the mid-1990s. Many players who came from other states somehow landed up playing for Jolly Cricketers, and he was no different. He playfully remembers how former players made life fun and difficult for them.

'The team was supported by Madhav and Vaman Apte and there was no way one could escape a game if one was in town. The team had a wonderful atmosphere. Cricket was played very seriously and yet winning was not the only criteria. The dressing room was full of cricket tales garnished with abundant jokes and banter. There were so many lovely moments. But two stand out as the most significant in my memory. One of them undeniably is the occasion of winning the title in 1980. It so happened that I had just returned from playing professional cricket in England. But the Jolly antenna had kept track of my arrival. It was the last match of the season and we needed a win to become champions. We fielded first and while attempting to catch a tail-ender at slips, the middle finger of my right hand got dislocated. It was the first time I had encountered such an injury and seeing a twisted, disjointed finger, my cry for help was quite demanding. We had in our side Dr Vishwas Raut who promptly came up, looked at it and clicked the finger joints together. Before I could even scream or make a tantrum, he tightly bandaged it and said, "Stop making a noise, you are perfectly okay."'

Singh continues, 'The time for me to bat was soon to come and my team was dependent on my performance. Even before the openers went in to bat, Doctor Raut made me wear my batting gloves. I had little idea that he did it because I might not have been able to put them on when my fingers swelled up later. In typical Bombay cricket style, there was no sympathy or mollycoddling from any of my teammates. They wanted runs and they wanted me to get them. When I came back from the match and took off my gloves, my finger had swelled up quite nastily. I was out of cricket for nearly two weeks after the incident. But after all this, all I can say is that it was definitely worth being a part of the Kanga League winning side. Yes, that day when I went out with my swollen fingers shrouded in my gloves, we won the match.'

Singh remembers his second unforgettable moment at a time when he should not have been playing cricket. 'By the mid-1990s season of the Kanga League, my cricket days were well over. It was a match in which Jolly Cricketers were playing Dadar Union and unfortunately, they were a player short. Frantic calls were made to me and they were laced with flattering and emotional blackmail at the same time. They all wanted me to play again. In our team was the legend of Bombay cricket, Madhav Apte. Apte was well past sixty and still shining. I could hardly make an excuse citing my age. Jolly were put into bat and soon we were in serious trouble having lost five wickets cheaply. I managed to survive at one end when in walked Mr Apte. With a combined age of over a hundred, the two of us oldies were to save our team. In the end, we went on to have a match-saving partnership. Madhav Apte batted resolutely to make his last half-century and I got out only in the eighties. Further, it was only because of exhaustion that we finally got out. I never played another Kanga League game thereafter, but the partnership, support, tips and enjoyment that I experienced alongside a true cricket legend and enthusiast during that partnership, was to me the grandest moment of playing the league.'

The image that stays with Singh and makes it the defining moment of Kanga League is that of two former cricketers well past their prime, tormenting the young, powerful champion side. It indeed defines the spirit of Kanga League perfectly. For Singh, what made Kanga League so crucial for a cricketer was the interaction between the young and the old. 'In difficult conditions, we rubbed shoulders with stalwarts, learning and listening to their words of wisdom.' Singh reiterates the one sentence that has been said again and again. And that is the fact that Kanga League is indispensable to the growth of a Bombay cricketer. And much more than that is the fact that it managed to be so crucial even when the general atmosphere of the tournament was one of sheer joy.

Vijay Nayudu, the grandson of Col. C.K. Nayudu and former Madhya Pradesh captain feels that the charm of the league is what makes it so unique. He states that the birth of the Kanga League can be traced to the first Presidency match that was played in July 1892 at Bombay Gymkhana between the Europeans and the Parsi XI. They had formed their club in 1848. The match was known as the 'Fire Engine match' as the fire brigade was used to remove water from the ground to make it suitable for the match to be played. Kanga League is full of such little quirks that make it incomparable to any other tournament and inimitable in any other space.

Nayudu says, 'The Kanga League has a special place in the heart and mind of every cricketer of Bombay who was part of it during the 1950s, '60s and '70s. Playing cricket during monsoon has its own charm and thrill that is completely different from playing on a good turf. When I look back, the memories are still fresh in my mind. I was asked to come to Prabhu Jolly ground at Azad maidan by my school captain Raju Rungta who was managing the then Rajasthan CC, a C Division team. It was a Sunday in 1959. As a fifteen-year-old boy, I found myself surrounded with players like Sunil Gavaskar, the captain of the team, V.S. Bahutule, Vilas Godbole, M.D. Vashist, Bhalya Varde and some others. They were all pulling each other's leg all the time and I had no clue of what was being discussed. I still remember the hectic knock of 100-odd runs played by Sunil Gavaskar in which he hit a few sixes over the road and later was seated on a chair completely exhausted. V.S. Bahutule did not spare anyone who misfielded or bowled badly and his Marathi "vocabulary" used to make players laugh all the time. The most enjoyable part was when he made a mistake. Then, all the players would be after him. Even amongst all this fun, there was seriousness and sincerity towards the game.'

Nayudu took some time to understand the format and the nature of the tournament. He had played for Rajasthan CC for three seasons before playing for Jolly Cricketers and Hindu Gymkhana during the period from 1959 to 1965 and again from 1975 to 1979.

'I feel playing the Kanga League had taught me many things about the game, especially playing on the back foot, the importance of stealing singles and fielding in close-in positions. The teams were placed between A and F Division.The standard of the game was very high for A Division teams while there was hardly any difference between B and C Division teams. Almost all the star players were involved in some team or the other. The tournament was enjoyed by people of all walks of life, who had fixed their loyalty to certain maidan clubs. The footpath, which has now been occupied by Fashion Street, used to be full of people watching the game at the Cross Maidan till the end.'

Nayudu particularly remembers the matches against Parsi Cyclists as always being full of thrills and excitement. 'Players like Behram Irani, Nowshir Tantra, Dadachandji, Farokh Engineer, and Mehil Irani were true characters and their no-holds-barred comments to each other used to be a topic of discussion and entertainment at the end of the game. They were always desperate to win matches from any situation and would fight till the end. They had the support of the local people and it was often difficult for outstation teams to win matches against them at Parsi Cyclists' ground.'

In those days, teams like Dadar Union, Shivaji Park, Hindu Gymkhana, Fort Vijay, Sunder, Jolly Cricketers and National had representations from the biggies of Bombay cricket. Sunday matches were comradely among teams, irrespective of the hierarchy of division system or class of players. 'Test and Ranji players used to meet and greet all and sundry especially during lunch break in various Irani hotels over mutton cutlet with gravy and paav (bread) which was available for Rs 2 or so. Vilas Godbole introduced me to the dish when I played my first Kanga League match, while Dilip Sardesai made me taste Russian salad for the first time at an Irani joint at Fort. There used to be many "informers" roaming all over the gymkhanas and maidans for the purpose of passing information about the proceedings of other matches at Matunga or Shivaji Park. This made some teams declare their innings after gaining the first innings lead for a possible outright win. Dilip Sardesai would always be keen to go for an outright win and often ended up almost losing the match.'

One of Nayudu's earliest memories of playing the Kanga League is throwing the ball to a young Sunil Gavaskar during lunch or tea break. 'Sunil would play the ball back to me on the uneven outfield. I wondered how he could play so straight and control his shots so that the ball came to where I was sitting on a chair. I never realized that I was watching a legend in his formative years. He must have been eleven years or so, four years younger than me at the time. He played his first Kanga League match within two years though his father was not too keen on it.'

Nayudu terms the Kanga League as a bowler's paradise and a batsman's nightmare. This analysis speaks very well of the Kanga League as not just an imitator, but a good leveller in the game of cricket since the accusation that cricket is batsman-centred is often made. Kanga League had a lot of aspects which gave advantage to the bowlers and gave them an equal footing by making them dangerous and difficult to play. It changed the entire grammar of playing cricket. It had its own heroes who could take wickets or score runs at will year after year.

To even get twenty-five runs was an achievement, he says. It did not involve continuous bashing of the bowlers by the batsmen, as often becomes the case in this age of tournaments like the IPL. Often we see that the boundaries are shortened nowadays and the fielding restrictions, power plays and indeed many, many rules are all directed towards letting the batsmen score more and more runs. It has to be said that at some point, so many runs make cricket tasteless. It seems that making runs is like a game of collecting candies and it doesn't give due credit to the intricacies that the disciplines of batting and bowling involve.

The Kanga League did not encourage bowler bashing. The bowler was not there only to be hit around the park by the batsman. The bowler was not on a defensive footing before the start of the match as is often the case now. The bowler attacked and attacked with confidence. Anyone scoring a fifty was considered a very good batsman in Nayudu's time. He recalls how, because of matches being extensively covered by the local media, anyone who made it to the headline on Monday would become a local hero for a week.

'The club secretaries who managed the teams were hard task masters, chasing every player to ensure that they all turn up on the following Sunday. The BCA had a dedicated team to ensure that the booklets containing details of the matches and past records were ready in time to be delivered to all clubs and players. The clubs in turn used to eagerly wait for the same.

Fielding was a difficult job with different matches going on the same maidan. Often the balls got mixed up when batsmen playing on adjacent pitches hit the balls in the same direction. The tall and thick grass near the cover area or a section of the boundary would make the ball disappear for a while and the batsmen continued taking runs with one eye on the fielder. They were always suspicious as to whether the fielder was pretending or the ball was actually lost. Teammates would shout for runs and the atmosphere was really funny.'

Nayudu, like many others, thinks that the Kanga League truly helped the technique of a cricketer. He says that it taught the batsmen to play close to the body. And it is true, as he suggests, that this skill remained the hallmark of all the star batsmen that Bombay produced all these years. Another important lesson that the Kanga League provided Nayudu was to be attacking while bowling and fielding. 'It is no wonder that Bombay has produced so many good fielders, both close-in and on the outfield,' he says. It is no wonder indeed; Kanga League was at the heart of much of Bombay's success.

A passionate club player and a famous cartoonist, Austin Coutinho has followed many events of Bombay cricket closely. Below he narrates the grand tale of why and how the '10-overs-per-hour' rule came to be implemented in the Kanga League. 'It was the season of 1984–85. Parsi Cyclists were playing a very strong Karnataka S.A. side at the former's home ground at the Azad Maidan. KSA scored a quick-fire, ninety-odd runs and declared to put the Parsi batsmen in on a drying wicket. B.S. Sandhu, Suresh Shetty and Austin Coutinho ran through the side. The hapless Parsi Cyclists' batting order capitulated for thirty-odd runs, Coutinho claiming six of the wickets.'

Vasudev Tumbe, the KSA skipper, wanted an outright win and thereby score full points. Thus, he instructed his batsmen to get quick runs. He then declared, setting the Parsi Cyclists a target of 100-odd runs. Coutinho remembers the veteran Mehil Irani as saying in typical Parsi style, 'I knew that Karnataka are a very good team but I didn't know they are greedy too!'

Shyam Nair, the Air India batsman, opened the innings and

scored twenty runs in the first two overs itself. Another 20–25 runs came in the next 3–4 overs. It is to be noted that Kanga League overs, till a few years ago, consisted of eight balls per over. Says Austin Coutinho: 'The KSA bowlers were at their wits end. But Tumbe, the shrewd tactician that he was, wasn't shaken. He instructed his bowlers, Shetty and Sandhu to take long run-ups and bowl not more than five or six overs in the one hour of play left. This was within the rules of Kanga League till then. Shetty started his 50-yard run up from the Bombay Gymkhana boundary line, while Sandhu started from the Prabhu Jolly wicket.

'When stumps were drawn, Parsi Cyclists were very close to the target, falling short by a few. But for the reduced number of overs, Parsi Cyclists would have won a famous match. Understandably protests spurted and the Kanga League Committee of Bombay Cricket Association decided to implement the ten-overs-per-hour rule, and eight-ball overs rule in the monsoon league.'

Perhaps the best anecdote of the circumstances and complications of the monsoon league is narrated by Hemant Kenkare. Maybe this light-hearted anecdote, one that has nothing to do with the birth of a genius or of matches or of victories and losses, sums up the spirit of the league as a whole for us. Kenkare remembers that the (late) A.M. Mamsa would always be the umpire at the Parsi Cyclists ground at Azad Maidan. 'Mamsa would often tell the story of how, once while umpiring an A Division game, an umpire on the pitch that was next to Parsi Cyclists' one adjudged a batsman out when a team fielder (who was playing another game) appealed. When Mamsa pointed this out to the umpire he was most ashamed.'

Whatever Kanga League was and is, one thing is evident. And that is that the league must have been a riot of fun for the people involved. Apart from the mischievous meddling of the weather gods that were taken in their stride by the league players, the matches being played on the Bombay maidans intersected each other leading to amusing circumstances. It created multiple labs and schools for cricketers of that era, all accessible on the same ground. No doubt, it was a lot of sweat and toil but it was also a labour of love, sweetened by the enthusiasm and fun due to the spirit in which the league was played. The stories of Apte, Kenkare, Nayudu, Yajuvendra Singh, Coutinho and others are only a few from the large corpus of sublime memories that together make the Kanga League. The league is a perfect example to show that fun and work are not necessarily opposites.

The Kanga League was played in the toughest conditions and perhaps that is the reason why humour was so important to its experience. It was played for the sheer joy of playing the game, for cracking jokes, for having a good laugh, for funny coincidences, and yet, it was played with a love for cricket that is unparalleled. The Kanga League is another example of how Indians have contributed to the sport of cricket: it is an ingenious contribution of Bombay to cricket.

Imagine the piquant scene of a batsman who wants to take a single but is not sure if the ball is with the fielder or not. The fielder is pretending that the ball is lost amidst the tall grass and is poised as if he is retrieving it from the grass. This makes for the perfect frame for the excitement and adventure that was the Kanga League. It set the pulse racing with every ball and no delivery could be dull in any way.

The Kanga League is everything that cricket in Bombay was

and is, only that it has more zeal, more commitment, more fun and more mud. The only thing that is lesser in the Kanga League than any other tournament is the stress that a cricketer has to suffer from. The constant worry about one's performance and the constant need to keep performing and thinking about one's future was not what the Kanga League was about, although it was a part and parcel of the sport. The Kanga League is not just any other domestic tournament that is played to get a ticket to an international team. It was not a ladder for anything. It was not a means to another end. It was played because of a certain respect for cricket. It was only about itself, only about playing the sport.

6

THE BEST BOMBAY XI

Let us sit back and think for a moment: if Bombay won the Ranji Trophy on forty occasions, how many great players would it have? Countless, truly! Bombay has been literally crammed with geniuses. There is enough evidence to claim that if Bombay fielded two sides in the Ranji Trophy, both the sides would make it to the finals. Bombay is certainly a dream team. But who has ever been satisfied in this world? The fortunate have other kinds of problems on their plate. With all this talent comes the problem of the lack of guarantee of one's place in the squad and eventually in the playing eleven. There are after all only eleven slots in a team! In a city where talent abounds, it is a rat race to get into the team, to fill one of the coveted eleven slots. Who gets to stay and who has to leave? Many great players had to bob in and out of the team because of the tough competition.

The very fact that an entire book is written to explore and explain the strength, domination and character of a single team at the national level, must in itself be evidence of the depth and talent of that team through the years. In the case of a team like

Bombay, a team that has won the coveted national championship, the Ranji Trophy, forty times, the problem only magnifies. From the 1940s through to the '80s the Bombay Ranji team was either the champion or at least the measuring scale for all talent and victories. Hence it is hard to fathom the amount of talent churned by the 'Khaddoos' team and its culture. Making an all-time eleven out of that pool is truly a daunting task. It is not a mere matter of statistics and arguments but also a matter of the heart.

But before we get into that, let us recall some of the great achievements of Bombay cricket over the years that renders this task so difficult. Perhaps the best way to do this is to take a closer look at not the Bombay team but at their opponents. It is here that we may find evidence of their excellence and depth. The fiercest competitor of the Bombay team was the Maharashtra team. Perhaps, having been in the same zone as their more heralded counterparts and having come across players from Bombay regularly both on and off the pitch, they faced the Bombay team sans the awe and fear that Bombay unfailingly inspired in all other teams. It is because of such exposure and their own tenacity that Maharashtra became Bombay's closest of competitors, at least through the 1950s and '60s.

There are a few match statistics and some stories that, despite the professionalism and the ruthless, 'Khaddoos' cricket that Bombay was known for, showed that Bombay could be beaten. Often, if not always, the hurdle before Bombay would be Maharashtra. As we shall see, these defeats, being few and far between, only go to show the strength of Bombay cricket.

On 5 November 1966, Maharashtra beat Bombay by one run. It was a closely fought match played in Aurangabad. Maharashtra's score was 327 and Bombay scored 326 falling short by one run. But under the zonal system in place then, only one team qualified from each zone. Even though Maharashtra beat Bombay, Bombay by virtue of beating other teams from the same zone qualified.

The 1940-41 match between Maharashtra and Bombay is another example of the rivalry and competitive face-offs between the two teams. The match was held in Poona. Maharashtra was captained by D.B. Deodhar. It was a five-day match played between 15 and 19 November 1940. Maharashtra scored 675 runs against Bombay's 650, leading to Maharashtra winning the match by twenty-five runs.

The third instance when Maharashtra defeated Bombay was in 1969-70 in a match played in the Brabourne stadium. Bombay was in a dominating position, having scored 220 runs for the loss of only two wickets. However, Maharashtra managed to effect a collapse of the Bombay batting line-up by bowling out the rest of the Bombay team for an additional 176 runs leaving Bombay with a total of 396. Maharashtra managed to cross this total for the loss of six wickets and went on to win the match based on the first innings lead.

Based on these performances, there was a heightened clamour that Maharashtra too must be allowed to play in the Ranji Trophy finals. Maharashtra, being the only team to intermittently challenge Bombay's superiority when other teams were not coming close, felt short-changed that they were not able to qualify for the Ranji tournament finals, despite beating Bombay, by virtue of being in the same zone as Bombay. They demanded that two teams should be allowed to qualify from each zone, thereby opening the door for Maharashtra to get in. Bombay on the other hand would manage to clear its path and get through the qualifiers, even after losing to Maharashtra, by beating other teams. Then, with its closest challengers pushed out, Bombay would ensure that its superiority remained intact.

This rivalry culminated in the 1971 Ranji finals when despite Bombay, Maharashtra managed to make it all the way to the finals. The result, if it was a win for Maharashtra, could have left a major decision in the hands of the administrators. It was not possible to allow two teams to qualify from only one zone. There had to be a level playing field for all the zones. However, the problem was that other zones did not have teams of the same calibre as these two teams, which would have led to a fall in the standards of the most prestigious national tournament. The face-off was an important one against this background.

In 1971, most of Bombay's first-string team was on national duty in the West Indies. Hence they were not available to play the finals of the Ranji Trophy for which they had qualified. A second string Bombay team made up of mostly college-level players faced a tenacious Maharashtra team. This was a good opportunity for the 'other' team from the West Zone to not only best their more reputed rivals but in the process bag the coveted Ranji Trophy. However, once again, Bombay got the job done.

The result also put paid to the demands for a second team from West Zone; in any case, if the demand continued to be raised, the administrators now had an excuse based on this match to deny it, given that Maharashtra had lost to a Bombay team that was mostly made up of collegians.

Apart from Maharashtra, Bombay's closest rivals were Rajasthan who made it to the Ranji finals seven times, never besting the 'Khaddoos' team on any of those occasions. Analysing these examples clarifies for us the difficulty in picking the

Bombay XI. Even their closest rivals were only able to beat them intermittently and that too after putting in their absolute best. It is not difficult to imagine the struggle that it must have been for teams from other zones to face Bombay.

Even when Bombay was being pushed to its limits, or being beaten, it was due to the talent from Bombay itself. Bombay's close rivals Maharashtra and the seven times Ranji finalists Rajasthan both had players from Bombay. And, if you are thinking that these players crossed borders because they were not good enough, think again. Amongst the players who crossed over include national players and prolific performers. Nari Contractor is a case in point. In the selection trial matches of 1951-52 he scored centuries but could not find a place in the Bombay team that was already brimming with talented candidates. The Gujarat captain who was present at the trials invited Contractor to play for the state and Contractor made a remarkable debut, scoring a century in each innings, for Gujarat against Baroda later that season. And Contractor went on to captain the national side. That such a player had to find footing elsewhere is a testament to the depth of the Bombay team.

I think now we have an inkling of the might and depth of the Bombay team – a team whose second string could strike awe and fear into the hearts of the opponents. Picking the best eleven from such a pool is a daunting task not purely because one is spoilt for choice, but also for the reason that it is a matter of the heart. Such a team, such a legacy rather, with its ruthlessness and winning habit also managed to inspire and sustain, for decades, the romance with cricket for lakhs of people.

I must confess that my heart and fingers tremble at the prospect of proposing the Best Bombay XI. How, indeed, can

I choose mere eleven players from a plethora of geniuses? And more importantly, what will be the parameters, yardsticks and principles for selecting the Best Bombay XI? Will it be talent or performance, average or strike rate? Match-winning knocks or match-saving knocks? How can statistics describe the situation under which the player performed? How can numbers ever tell us what a win meant? Can the emotion, the faith that a player brought in the team and the viewer be ever felt by people who aren't of that era?

However, since I have undertaken the task, let me put my cards on the table straightaway. I will assert that there are two positions in the team which cannot be challenged. They are the openers Vijay Merchant and Sunil Gavaskar. It's not to say that there were no other contenders for this spot, but these two have to be given their due.

The misery of life is that each selection is accompanied by rejection. As the clichéd saying goes: 'One man's gain is another man's pain.' Selectors have the thankless job of segregating wheat from chaff. But it is not always that simple. There is no plain distinction between wheat and chaff all the time. If the difference in quality was too obvious, there would be no dilemma for the selectors. A combination of style, technique, temperament and contexts lie at the root of such a dilemma. Players are not numbers, they are made of very complex talents, all of which come together to make them a performer. To analyse which player with which combination of talents is better suited at a particular point of time is indeed one of the most difficult mental tasks. And yet, it is not always about calculation. At times it is pure intuition. One looks at a player and is driven to certain judgements or expectations; the source of which cannot be quite identified. However, intuitions don't always work and thus we are all thrown into this deep abyss of constantly negotiating between calculation and intuition. Choosing one player is as difficult as choosing the last one. All this is to say that there are no set formulae for choosing successful players.

Selection entails rejection and the pain of rejecting deserving players is truly greater than the joy of selecting some. As important as selecting the best team is talking about the people who just missed the mark and why. One player who would have succeeded immensely if he hadn't had to leave India was K.C. Ibrahim. He migrated to Pakistan post-Partition and retired in 1952 itself. The right-hand batsman played four Tests for India against West Indies in the 1948-49 series at home, and scored a humungous number of runs. Ibrahim had made his first-class debut in 1938 and was known for having made a lot of runs in domestic cricket. He began the season of 1942 with an unbeaten 230. In 1947-48, Ibrahim was uncontrollable with his bat. He scored 1,171 runs at 167.29 which consisted of four hundreds. This won him the Indian Cricketer of the Year award. His scores read as follows 218*, 36*, 234*, 77* and 144*, which makes for a total of 709 runs without being dismissed! However, his performance drastically dipped towards the end of the series. His last innings scores read two, two and four. Moving to Karachi in 1950 proved to be the end of his career.

Madhav Mantri who used to open with him for Bombay said: 'He was very confident in playing seam bowling on a matting wicket. A consistent player for the Muslims in the Pentangulars, he once single-handedly won a game for his team by scoring 137. It was a great exhibition of batsmanship. A fine captain, he backed his players and would discuss team strategies with them.' KC was the captain of the victorious Bombay team in the Ranji Trophy of 1949. The knockout format that existed then required each and every match to be won to stay in the competition. In the timeless seven-day Ranji final of March 1949 at the Brabourne stadium, he opened the innings and batted for ten hours to score 219 against Baroda. The knock was as responsible a captain's knock as one will see. Old-timers never stop quoting it.

As a teenager, Ibrahim was known to be supremely intelligent. Studying at the St Xavier's College between 1937 and 1941, he would solve complicated problems in a jiffy and scored brilliant marks in mathematics. But on the cricket ground, it would be difficult to believe he was the same studious boy. He would be at his attacking best, scoring runs with panache and confidence. He easily got a ticket to the national team and a life of glory awaited him. But the circumstances were such that he had to move to Pakistan. Sadly, India lost a gem and so did the world of cricket.

The case of Madhav Apte is intriguing. He was technically precise. His first-class career began with a bang. He scored a century on debut as an opening batsman against Saurashtra in 1951-52. Within a year, he was on the tour of West Indies where he got scores of 64, 52, 64, 9, 0, 163*, 30, 30, 15 and 33 – all while opening the innings. But as soon as he came back to India, he was dropped. It was shocking, but that is the way things worked. Apte, however, seemed unperturbed and went on to score 2,070 runs in the Ranji Trophy (average: 39.80). He continued to play with exuberance till the late 1960s.

Another close contender for the all-time opener spot is

Madhav Mantri. Everything he did – in front of and behind the stumps – was with the right amount of confidence. He was always confident but never flamboyant. He scored 2,787 runs (average: 50.67) in the national competition during a first-class career that stretched over twenty-five years. His highest score was 200 for Bombay against Maharashtra in 1948-49, the third of three centuries in successive matches. In first-class cricket he had 193 dismissals, 137 of them came out of caught behinds.

Mantri was a genuine opening batsman who read swing well and negotiated it confidently. The precision of his technique can be gauged by the fact that in the fifty consecutive years of the treacherous Kanga League that he played, he never got injured. This league, it must be remembered, was played in the monsoon without a helmet or other protective gear. Connoisseurs of the game feel that Mantri would have been an asset to the team if he had played more Tests.

Dilip Sardesai and Ashok Mankad were important openers in the Bombay team too, but by and large they were middle-order batsmen. Farokh Engineer shifted to opening midway through his career. Bombay was thus blessed with many openers, but even amongst all of them, the two stand out beyond doubt. There cannot be any argument that Vijay Merchant and Sunil Gavaskar would be the best opening pair. It was often said, and not wrongly, that beating Merchant's defensive bat was as commendable as claiming his wicket.

Vijay Merchant had a Test average of 47.72 and a first-class average of 71. He gathered thousands of runs on home pitches and scored over 4,000 runs in his two tours of England. His style of late-cutting the ball made people marvel. Merchant made forty-four first-class centuries, eleven of which exceeded 200 runs and one of them was of 359 runs! Merchant is often called the person who brought in the era of safety-first batting in India. In 1936, he was crowned the Wisden Cricketer of the Year while C.B. Fry exclaimed: 'Let us paint him white and take him with us to Australia as an opener.'

Merchant and Gavaskar, however brilliant, were different types of players. Merchant was defensive and had the technique and patience to bat on any pitch for two days. Gavaskar was much more natural. Though his technique was perfect, he negotiated the new-ball attack with a lot of confidence. Even as a schoolboy, he scored a century with strokes flowing in all directions. Seeing him leave the ball against fast swinging deliveries on seaming wickets was a treat to watch.

In an era of really quick international bowlers, Gavaskar batted like a champion. However, one could see that Gavaskar slowly tamed himself and the aggression turned to caution with time. He knew that he was an important batsman and things will get difficult for the team if he played recklessly.

Ninety-two-year-old Russi Cooper puts the comparison between Merchant and Gavaskar up front. 'By today's standards, Merchant's batting was boring. He would nudge the ball here and there and mainly play on the patience of the bowler. For bad wickets he had very good technique. He would watch the ball till the last second. He simply loved to bat. Gavaskar on the other hand had shots all round the wicket.'

Now we come to the trunk of the team, the middle order. The middle order is perhaps the most difficult spot to choose. Only runs cannot explain the success of a batsman. The middle order has to stay strong and tight and lay the base of the innings. Openers can shine or fail and it is the middle-order batsmen who will have to take the brunt of the opener's play when they fail. It is an uncertain position also because at the start of the game you have no idea what to expect and no idea about what you are expected to do. If the openers shine, the task of the middle order is to complement by being flamboyant and aiming for a huge score. If the openers fail, however, the middle-order batsman finds himself on the pitch knowing that he is the sole link to success or failure of his team in the match. The pressure can be immense.

Bombay has been fortunate to have many contenders who have been brilliant middle-order batsmen. For the purpose of the four spots in the middle order, I have shortlisted more than a dozen genuine competitors and each has a unique record. Unlike Merchant–Gavaskar duo who had little competition, the competition is stiffer for the middle order, especially with the retirement of Sachin Tendulkar now.

The players whom I struggled between are as follows: Khandu Rangnekar, Ajit Wadekar, Dilip Sardesai, Vijay Bhosle, Vijay Manjrekar, Manohar Hardikar, Ramnath Kenny, Ashok Mankad, Dilip Vengsarkar, Sandeep Patil, Sanjay Manjrekar, Sachin Tendulkar and Vinod Kambli. All of them are pure middle-order batsmen. One can put the likes of Vinoo Mankad, Dattu Phadkar, Polly Umrigar, G.S. Ramchand and Bapu Nadkarni in the all-rounder's category.

Another clarification that I have to make is that I possibly cannot select them in the batting slots that they usually batted in. Wadekar, Rangnekar and Kambli, the three left-handers in the list were all stylish attacking batsmen. Rangnekar initially played for Bombay but later moved to Maharashtra and Holkars. He was a favourite of Col. C.K. Nayudu because he used to attack in any situation. He was a player of big innings and fielded extraordinarily. Their batting numbers weren't too rigid when they were young, like many other Bombay batsmen. Rangnekar preferred to bat higher up but was shunted in the middle order instead.

Seeing the stylish Wadekar walk in at the fall of the first wicket became almost like a ritual for Bombay fans. Wadekar was devastating at number three. Wadekar drove with disdain; he was severe on anything that was fractionally short and cut it square. His best innings of 323 in the Ranji Trophy came against world-class spinners B.S. Chandrasekhar and E.A.S. Prasanna at the Brabourne stadium. Wadekar exuded high-class batsmanship.

Vinod Kambli was perhaps more aggressive than the above two. He was immensely talented. At the Test level, he bagged two double hundreds, one of which came against England. Kambli scored 6,459 runs for Bombay with a great average of 67 while Wadekar had average of 58.51. On the other hand, while Kambli had an average of 54.20 in Tests, Wadekar wasn't successful in Tests as a batsman.

Nari Contractor was one person who played a lot with Wadekar and watched a lot of Kambli. He opines: 'Kambli was definitely better as far as talent was concerned. However, I have watched Ajit play some fantastic knocks. Kambli may have a better average playing for Bombay and India and had Wadekar mentored Kambli well, he would have been a very good batsman internationally.' Similar opinion is echoed by quite a few former international players.

Chandu Borde, however, differs. 'The major difference between Wadekar and Kambli was that Wadekar hooked well. Kambli was sorted out against short stuff. I would still prefer Wadekar at three and not Kambli.' One explanation that favours Wadekar is that he got to play international cricket quite late in his career. He ought to have played for India when he was in terrific form during university days. But there were many who were picked ahead of him. Had he been picked when he was in form, his statistics might have looked better. However for me, Wadekar is the one who will bat at three for The Best Bombay XI.

The slots of Nos. 4, 5 and 6 have Rusi Modi, Vijay Manjrekar, Ramnath Kenny, Manohar Hardikar, Dilip Sardesai, Ashok Mankad, Dilip Vengsarkar, Sanjay Manjrekar and the great Sachin Tendulkar as contenders. Each one of them contributed immensely to Bombay cricket and each was a gem in his own right.

Take the example of Rusi Modi. His record is amazing indeed. He was a wristy stroke player whose elegance was supplemented with a voracious appetite for runs. Modi was the first batsman to score 1,000 runs in a season in the Ranji Trophy. His record was surpassed only forty-four years later by W.V. Raman. Modi scored 215 for Parsis against Europeans in the Bombay Pentangular and a 203 not out against the Australian Services team in 1945-46. He bagged 560 runs against West Indies. It was in this series that he got his only century in Tests: the 112 at Bombay. He continued to play for Bombay and be a shining asset. In a first-class career that spanned almost twenty years, he scored 7,509 runs (average: 53.63) with twenty centuries.

Vijay Manjrekar was yet another adored batsman. Mansur Ali Khan Pataudi felt that he had the best technique amongst

Indians. He scored 133 in his first Test in England in 1952. It was a knock of supreme quality. The series against New Zealand and England were his best performances. Among his seven Test centuries, the highest of 189 came against England at Delhi in 1961-62.

The remaining gems in our bag – Ashok Mankad (average: 76.08), Dilip Vengsarkar (average: 74.18), Sanjay Manjrekar (average: 68.44) Ramnath Kenny (average: 62.48), Manohar Hardikar (average: 50) and Sachin Tendulkar (average: 87.44) – have the best credentials. Vengsarkar and Tendulkar surely deserve two out of the three slots. The remaining slot has to be contested between Sardesai, Kenny, Hardikar and Ashok Mankad. Sardesai has an average of 54.55 in sixty-one matches and Mankad played ninety-three matches at an average of 76.08. While Mankad scored 6,619 runs with twenty-two centuries, Sardesai scored only nine. On the sheer weight of the performance for Bombay, Ashok Mankad is way ahead of Sardesai.

We have half of the team at our disposal at the moment. Our team at present comprises Merchant and Gavaskar as openers, Wadekar at three, Tendulkar at his customary four, Vengsarkar at five, Ashok Mankad at six. Perhaps we can debate about Rusi Modi and Ashok Mankad and compare their credentials further.

Now, extremely crucial in the grand team of all-time Bombay XI are the two slots of all-rounders. The contestants for these slots are Vinoo Mankad, Dattu Phadkar, Polly Umrigar, G.S. Ramchand, Bapu Nadkarni and Ravi Shastri. Out of these, Vinoo Mankad,

Bapu Nadkarni and Ravi Shastri were left-arm spinners and good batsmen. Phadkar, Umrigar and Ramchand used the new ball and were great with the bat.

All these great players have the most phenomenal of records. However, having Umrigar at seven and V. Mankad at eight seems to be a good combination. The thing is that if we have Modi or Ashok Mankad at six, it would disturb this combination. With the kind of record that Umrigar possesses, he can be brought in at six. Umrigar is easily one of the all-time greats. Umrigar was an all-rounder of merit. Handsome as he was, Umrigar was a commanding figure at the crease with whatever he did. Batting, bowling or while directing operations as captain, Umrigar towered over the field even when he simply stood in his usual position at first slip.

It was Umrigar that held the record of the highest score by an Indian on tour for three decades! His 252 not out against Cambridge University in 1959 was priceless. As a bowler, his finest hour was when he took four for twenty-seven while helping India to defeat the mighty Australia at Kanpur in 1959. A shrewd captain, he led India in eight Tests, losing only two before he resigned from captaincy because of a misunderstanding with the selectors. Umrigar is one of the only two Indian cricketers (Vinoo Mankad being the other) who have scored a century and also taken five wickets in an innings. To top it, this achievement was bagged by Umrigar overseas against West Indies in 1962. Umrigar is also to be remembered as the very first Indian to hit a Test double century. So Umrigar comes at six.

Vinoo Mankad is definitely another must. He makes for the ideal No. 7 player. He can easily be called one of the greatest all-rounders that India has ever produced. In Tests, he scored a 2,109 runs with an average of 31.47 and took 162 wickets at 32.31. Mankad scored five centuries and on two occasions in his career, he took eight wickets in an innings. He holds the record of a 413-run partnership for the first wicket with P. Roy. He scored a blistering 231 in this match and maintained an average of a whopping 105 in that series!

It was Mankad who was the key bowler – twelve wickets in the match – in India's stupendous victory over England in 1951 at Madras. This was India's first victory against England. The best example of his all-round brilliance is perhaps the Test at Lords in 1952 when he scored 72 and 184. His calibre and charisma have to be understood by the fact that in the entire match he ended up bowling ninety-seven overs taking five for 231.

Eventually, it was England who won by eight wickets, but Mankad's performance won everyone's heart. His effort in that match can easily be given the title of the greatest effort by a member of a losing team. In the forty-four Tests he played, India won only five. Yet, he continued to play his own part well.

Now we face ourselves with the question of the wicketkeeper, i.e., slot No. 8. The play-off is essentially between the greats Naren Tamhane and Farokh Engineer. Old-timers were always charmed by the technique and 'safety-first approach' of Naren Tamhane. His movements were swift and he was always in the mindset and position to effect a dismissal. On the other hand, Engineer was flamboyant and loved leaping and diving to both sides. As far as batting is concerned, Engineer scored in an attacking way, but Tamhane was not a batsman. In fact, later in his career, Engineer started opening the innings and a slot in the middle for an all-rounder was created.

Farokh Engineer was the best in what he did. What more can be said than the fact that he was chosen as the first-choice wicketkeeper for the Rest of the World XI series in England and Australia in the early 1970s. Engineer's diving tactics needed extremely sharp reflexes, especially considering that he was the keeper to the legendary spin quartet of Bedi, Prasanna, Chandrasekhar and Venkataraghavan. At Madras against West Indies he made a quick ninety-four, his highest and finest score as a batsman. Engineer makes for the ideal wicketkeeper for Bombay in every case. The number eight slot belongs to Farokh Engineer.

We have finally come to the last lap of the team: the bowlers, who are the only ones who can win a game in the end. Bombay has a bad name for having bowlers who do not capitalize on their potential. I have devoted an entire chapter (see Chapter 4)in this book to the fact that the bowlers of Bombay do not match the brilliance of its batsmen. While Bombay has had a range of great batsmen and to choose amongst them is a terrible headache, the bowlers are fewer. However, though they do not match up to the batting, the bowling department was certainly good by itself. After all, it was the team of Bombay; its bowling has won many matches for its batsmen. There are many bowlers vying for the three prestigious slots. In my analysis for the last three slots, Phadkar will share the new ball with one of these five: Ramakant

Desai, Karsan Ghavri, Abdul Ismail, Abey Kuruvilla and Paras Mhambrey. All of them have done remarkably well and given Bombay the biting edge that any team needs to feel unbeatable.

Ramakant Desai was fascinatingly quick. When he was nineteen, he took four wickets for 169 runs against West Indies in Delhi. He was the one who assumed the form of a leader in the 1959 tour of England. He put England in a precarious situation at Lord's where he had figures of five for eighty-nine in the innings. However, within a couple of years he lost his pace because of being over-bowled. But he made sure he reinvented himself, became a cunning bowler and relied more on variations and cutters.

Abdul Ismail has 244 first-class wickets to his credit while Abey Kurvilla has 290 and Paras Mhambrey 284. However, the record of Karsan Ghavri beats all four. In thirty-nine Tests he has 109 wickets, besides 450 first-class wickets and 4,500 first-class runs. Ghavri was a Rajkot-born all-rounder who took senior Bombay cricketers by surprise when he made them hop in the Ranji Trophy match. Ghavri had just returned from the Indian Schoolboy's tour of Australia and it was Dilip Sardesai who offered him a job in the ACC. Playing with the likes of Umrigar, Nadkarni, Sardesai, Ramakant Desai and Vijay Bhosle, Ghavri's skills improved dramatically and he put those skills to best use for Bombay cricket. With his all-round ability, he could have been the perfect partner to share the new ball with Dattu Phadkar but as a pure fast bowler with effective bouncers and accurate yorkers, Ramakant Desai is ahead of others.

Standing strong in our prospective list is Padmakar Shivalkar who has a tremendous record indeed. However, it has to be said that neither Shivalkar nor Baloo Gupte matches up to Subhash

Gupte who mesmerized batsmen all over the world with his guile and I have no hesitation in asserting that no other bowler stands a chance in front of him. He was showered with praises by none other than the great Sir Garfield Sobers. Subhash Gupte was a world-class leg-break and googly bowler. Though he was not one of the people who got instant success, his Test career spiralled immensely in the West Indies in 1952-53, where he took fifty wickets at an average of 23.64. But these figures can hardly describe the conditions under which he took those wickets. In fact, he took twenty-seven wickets in Tests on perfect batting wickets; moreover he was bowling to the three 'Ws' – Clyde Walcott, Everton Weekes and Frank Worrell – and Alan Rae, Jeffrey Stollmeyer and Bruce Pairaudeau.

Gupte proved to be the best bowler in Pakistan as well; and later, against New Zealand, he was pretty much unplayable. He held the record of bagging thirty-four wickets in the series, a record that was surpassed only twenty-seven years later by Chandrasekhar. The high point for him was when he bagged nine wickets for 102 runs against West Indies in Kanpur. It was for that effort that he got the great appraisal by Sir Garry Sobers who said he rated Gupte higher than Shane Warne. In his first-class career, Gupte ended up taking 530 wickets at an average of 23.71. He has also been famous for wiping the entire batting line-up of Pakistan Services and Bahawalphur CC sides in 1954.

The comparative study of these three bowlers will be a tough but a fascinating job for us. Compare we must, because that is the only way to reach a coherent argument and basis to judge their aptness in our team. In thirty-six Tests, Subhash Gupte took 149 wickets. We also have to account the 530 first-class wickets that Subhash took, with twelve five-wicket hauls in Tests and thirty-six in first-class matches. His brother, Baloo Gupte, played a couple of Tests and has 417 first-class wickets with twenty-three five-wicket-hauls to his credit.

However it has to be said that Padmakar Shivalkar has been the most unfortunate. A mention must be made here of his accomplishments. He took 589 first-class wickets including forty-two five-wicket hauls and thirteen ten-wicket hauls and yet didn't get to play a single Test match. It was a travesty of justice and yet it is true that it happened.

Our team is near-perfect at this point. We have done our job of selecting each and every slot for the team. The great team of Bombay XI has been compiled. But having done this, I have to say that this can by no means be a perfect assessment of all the greats that have walked on the Bombay pitches and given their heart out for the sake of Bombay. On the other hand this has been a humble attempt on my part to attempt to consolidate all greats into a single team.

Let us look at what we have on our plates. Firstly, we have a solid pair to open: Merchant and Gavaskar. This is followed by the stylish Wadekar. Any discussion cannot rule out Tendulkar's right to have the number four spot to his name. Because of his international commitments he may have played less for Bombay, but his average for Bombay is phenomenal. I did not discuss his name at length because for me this requires no debate whatsoever. I sincerely doubt any cricket lover would think otherwise. Sachin belongs in the Bombay team without reconsideration. He truly belongs to the team and at the number four spot that suits him best. At number five, the great Bombay team will have Dilip Vengsarkar. Like Tendulkar, he was another person who hardly got to play for Bombay; he played less than fifty matches. But he has shown his value enough in these few outings to belong in the dressing room of the Bombay greats.

Though we can have one of the two prolific scorers, with Rusi Modi and Ashok Mankad competing for the number six slot, we need balance more than aggression here. The all-rounder Polly Umrigar would be the best person to bat at six. If either Modi or Ashok Mankad bats at that slot, there will be one less slot for an all-rounder.

We are halfway through the job. At number seven, the great Vinoo Mankad will walk in, another all-rounder and a great left-arm spinner. He will be followed by wicketkeeper Farokh Engineer at number eight. At nine and ten, we have left-arm fast bowler Karsan Ghavri and Ramakant Desai. The last slot automatically goes to the great leggie Subhash Gupte.

Our team is complete; we have picked out eleven from a vast sea of cricketers who have worn the Bombay lion crest. I have considered every candidate in every era, shortlisted a select few among the rest and further handpicked players for each and every slot with much care and thought.

Any team remains incomplete without a cohesive factor. Often it is the captain who becomes this factor. We have chosen the team; put together a series of greats like a pack of cards. But the most important question that remains is who should lead the team? To whom do we bestow the mantle of the great legacy of Bombay? At such junctures, seniority will be a trivial issue for selection. Merchant led Bombay for more than a decade and won many matches; so did Ajit Wadekar. Should we give the mantle to one of them? However, I feel that there is something in Polly Umrigar that makes him the person for the job. His astute leadership skills and tactical acumen make him a natural leader. I will thus make the decision to bestow captaincy on him.

So, here is my choice for The Best Bombay XI:

Vijay Merchant
Sunil Gavaskar
Ajit Wadekar
Sachin Tendulkar
Dilip Vengsarkar
Polly Umrigar (Captain)
Vinoo Mankad
Farokh Engineer
Karsan Ghavri
Ramakant Desai
Subhash Gupte

I am aware that the fate of the great team of Bombay XI that I have picked is being put to question and is being scrutinized. It will be subjected to immense scrutiny and perhaps criticism. There will be debate on the non-inclusions of Nadkarni, Sardesai, Rusi Modi, Ashok Mankad, Padmakar Shivalkar, Naren Tamhane, Dattu Phadkar, Baloo Gupte, Manohar Hardikar and Vinod Kambli. And indeed, all these players are the best of the best and all debates and dissatisfactions are valid. Debates only go on to show that Bombay has too many perfect XIs.

However, in my defence, it should be kept in mind that I have tried to forge together a team. As much as individual merits, I have paid close attention to the combination of the team. We should not forget that it is not just a collection of great individuals that make a great team but individuals that complement each other. I have tried to make a team of Bombay XI, a team that can truly play on the field and enchant the opposition.

Perhaps there is no need to make such a team, for teams and teams from Bombay have actually been doing this in reality. Bombay teams have achieved the zenith of success, reached where no team has. The Best Bombay XI is a reminder of all these teams of Bombay. It is a reminder of the rich legacy of Bombay cricket and the different variety of gems that this city has churned. Each of the eleven players of the team that I have picked has a story behind him. Each player is made by his circumstances, his friends and his hard work. In the stories of these eleven players are encompassed the stories of the thousands of aspirants and lovers of the Bombay cricket team. All of them form the perfect eleven in different ways.

7

GAVASKAR AND TENDULKAR: THE TWO LEGENDS

W hy can we just not watch matches, enjoy them and leave it at that? Why do we have to compare them and rank them? Sport is never only about winning and losing. If it was that, a mere glance at the statistics would inform us of who our heroes should be and that would be the end of it. But we all know too well that that is not the case. We are interested in knowing the many factors that combine to contribute to a player's performance or to frame his or her career. We are interested because we feel that the foundation on which we argue and choose our heroes reflects on us and defines us. Hence sports become a metaphor for many things in the world beyond the grounds. In a country like India, where cricket has singularly captured the sporting imagination of the country for the better part of the last half a century, debates to pick the greats of the game are many.

As stated, many factors contribute to our understanding of the players and their performances. However, we may at this point

139

wonder what we hope to gain by indulging in such comparisons? Comparison between players is like sweet poison. It kills the charm of two lives but at the same time it is too tempting to resist. Comparisons are particularly odious when two persons of great calibre are considered. But it is precisely when two people are great contributors to the game that comparisons become enticing, like a guilty pleasure. Comparison, evil as it can be, becomes necessary and inevitable at times. As soon as you start talking about a match, you enter the terrain of analysis and once you start analysing, comparisons are a must.

Comparisons have been inevitable in cricketing history. And, if you need proof of this, consider the following. Let me remind you of a time in cricketing history when island politics was at its rise in West Indies. Cricket lovers of British Guyana would say that Rohan Kanhai was a notch better than Sir Garfield Sobers who was a perfect three-in-one; a great batsman, a great bowler and a great fielder. These arguments went on often, particularly during matches when Kanhai would, during a brilliant innings, often outclass Sobers with his majestic stroke play. Such is this task that even the great Garfield Sobers came second at times. Hence anyone who undertakes such an analysis is burdened by the opinions, memories and emotions of all the lovers of the sport who take pride not only in their favourite players and performances but also in how they regard these players and performances.

Another case in point was the debate among South Africans, who bothered themselves a lot wondering whether the left-handed Graeme Pollock was more aggressive than his West Indian counterpart, Sobers. With minimum of back lift and precise footwork, Pollock would bisect the field with superbly timed shots. However, Sobers was excellent in whatever he did on the field: batting, bowling medium pace and spin and picking catches. Had Pollock and Barry Richards not been affected by the apartheid policy of their government, perhaps they would have done well against the likes of players that West Indies possessed.

Can we hypothetically compare how Pollock and Barry Richards would have fared against Australia and England? Richards did exceedingly well playing for Hampshire and smashed West Indian bowlers in several innings on county circuits. Or consider the fact that while playing in the Sheffield Shield in Australia, Barry Richards hit 356 in a day against the raw pace of Dennis Lillee. The faster Lillee bowled, the quicker the ball reached the fence.

But eventually Test matches are a different ball game. World cricketing history is full of comparisons and they will always be. But now to another important question: comparisons are fine, they are inevitable and needed but what is a just marker of comparison? Is it fair to compare great players with the aid of statistics? Well, to be fair I have to say no. It is true at the same time that statistics make comparison possible. They are perhaps the only way to relive the matches that are not possible to witness in a single lifetime. However, analysis is not merely about smacking a doughy batter of numbers.

Cricket, as I briefly touched on in the first chapter, is a game of nuances. The romance of a 'sleepless' city like Bombay with this sport that moves at an aristocratic pace is because it lends itself to literature, to storytelling, as perhaps no other sport does. Hence, analysis of cricket requires keen surgical incisions into the statistics to reveal what they contain and what they mean. Hence, no comparison with statistics alone can ever be perfect.

I do not think anyone who follows the game disagrees with this point because sports are not only about the numbers. A tiny thing can make a huge difference in sporting careers and to add to that, the rules of the game change with each era. How can we compare success in a game when the rules itself have changed over time? The playing conditions, the no-ball rule, the quality of equipment, the protective gear and many more factors have to be considered.

We have to carefully account for the factors considered to draw the comparison and what those particular factors reveal about the players in relation to each other. In a cricket-crazed country such as ours all observations are consumed with a liberal seasoning of passion. This stretches across the entire breadth of the emotional spectrum. The slightest tinge of criticism draws the rage of fans while even a technical observation is often stretched to elevate our players to the highest pedestals. Analysis is not a mere formality undertaken to sing praises of one player and deride another.

Consider the time when Sir Don mentioned in the media that he told his wife that he saw himself in Sachin Tendulkar. All of a sudden the films of Sir Don were unearthed from locked cupboards. Stroke by stroke, each of his shot was compared to Tendulkar's. And the two did look similar to the connoisseurs of the game. However, what does that tell us about the players apart from just that: that there exists a similarity in their stroke production? They differed in statistics, where Sir Don was streets ahead of Tendulkar. Apart from talent, a lot of other factors have to be considered.

Bradman played in the era of the back-foot rule which allowed bowlers to drag their back foot. This was certainly unfair to batsmen, and tall bowlers certainly looked menacing. Also, bodyline bowling made the bowler with the fielders in the leg cordon look dangerous. But Bradman reigned in the era of the bodyline series.

The question for us, those who compare, is this: Did Tendulkar have to encounter similar playing conditions? No. Sir Don only referred to the similarity in Tendulkar's stroke production in relation to his own style. He had not compared any other factors. It was not his intention to run him down. However, Tendulkar felt honoured and his followers relished the grand compliment. After all, any emulation of Sir Don seems worthy of celebration especially when recognized by the great batsman himself.

The example of comparison between Bradman and Tendulkar is still a one-off thing. In India, we have debates that have been on for years together. And even though not many of those debates, if any, have reached any semblance of a conclusion, it can be safely said that these comparative debates will continue. And, no matter what happens in the game, comparisons will always be made between Sunil Gavaskar and Sachin Tendulkar. After all, both were crucial in starting a new legacy of Indian cricket, at different points of time. One is an accomplished opening batsman and the other is an extremely aggressive middle-order batsman. Their styles of play too have been different.

When Gavaskar used to open the batting, the Indian batting line-up was brittle. He had to change his natural approach to batting to suit the scenario. He had an array of shots and used to be an aggressive batsman during his under-nineteen days. In fact, towards the end of his career, the beaming deliveries of Holding, Marshall and Davis were hit all over the park by him. This was while equalling Sir Don Bradman's record of twenty-nine Test centuries. It was an exhibition of controlled hitting. Similarly, he outclassed Srikkanth against New Zealand in a World Cup match of 1987 at Nagpur.

Tendulkar on the other hand has always been an aggressive player. Stockily built, he has had his ways of reading and dealing with situations. Fall of wickets has never been his major concern. Unlike Gavaskar, he had a good batting line-up to follow him. Sehwag, Dravid, Ganguly and Laxman in the middle-order brought a calming stability in the batting. And Tendulkar used it to his complete advantage by consistently attacking the bowlers.

This debate is complex and not conducive to being resolved easily. Kapil Dev is one person whose opinion in this debate will hold huge importance, since he played with both Gavaskar and Tendulkar. Here is what he has to say: 'Gavaskar was the most complete cricketer that I ever came across. I have seen players like Viv Richards who was completely ruthless. I have never seen Don Bradman, so I can't talk about him but I have seen that Sunil Gavaskar was a complete cricketer. Maybe he was not like Gary Sobers who could hit a ball outside the off stump on to the leg side. A player who could do that was Mohammed Azharuddin who used the bat in a different manner from Gavaskar. But Sunil Gavaskar, I observed, was very strong in his own way. The most important aspect of his batting was that he knew where his off stump was. Not many knew it.'

Kapil Dev continues: 'It may sound harsh but Tendulkar was one cricketer who had more talent and ability than even Sunil Gavaskar. He had the ability to destroy the bowling attack on his own. As he kept on playing, I noticed that he wanted to play more like Sunil Gavaskar. I think he had more talent than anybody else but he went into that Bombay shell wanting to play correct cricket. When he started he could hit the best of the best balls. Even Sunil couldn't do that.... Sunil was always very perfect but somewhere along the line, I feel that Sachin hasn't done justice to his talent. When I look back at his performance, I observe that though he scored a lot of centuries, he did not convert those centuries into 200 or 300-plus score like Lara did. Once Sachin got a hundred, he should have hit a boundary every over, but he starts playing like a typical Bombay player and that's the reason he hasn't scored big knocks.'

Kapil's assessment might sound harsh as he said but the truth is that I know many who would agree with the assessment of Kapil Dev. Adding to his valuation of how Tendulkar could have performed differently, Kapil adds: 'Tendulkar didn't grab an opportunity when the bowler was down. He did not think, "I will go after him". He used to go to the non-striking end with a single after scoring a hundred. That is more like Sunil Gavaskar. Sachin can be thought of in two phases: one when he started – his first ten years – and the other post that mark. He did not accelerate after the first ten years. I cannot even compare some of his earlier innings to the later ones. Only he can answer why he changed his style. When we look back at his performance, I would say that he had done more than anybody else. However, if he had played the way he played in the beginning, he might have scored 300–500 runs less but in my eyes he would have been a cricketer we all would have remembered.'

Kapil Dev here mentions that even if a few hundred runs were missed by Tendulkar over the span of his career that could have been discounted in lieu of the style with which he could play by trading those runs. He justifies the emphasis on the style of play rather than only accumulating runs, by stating that the fate of games can be determined by style. 'I don't agree with people who claim that Sachin was a mature cricketer at the age of fifteen. That was talent. He matured much later. The difference between Sunil and Sachin is that nobody expected Sunil to win matches. His game was not suited to it. Sachin's style, on the other hand, was perfectly suited to win matches. Then, why did he change his style?'

What then are we to understand from Kapil Dev's analysis? On what grounds do we compare these two players or differentiate between them? Kapil makes the question of comparison slightly easier for us when he says, 'All eleven players in a team cannot be match-winning players.' However, he says, 'Sachin had the ability to win matches single-handedly and destroy attacks. Unfortunately, he changed his style. Players like Yuvraj, Dhoni and Sehwag were the ones known as match winners in that team. On the other hand, players like Gavaskar and Shastri contributed in saving matches.' A player's approach to the game is as important as his talent and aptitude.   And ultimately it's the style that would determine this approach. As Kapil Dev rightly pointed out, Gavaskar's style was not suitable for winning matches. Statistical analysis indicates that while only six out of Gavaskar's thirty-four Test centuries were match-winning innings, he has helped India draw Test matches on twenty-two occasions.

This effectively means that a good 64.70 per cent of Gavaskar's centuries were match-saving centuries. It is worth noting though that, one of his six match-winning centuries was at the Port-of-Spain in 1976 when India chased 404 runs in the last innings.

Also, more than numbers can say, this is an astonishing record considering the role Gavaskar played against formidable fast bowlers of the opposition. And not to forget, all this was done without a helmet. To his credit, Gavaskar played on uncovered pitches which are more bowler friendly than covered pitches. Also, thirteen of his centuries came against the mighty West Indies. The conditions under which Gavaskar played make his performances twice as unbelievable as they seem.

Chetan Chauhan, former Indian opener, describes the batsmanship of Gavaskar well: 'I first saw Sunil Gavaskar when he played for Bombay University and I, at the time, was playing for Poona University. Subsequently, we both played for West Zone in the Vizzy Trophy and became very good friends. He was an absolute professional and worked on his technique and his game.He would think a lot about his cricket. The one thing I learnt from him was to never to throw away my wicket. Gavaskar was very mean when batting was concerned and always made the bowlers slog to earn his wicket. When he was on the ground, his entire focus would be on cricket. I was amazed at his appetite and focus for runs right from the university days. He would take time to become friendly and would not easily speak his thoughts and views to many people. But once he became sure that the person was harmless, he made for great company after the game. I opened with him for India in thirty-five Test matches and had an excellent understanding with him on the ground as well as outside it, when the game was over. I think I was one of the very few people in whom he confided regarding the team and the players.'

A facet of Gavaskar's batting, apart from his appetite for runs, which is often pointed out with admiration, is the way in which he scored those runs. Chauhan too provides testimony to the same while illuminating further on the relationship they shared on the pitch. 'Gavaskar was a typical Bombaywalla and would go out of the way to support a player from Bombay. While batting together, he gave me great support and advice and would even caution me when I played loose shots. I was one of the very few cricketers he would ask between the overs, if he had committed any mistake while playing. We would encourage and motivate each other because we knew that as openers, the team depended on us. He would always stay on at the wicket as long as possible, so that it became easier for the later batsmen who would follow. Needless to say that because of our understanding, help and motivation for each other, we had nine or ten century partnerships for India.'

There are different reasons attributed to Gavaskar's style of play. Some believed it was the mental make-up of Gavaskar that led him to sculpt his game in the mould of a grafter. Others believe it was the era in which he played that contributed to his style of play. Since Gavaskar didn't enjoy the luxury that Tendulkar possessed through the better half of his playing career, of having Ganguly, Dravid, Laxman and Sehwag all backing him, the opposition attacked Gavaskar venomously. They were aware that once they saw the back of Gavaskar, their job is as good as done because they were unlikely to face much resistance from other batsmen. Hence, Gavaskar curbed his shot making to serve the purposes of the team, even though he possessed all the shots and was an aggressive batsman in his younger days. This was not a restriction that Sachin Tendulkar had to abide by for most of his career.

Here we see that although the comparison started out between the two players, the factors have already broadened to include the abilities and styles of other players, batsmen, in the

Bombay Gymkhana: A venue for the first ever Test match played in India against England in 1933

(left) **Vijay Merchant:** Father figure of Bombay cricket, Merchant had a first-class average of 71 and was the Wisden Cricketer of the Year in 1936

Vinoo Mankad: One of the greatest all-rounders that India has ever produced

Subhash Gupte: World-class leg-break and googly bowler

Bombay Presidency (Proper) Cricket Association

THE formation of the Central Board of Control for Cricket in India and the organization of local cricket associations followed almost automatically as a result of the visit of the M.C.C. Team to India in 1926-27. That tour had been arranged, very successfully and ably, by the Calcutta Cricket Club, and although the programme was in every way a most satisfactory one, it became evident that if such visits were to be repeated in the future, it was putting too great a strain on one club to expect it to continue arranging tours of such importance. Consequently correspondence took place between the various provinces with a view to the formation of a body sufficiently strong in finance and backing to assume the responsibility for India's cricketing future. Under the then existing circumstances everything seemed to point to Bombay, with its already existing Quadrangular Committee, as the most favourable site, and to that committee as the most satisfactory nucleus for such an all-India Board.

The project actually took shape as a result of the interest in this matter shown by Sir Leslie Wilson, the then Governor of Bombay, and under his patronage a committee was formed which for some time functioned in Bombay and whose executive members were more or less the members of the existing Quadrangular Committee.

In 1928 it, was, however, found that without a paid secretariat it was not possible to carry on the work involved, and it was decided to ask Col. Rowlandson of the Army Sports Board to take charge of the direction of this Board of Control for Cricket in India and to keep the offices of the Board at Delhi. This move was carried out with the result that from that date the control of cricket in India has been worked from Delhi rather than from Bombay, which many people considered to be the true centre of Indian cricket.

In the meantime other provinces had been busy forming local and provincial cricket associations which had a voice in the direction of the affairs of the Cricket Board of Control at Delhi. In view of this movement it was resolved, in 1928, to form a cricket association for the Bombay Presidency which should have control of all cricket in the presidency and which should gather in one corporate body all the leading cricketing clubs of the presidency. Having achieved this it then became essential for this body to associate itself with the Board of Control for Cricket at Delhi and thus to secure a place on the Managing Committee of that body.

WINNERS OF RANJI TROPHY

The Bombay Presidency (Proper) Cricket Association XI who were the holders of the Ranji Gold Cup Championships in 1935.

A combined group of the Bombay Presidency (proper) Cricket Association winners of the first Cricket Championship of India and the Cricket Club of India—1935.

Combined Bombay Presidency and Madras Teams in final of Ranji Trophy Championship 1936. Bombay were the winners.

(above) **Vijay Manjrekar:** Much acclaimed Bombay batsman with the best technique among Indian cricketers

(left) Polly Umrigar: Astute captain, he believed in winning matches

Naren Tamhane: Wicketkeeper and captain with an excellent technique and a 'safety-first' approach

Ramakant Desai: A fast bowler who relied on sharp bouncers and accurate yorkers

Dr H. D. Kanga, President
Bombay Cricket Association

FROM :
BCA Annual Report for the year ended 31st March 1946

Dr. H.D. KANGA :

It is our great misfortune to have to record the sad demise
of our President Dr. H.D. Kanga during the year. Dr. Kanga was
at the helm of the Association from its very inception, as
President from 1930 to 1034, then was the Chairman of the
Managing Committee from 1935 to 1944. On the retirement of Sir
John Beaumont Dr. Kanga was elected President, which office he
held till his death. Dr. Kanga served the Bombay Cricket Associatio
and the Board of Control for Cricket in India for a number of
years. His great faith, enthusiasm and unceasing interest in
cricket helped to raise the standard in Bombay to which it is toda
and for this great service Bombay will ever cherish his memory
with gratitude.

To commomerate the memory of the late Dr. H.D. Kanga, the
Associ tion is contempleting to institute the League Cricket
Tournament and to nameit after him. It has also decided to collect
funds for Dr.H.D. Kanga Memorial Fund towards which an amount of
Rs.2,629/2/- has alrwady been contributed with further contributic
expected to come in. The Committee is also considering to establis
a Sports Library, and to name it after him. A full size oil-colour
Portrait of the late Dr. H.D. Kanga id also ready for being
unveiled very shortly.

Madhav Mantri, captain of the Bombay team in 1957,
receiving the Ranji Trophy from President Rajendra Prasad
at Rashtrapati Bhavan.

Mansur Ali Khan
Pataudi and Polly
Umrigar at Port-of-
Spain in 1961

Farokh Engineer: Flamboyant wicketkeeper

(top) **Ashok Mankad:** Prolific run-scorer for Bombay and a thinking captain

(left) **Ajit Wadekar:** Stylish left-hand batsman and India captain

**Wankhede
stadium:** Named
after Bombay Cricket
Association president
Seshrao Wankhede, it
was built in 1974 and
the first Test match
played here was in
January 1975 between
India and West Indies

The Bombay Cricket Association

Managing Committee (1972-73) :

President : Mr. S. K. Wankhede

Vice-Presidents : Mr. K. M. Rangnekar
and M. W. Desai.

Jt. Hon. Secs. : Prof. M. V. Chandgadkar
and S. V. Kadam.

Hon. Treasurer : Mr. R. M. Dadachanjee.

Committee Members : Mr. S. C. Sheth, Mr. V. B. Prabhudesai, Mr. S. D. Kotnis,
Mr. R. V. Gavaskar, Mr. P. S. Bhesania, Mr. V. V. Godbole, Mr. R. D. Jukar,
Mr. B. V. Mahaddalkar, Mr. S. J. Diwadkar, Mr. P. R. Umrigar, Maj. R. G. Salvi,
Mr. R. C. Purohit, Mr. D. K. Abdulla, Mr. M. Pandey, Mr. K. B. Mehta, Mr. J. B.
Braganza.

Dr. H. D. Kanga League Committe:
Mr. M. K. Mantri, Mr. M. S. Hardikar, Mr. M. D. Irani, Mr. S. D. Kotnis,
Mr. P. S. Bhesania, Maj. R. G. Salvi.

Dr. H. D. Kanga League Silver Jubilee Souvenir Committee:
Mr. S. D. Kotnis, Mr. G. K. Menon, Mr. A. J. Dossa.

Sunil Gavaskar: One
of the greatest openers
ever. Could build an
innings under pressure

Dilip Vengsarkar: With an upright stance, he preferred to play the ball on the up

Karsan Ghavri: Let-arm fast bowler who in his day would make batsmen hop

Sandeep Patil: Ruthless striker of the ball, he believed 'attack is the best defence'

(top) **Brabourne stadium:** Owned by
the Cricket Club of India, it was built
in 1937. Its North Stand houses the
headquarters of the Board of Control for
Cricket in India (BCCI)

(facing page) **Sachin Tendulkar:**
Batting legend, he has monopolized all
the batting records in Tests

(above) Kanga League match in progress at Azad Maidan

(below) Dilip Vengsarkar, Madhav Mantri and Vasu Paranjpe at the
Dadar Union club.

teams of their respective eras. Hence, the process of comparative analysis is inevitably and uncontrollably inundated with many hypotheticals that add to the complication of analysing the available facts.

One illustration of such complexities in the comparison between Gavaskar and Tendulkar would be the recurring question: would Viv Richards have been as devastating as he was if he had played against the ferocious attack of West Indies, the pace quartet of Roberts, Holding, Marshall and Garner – not to speak of the other equally fast bowlers of the West Indies during the 1970s and '80s? The encounters would have made for great matches but we can safely say that Richards would not have been able to look so pervasive.

And this is the exact reason why Gavaskar scores over others. In the above hypothetical conundrum, the truth of which is not possible to ascertain, we find a reason why Gavaskar must be regarded very highly as a player. He scored thirteen of his hundreds against the very same brutal attack of the West Indies. Moreover, Gavaskar did it in an era when they would put all their energy in attacking him. That age had no neutral umpires to check no-balls, no limit on the number of bouncers and the pitches were uncovered. And last but not the least, there were no helmets as well.

The one major difference between Gavaskar and Tendulkar is that Gavaskar opened whereas Tendulkar batted at four. Facing the shiny new ball, which would be swinging and bouncing consistently at a speed of 150 km per hour, is the toughest job in the world. Fast bowlers used to bowl in short spells to preserve their energy. Facing such spirited bowlers was definitely more dangerous than playing at number four. However, it has to be said that at that slot, Tendulkar was as effective as any other batsman in the world in combating quick bowlers.

Anshuman Gaekwad used to open the innings with Gavaskar. He remembers the unique challenges the cricketing community posed to batsman of that era, especially the openers. He recounts it for us to help us imagine the milieu Gavaskar had to play in: 'The team required Gavaskar to stay put and bat as long as possible. Usually the role of an opening batsman was to see the new ball off. In the case of Sunil, the team wanted him to block one end. To his credit he curbed his shots and when required, he attacked. Having played with him, I observed that he had the gift of concentration. And he was a very good judge of leaving the ball. On the other hand, Sachin was a genius. As a coach I watched him closely. His preparation was meticulous. People often say that Gavaskar didn't play with a helmet while Sachin did. That is quite crucial, but it has to be said that the rate at which international matches were played from the 1990s, there was no sense in risking playing without a helmet.'

The circumstances and certain specifics obviously differ from each other. However, those factors are a condition of time. An individual player for the purpose of aiding comparison cannot stop time or freeze the changing conditions and rules. We have to concede that both players made their choices, the reasons for which are rooted in the circumstances of their respective eras. If we demand Sachin to play without a helmet, how ridiculous would that proposition sound? While we have to factor in Gavaskar's bravado for playing without the helmet, we cannot hold that against Tendulkar and vice versa. However, with these contexts in mind we may now consider something that is mostly under the control of the players: statistics.

Even for the comparison of numbers we have to make an attempt at equating the two sets of statistics. Gavaskar played 125 Tests whereas Tendulkar played 200. Thus, if one has to compare them, the base has to be of 125 Tests. It will be unfair to Gavaskar if his record is compared to 200 Tests of Tendulkar. Here is a comparison based on the first 125 Tests of both.

Gavaskar					
Tests	Innings	Runs	Avg.	100s	50s
125	214	10,122	51.22	34	45

Tendulkar					
Tests	Innings	Runs	Avg.	100s	50s
125	201	10,281	57.12	35	41

We can see that apart from the difference in averages, there is hardly any difference between their scores. If Gavaskar scored thirty-four hundreds, Tendulkar's tally exceeds by no more than one. The statistics indicate a marginal difference. In 214 innings, Gavaskar scored 10,122 while in thirteen innings less, Tendulkar scored 10,281. This means Tendulkar scored 159 runs extra in thirteen innings less. Again, there is no major difference in the scores.

However, the playing conditions of the era of pre-covered pitches made all the difference. This is not to say that Tendulkar would have struggled in that era. A genius finds his way in any conditions, but if we consider people who played in that era, the conditions, and the no-ball rule, all of it made it very difficult for the batsmen to excel. This was true especially in

England where conditions changed when play resumed after abrupt rains. The pitch would change its behaviour and a batsman who was playing well would begin to struggle on the rain-affected pitch. After the practice of covering pitches was institutionalized, the extra advantage that bowlers would have had was mostly nullified.

The morning dew was a blessing to fielding sides on uncovered pitches. A captain would hardly ever throw the ball to a spinner to start the proceedings in those conditions. Merely an hour and a half of the mornings in dewy conditions plus skilled fast bowlers would rattle batsmen. Those ninety minutes then were good enough to determine the fate of a five-day Test match. This, again, was especially true in English conditions or even in the subcontinent conditions in winter. Gavaskar was really sure of his off stump and would keep leaving the ball with superb judgement. Now that the pitches are covered, there is hardly any dew on the pitch in the morning. This is one of the key reasons why fast bowlers hardly look menacing in the current era.

Gavaskar again shines in this regard. As an opening batsman, Gavaskar was often India's shield against the barrage of fast bowlers on such mornings, in those challenging batting conditions. If we add to it the quality of pace bowling and uncovered pitches prevalent in that era, Gavaskar's numbers gladden the reader's eye. Speaking of the quality of pace bowling during the 1970s and '80s, it does not take much for anyone remotely familiar with the bowling attacks of those decades to appreciate any batsman who would play without a helmet. This must be factored in to illuminate the quality of Gavaskar's statistics. This is especially true in the case of his hundreds, more than one-third of which were scored against a team widely regarded to have the best battery of pace attack in any era of cricket.

The introduction of helmet was a big move in increasing the confidence of batsmen. Nari Contractor was hit on the head by Charlie Griffith's delivery and managed to survive. He says: 'I would put it this way. Those who are playing with the helmet get hit but they are up and playing. During my days when batsmen like me were hit on the head, they either went out of the game or were not the same batsmen any more. In fact, some kept playing but weren't comfortable against bouncers. It's a question of confidence. When a batsman is hit on the helmet, he isn't worried. He takes off the helmet, checks whether it's OK and starts batting again. Get hit on the head and you won't know whether you will survive, which is what happened to me. And mind you, during my time there was a back-foot no-ball rule. The fast bowlers would drag their back foot. This was dangerous.'

Gavaskar may have got hit only once while Tendulkar was hit several times on the helmet. Again and again, the Indian public was tired of hearing about the several injuries of Tendulkar. It almost felt like Tendulkar had taken the pressure of the entire country's aspirations onto his body which was wilting more with each passing day due to the demands of the international cricket calendar. The incident of Tendulkar's tennis elbow comes to mind. It was a phase when his career seemed all but over. Many including Greg Chappell doubted Tendulkar's ability to continue to play. He was even advised to quit the game but he was tough mentally and refused to give up. Instead, he became focused and positive. When he came back to international cricket, he had changed his approach. He was more circumspect and that childlike flamboyance he had always had was missing. He seemed like a typical English professional who was out there to pile on runs.

On his second coming after recovering from the ghastly injury, Sachin looked like a person who had defined a set of goals for himself. His preparation had more method. He was not there to entertain the masses any more and, for the first time, it looked like Sachin knew his limitations. He seemed to be listening to his body. His arc of shots conformed to geometrical precision. He knew when to attack and when to retreat. The brilliance of the old Sachin was still in him but he no longer changed gears at the crease quickly. Sachin had, in fact, raised the bar after his injury. He made mental notes of old and new bowlers on the international circuit. He also knew that he was going to receive a lot of short stuff and that it would be directed to his ribcage. But Sachin knew that there was no scope for error. He was tying up all the loose ends, leaving no space for mistakes.

Then came the IPL and Sachin became the 'icon' player for the Bombay team, Mumbai Indians. Sachin knew that he had to play as the form demanded and that he wasn't getting any younger. He pleaded with cricket lovers to not expect vintage cricket from him. In the IPL he became more of a guide to the younger players. This was equally true in the national team too. Especially after both Ganguly and Dravid quit international cricket, Sachin's presence in the team meant a lot to a generation that was otherwise enamoured by the quick pace of T20 cricket.

The great Sachin Ramesh Tendulkar has to be understood against this daunting background. His fight against the injury that threatened his career is no mean struggle. The wisdom with which he changed himself in order to sustain himself for a longer duration at the international stage defied odds. However, his pursuit to play the sport he enjoyed was mistaken as playing for records. In fact, I will go on to say that no sportsperson can ever play for records because records are always broken sooner or later. In every passionate case, it is the journey that is important and that can be the only motivation for any player to give his heart out on the field. Things like records can hardly motivate a person to spend a lifetime in devotion to a sport. Those who accuse sportspersons of playing for records should introspect and wonder if anyone can really struggle day in and day out, waste litres of sweat on the ground, only for a few numbers.

One of the last domains we have to include in this discussion is the captaincy of these two greats of the game. Gavaskar and Tendulkar were both leaders in their own right. However, as far as captaincy is concerned they had very different styles. Gavaskar was astute. Realizing that international oppositions were bowling at a slow over rate and that India had many spinners, Gavaskar slowed down the game but within the rules. He invited the wrath of foreign media but was prepared for it. Aware of its limitations, he moulded his team to think in a novel way. He was blessed with Kapil Dev in his team, as a fast-bowling all-rounder. Gavaskar put Dilip Doshi's experience in handling situations to good use. Then there was Karsan Ghavri in the team, who on his day would make batsmen hop.

Tendulkar too was blessed with a good side, yes. But he

had set high standards as well. Tendulkar would tend to get a bit aggressive while marshalling his resources. He gave the impression that he expected bowlers to take a wicket every ball. Eventually, the exercise didn't go well with his temperament and becoming frustrated, he quit captaincy. Perhaps, the difference between Sachin's and Gavaskar's teams was that while Gavaskar got the players he wanted in his side, Sachin didn't.

Chandu Borde, once chairman of the selection committee, has a different perspective to offer us: 'Sunil would come prepared for a selection committee meeting. His cricketing logic was sound. He never gave the impression that he was pushing for an undeserving player. As a chairman I always backed the captain because eventually he has to get the best out of the players.' Balvinder Singh Sandhu analyses the mindsets of both as captains: 'I played under Gavaskar a lot. He hated losing. His approach was safety first. He knew the strengths and weaknesses and was a good strategist. He would go for a win only when he was convinced that there was an opening. One could argue that this was a defensive move but he knew that just with one great bowler, Kapil Dev, he just couldn't attack always. Tendulkar was aggressive by nature. He led the team with the same approach as he batted. He believed in the motto: if we can't play to win, why play at all? This led him to putting pressure on his bowlers. He set high standards for them and when they didn't deliver he used to get upset. Sunil always trusted his bowlers. He gave them their field and whenever there was some disagreement in field setting, he would go by what the bowler wanted. Tendulkar on the other hand set the field for the bowlers himself and he wanted the bowlers to bowl accordingly.'

We have a multitude of incidents and anecdotes at our

disposal. But I must say that to choose between the genius of Gavaskar and Tendulkar now is as difficult as it ever was. However, one thing that is for certain is that both played on unequal fields. Tendulkar was attacking and Gavaskar was defensive. But do we attribute this quality to each of the player's own genius or their environment that allowed or, at other times, dictated their style of play?

It is difficult to reach a decision. However, undertaking this exercise seems futile without providing a conclusion. I will go ahead to reiterate that if Gavaskar had the backing of Sehwag, Dravid, Ganguly, Laxman and Kumble, Gavaskar too would have been an attacking batsman. He had every shot in the book and could well have been a dangerous batsman. But Gavaskar played at a time when the Indian team had a long tail and the spinners could hardly hold the bat. Vishwanath, Vengsarkar and Mohinder Amarnath were not consistent.

If we are willing to be brave enough and tabulate the calculation, Gavaskar was certainly a better player. This opinion is debatable and rightly so as we cannot ever fully resolve the competition between these geniuses. But as far as this analysis is concerned, Gavaskar shines brighter. He will always be the first batsman to score 10,000 runs in Test cricket. He will always be the batsman who gave India the strength to dream, at a time when dreams did not come easy. The struggle of Gavaskar is the story of India's cricket team and its gradual rise in the cricketing world. It would be fitting to recollect Gavaskar's century contribution in chasing down 404. The Indian team that shines bright and fresh today is the product of coarse tanning of many years. It is through people like Gavaskar that Tendulkar's team came into being; every bit of the struggle contributed to the team that could one day attack without any fear. Gavaskar was the first brick of the foundation.

All this said and done, it doesn't discredit Tendulkar's worth in any remote way. Tendulkar's fortunate flaw was that he played among many greats; he played amongst spirited players like himself who were fresh and full of life and ready to transform the story of Indian cricket into a fairy tale. He played at a time when Indian cricketers were no longer satisfied with just saving matches, with just playing well once in a while. While Gavaskar shines as an individual in his times, in being a person who gave the obscure Indian team a veneer of respectability on the international scene, Tendulkar stands as a true representative of his time. He shone among an array of geniuses and his contribution can hardly be judged independently because that was the age of the outburst of Indian cricket on to the world scene, the age when India 'arrived'.

I started the comparison of these two players with a set of disclaimers. Comparisons are inevitable and yet futile. At the end of the chapter that thought has not changed. I consider Gavaskar to be a better player than Tendulkar not because of individual analysis alone but because Gavaskar played in an age of little support. At the end of this, the only thing we can surely assert is that cricket is not about the individual; the team makes the player. The situation makes the player. Situations, if conducive, can make one the best player, as in Tendulkar's case, or they can make one the better player by being adverse, as in the case of Gavaskar. That underlines why such an exercise is undertaken repeatedly, albeit with the awareness of its futility. These exercises tend to be slightly misleading. At the beginning it seems the point should be to reach an airtight conclusion.

However, just the process of undertaking such a task clarifies the contexts of the accomplishments of our heroes, thereby making their images sharper in our memories. It is what sustains our romance with the sport.

8

INTERESTING MATCHES
FEATURING BOMBAY

ompetitive sports are not merely about the spirit in which a game is played or the cultural inspirations for the sportspersons of a region. These are all factors that we love about sports. These are the reasons that elevate sports beyond a spectacle on the field to an activity that inspires us, moulds our perspectives and shapes our aspirations and character. However, at the end of the day, competitive sports are about victory and defeat. It is another matter that we have to learn to accept the two in the same spirit.

It is during a match, in competition and in competition alone, that we learn the efficacy of the cultural influences that have formed Bombay's Khaddoos brand of cricket that we have been talking about. It is only under the pressure of a match hanging in balance that the true character of any team and in the case of Bombay, the character of their legacy is revealed.

We already know the rigour with which Bombay players

attended practice sessions. The professionalism that Bombay brought to practice sessions set the benchmark for professional practices in Indian cricket. Bombay players are said to have approached every match, be it club, state or zone matches, with the same ruthless professionalism. However, all this is merely the background to the central issue.

The point of professional sport, I reiterate, is competition. All the practice that is done for hours every day for years together may be rendered useless if those skills are not executed on demand, on the pitch during competition. Even the most skilled players may fall short sometimes, and surprisingly so, due to the pressure imposed by the competition.

How then did the Khaddoos spirit of Bombay cricket handle such competition and pressure? By now we already know that Bombay enjoyed tremendous success at the national level and for most of the three decades from the 1940s to the 1970s monopolized the top spot in Indian cricket. Each team's performance and their success were measured against the Bombay cricket teams of those years. After all, they did win the Ranji Trophy forty times; nearly six times as many as their nearest competitors.

But as has been mentioned repeatedly in this book, sports narratives, even success stories cannot be captured merely by numbers. It is the fire of competition that brought out the best in Bombay even when they were being dominated during the course of a match. Let us take look at some of those performances that best exemplifies the Khaddoos spirit of Bombay cricket; a winning brand of cricket.

Bombay vs Madras, Ranji Final
Venue: Brabourne Stadium
16 to 20 February 1968

With Bapu Nadkarni, Ajit Wadekar, Dilip Sardesai, Ramakant Desai and Umesh Kulkarni on the tour of Australia and New Zealand, the Bombay team which included a few young faces was led by the tenacious and shrewd Manohar Hardikar.

There were only two senior players, skipper Hardikar and opener Madhav Apte. And there was a bunch of youngsters by the names of Ashok Mankad, Sudhir Naik and Eknath Solkar. They would go on to be great servants of the game for a long time to come, but that was in the future. At the time of the match, Bombay faced an uphill task and the trail was only to become steeper when the spinners were employed by Madras on day five. Bombay lost five quick wickets against the spin duo of Venkataraghavan and V.V. Kumar before lunch on the fifth day. Hardikar had only the nineteen-year-old Eknath Solkar with him for company. The honour of Bombay was in the hands of the inexperienced tail.

The pitch had uneven bounce which was being exploited by the two spinners. But Hardikar and Solkar negotiated the attacking bowling using good pad play and saved the game for Bombay. Bombay won the Ranji Trophy on the virtue of having taken the first-innings lead. Solkar came out as a player whose temperament had been tried and tested. Temperament indeed was the key thing that selectors looked out for. Whenever a player was found wanting in temperament, he was dropped and no amount of runs or wickets helped him get back in the team.

On an early morning, on a damp pitch in Brabourne stadium,

Hardikar won the toss and put Madras in. By lunchtime, medium pacer Arun Varde's outswingers had Madras struggling with scoreboard reading seven down for eighty-one. As the pitch improved, C.K. Bhaskaran and Prabhar Rao began to use the long handle to attack the Bombay spinners. They added ninety-seven for the nineth wicket and Madras was all out for 258. Madras fought back and by the end of play they grabbed two wickets for seven runs.

Next day, Ashok Mankad joined opener Madhav Apte who got out for ten and the scoreboard read three down for thirty-one. Now something happened that had an impact on the result of the match. In fact, the captain of Madras, Venkataraghavan, still maintains that had that incident not occurred, Madras would have won the Ranji Trophy.

Mankad played one delivery from Venkat early and played straight into the hands of the mid-on fielder A.G. Satvender Singh who accepted the dolly catch gleefully. The catch was so easy and simple that he didn't feel the need to appeal. Mankad quite shrewdly began to tap the spot where the ball had landed. Neither Satvender nor the bowler, Venkat, appealed and the umpire didn't give the batsman out. Mankad went on to score a brilliant knock of 112 and Bombay took the score to 312, a lead of fifty-four.

The pitch was good for batting. The opening pair of Madras, P.K. Belliuppa and K.R. Rajgopal put on 121 runs. Each batsman was contributing and there was a discussion among the journalists and commentators that if Madras took the lead to over 250, the fourth-innings chasing that score against Venkat and V.V. Kumar would be difficult.

After the second-wicket partnership of seventy-six runs between experienced Madhav Apte and Vijay Karkhanis, Apte was bowled by V.V. Kumar. Apte was followed by Karkhanis, Mankad and Bhosle. From one down for ninety-one Bombay collapsed to five down for 109 by lunch.

The fifth-day pitch had uneven bounce which was being exploited by the two spinners. Except skipper Hardikar there was no batsman left in the Bombay team. When teenager Eknath Solkar joined Hardikar, he was surrounded by half a dozen close-in fielders. With Venkat and Kumar spinning the ball a great deal on a favourable pitch it was difficult for batsmen to negotiate their bowling. When it looked as if the end was imminent, Hardikar used tactics which were employed by England's Peter May and Colin Cowdrey against the mystery bowler Sonny Ramadhin of West Indies. They thrust their pads and smothered the spin and the turn.

When Hardikar began to do it against the spinners, they felt frustrated. When spinners would pitch it up he would take a single. Solkar, learning from the master, began to use pad play. The two knew that they had to bat from lunch till the end of the day. One wicket and Madras was through. Both batted like champions and Bombay scored 225 for five. Hardikar and Solkar remained not out with sixty-two and fifty-five respectively.

Had Madras appealed and Mankad been out on the second day, perhaps Bombay would have lost the chance to win the championship. At the end of the season, Hardikar, Madhav Apte, Baloo Gupte and Ramakant Desai retired from first-class cricket.

Bombay vs Maharashtra, Ranji Trophy Final
Venue: Brabourne Stadium
2 to 7 April 1971

This time, the Bombay team had to accept that the Maharashtra team led by Chandu Borde was too good for them. However, complacency breeds complacency and though the Bombay team was without Wadekar, Sardesai, Solkar, Mankad and Gavaskar, magic unravelled on the field nevertheless, and Bombay ended up winning the thrilling final. By now, this must be of no surprise to the readers.

Bombay won the toss and elected to bat. The Brabourne pitch has always been a batsman's paradise after the morning of the first day and skipper Sudhir Naik was more than keen to put up a good score. But when Bombay lost Sudhir Naik, Vijay Bhosle and Mahesh Sampat for only twelve on the board, putting up a score of 300-plus seemed impossible. Anwar Shaikh and Sadanand Mohol were moving the ball on a pitch which had early morning moisture. However, the diminutive Ramnath Parkar didn't curb his shots and was playing all round the wicket. When Parkar was at seventy-two, he played a shot that is etched in my memory till date. The left-arm spinner Vithal Joshi bowled a 'chinaman' and Parkar picked it up early, swept in a Rohan Kanhai style, falling on the grass with both legs in the air. In the company of Ajit Naik he added 142 runs to Bombay's tally.

But just as things were going smoothly, Naik jumped out to leggie Nicky Saldanha and was stumped. Parkar, who had completed his century, lost his wicket on the same score as well. Bombay then lost four wickets for thirty runs because of Saldanha's tantalizingly flighted deliveries. Saldanha says, 'Bombay batsmen always thought I was an overrated bowler. They would feel that my flight was easy to hit. Even after Ajit Naik was stumped, other batsmen were trying to hit me out of the ground but I kept flighting the ball. I got six for sixty-six.'

When Bombay came to bowl, Abdul Ismail and Ajit Pai were

moving the ball well. Pai would bowl big inswingers and Ismail had mastered the outswing and both the openers were sent back to the pavilion with the score reading twelve. Borde was batting fluently but Bombay bowlers were bowling a great line. Hemant Kanitkar was very cautious as usual.

When Borde was on forty-eight, medium pacer Ajit Naik placed Ramnath Parkar, the best fielder, right behind the square leg umpire. Two balls later, Ajit Naik bowled a bouncer, Borde mistimed the shot trying to hook it and Parkar held a good catch. Borde was soon followed by Kanitkar who was beaten by an off-cutter by Pai. Saldanha came and began to play his shots. He was a person who had always relished the pressure of playing against Bombay. Padmakar Shivalkar and Milind Rege were accurate and though left-hander Vithal Joshi gave company to Nicky Saldanha, Maharashtra's end looked imminent. Eventually, Maharashtra conceded a lead of fifty-seven runs.

Bombay's second innings was almost a repeat of the first. This time, Bombay lost three quick wickets for twenty-one. Vijay Bhosle began to play bowlers with confidence, in the company of Mahesh Sampat. Sampat blocked one end up but kept rotating the strike while Bhosle, a brilliant player of spin bowling danced down the wicket to play beautiful shots against the spinners. Borde shrewdly introduced offie Chetan Chauhan who trapped Bhosle in front of the wicket when he was trying to play across. Bombay was folded up for 196 despite Milind Rege's lovely drives. Maharashtra had a target of 254 to win the Ranji Trophy.

However, instead of the usual Chetan Chauhan, it was left-hander Swaroop Kabadi who opened the final and decisive innings with Madhu Gupte. That day, Abdul Ismail was bowling at his very best; his outswingers were on target and he bagged two wickets. Maharashtra was three down for thirty-one. Borde arrived on the scene and played a gem of a knock. His on drives and cover drives were a treat to watch. But just as he was gathering momentum, Borde was caught off a Shivalkar delivery. Rege had taken a blinder in the slips. The grand old man of Maharashtra cricket, Prof. D.B. Deodhar, squealed, 'Oh no!'

That night when the Maharashtra team went to sleep, they knew that they needed 110 to win with five wickets in hand. Saldanha recollects, 'I was unbeaten and the officials kept coming to my room to give advice. They just wouldn't go. After some time, Borde summoned me and said that I should play my natural game. Anwar Shaikh was spared because he wouldn't have paid heed to such advice.'

The next day, the gang of Maharashtra team had visibly swelled on the first floor of the CCI. Sensing victory, a big room in a five-star hotel was booked for the celebration. Meanwhile on the field, Saldanha was playing responsibly, while Shaikh was taking risks. Shivalkar, however, was in fine form on the day and was turning the ball square on the fifth-day pitch. When Shaikh jumped out of the crease to loft Shivalkar, he was bowled. Saldanha had only Joshi and Kirtane but Kirtane was run out in a terrible muddle. The Maharashtra team was rudely woken up from its slumber. Pressure was now mounting with the score reading 153 for seven.

Saldanha was caught in the gully brilliantly by Sampat. It was again a Shivalkar delivery. The dejection on the face of the Maharashtra supporters was evident. The chance was slipping away, and it did. When Shivalkar trapped Akhlaq Khan a lbw, Bombay won the Ranji Trophy by forty-eight runs. Maharashtra had only managed to make 205. Perhaps they had sensed victory a little too early. That turned out to be their gravest mistake. Bombay rose to the occasion brilliantly, holding on to whatever catches came their way and never pressed the panic button. One wonders how Maharashtra's five-star party booking finally turned out to be. The star-studded team was better than Bombay on paper, but had become too complacent too soon.

Bombay vs Baroda, Ranji Trophy West Zone League Match
Venue: Baroda
22 to 24 January 1972

When I boarded the Baroda Express late in the evening of 20 January 1972 for my first visit to Baroda, I was little concerned with covering the game. Instead, I was looking forward to visiting the house of Vijay Hazare and spending some time with him. In the train with me were Bombay players Vijay Manjrekar and Sudhakar Adhikari. One played for Rajasthan and the other was a faithful former Bombay opener, ragging me in typical Konkani sarcasm. Baroda is a city which breathes education. With the patronage of royalty, Baroda managed to put itself on the cricketing map. It had players of the stature of Vijay Hazare, Dattajirao Gaekwad and Chandu Borde. These are players who have had a crucial role in the development of Indian cricket.

The trio of Abdul Ismail, Sharad Hazare and Ajit Naik were called 'The Mukti Fauz' after the Bangladesh war of 1971. They could not stop laughing on the train, till someone shouted '*sojao, ek baj gaya*' (Sleep, it is one o'clock). I just couldn't sleep thinking of Vijay Hazare and his exploits all the time.

At dawn we reached Baroda. Though we were adequately covered to combat the biting cold of Baroda, the weather was making parts of my body numb. At noon the Bombay team was at the Motibaug Palace ground for practice. The Maharaja of Baroda, Fathesinhrao Gaekwad, was exchanging pleasantries with Vijay Manjrekar. The scenery was as picturesque as it can get. The field was surrounded by trees with the Laxmi Vilas Palace in the background.

Baroda won the toss and made Bombay bat on a pitch that looked full of runs. Why did Baroda not bat then? The question was somewhat answered in the next forty-five minutes. Bombay had lost three wickets with twenty-four on the board. Playing without the injured Ajit Wadekar, Bombay lost openers Sudhir Naik and Ramnath Parkar and then Eknath Solkar in quick succession. It was the tall and slim Anthony Fernandes sharing the new ball with Narayan Satham, a bowler who had always been competitive. The cold conditions and heavy atmosphere proved to be ideal for swing bowling as this duo hit the right lengths and got the ball to swing prodigiously.

Dilip Sardesai and Ashok Mankad moved the score slowly before both were consumed. It was then the turn of debutant Suresh Deobhakta, the sixer specialist in the maidans of Bombay. When he was walking gingerly to the wicket, Manjrekar, sitting with the team, had already asked the next batsman Ajit Naik to be ready. Manjrekar was an astute reader of body language and an accurate predictor of consequences based on symptoms. And yes, Deobhakta was soon walking back to the pavilion. As Ajit Naik was walking to the wicket, Manjrekar pointed out to Sudhakar Adhikari, 'Look at his drooping shoulders. No way will he stay there.' Adhikari asked him to keep quiet. But Naik too departed from the middle.

After Atul Mehta fell to the Fernandes brothers, with the

wicketkeeper Leslie taking sharp catches off Anthony, Bombay's score was eight down for eighty-one. When wicket keeper Sharad Hazare began his walk to the wicket, Manjrekar kept staring at him. The stare itself spoke more than a hundred words. However, lunch was called in soon and Skipper Sardesai bellowed in the dressing room. 'Is this the Bombay team? Is this the way to bat?'

However, Manjrekar's stare meant that 'if we had lunch, we would have had it'. Remembering this situation, Sharad Hazare said, 'When we were seven down for nothing, I told Abdul to hang on. "Look," I told him, "if we don't win this game people in Bombay won't spare us." During lunch, Sardesai was shouting and Manjrekar was extremely critical. And we were not given anything to eat. We took the score to 114 and then were all out for 129.'

Funnily, when the Bombay team is down, it's the most dangerous team. It has a strange knack of rising from the depths, as if doing it other times is too boring or too bothersome for them. They have always become stronger when there is a threat to their position. As it turned out, Abdul Ismail and Ajit Naik were devastating and the Baroda batsmen began to tumble. The atmosphere became festive and after every wicket the Bombay team would sing the popular song from the film *Amar Prem*: 'ye kya hua, kaise hua' (What's happened? How did it happen?). Said Abdul Ismail, 'The pitch was good for batting but conditions were conducive to swing bowling. Whenever a new batsman would arrive at the crease, we all would sing the song. That did unsettle them.' Baroda collapsed: nine down for nineteen. Just then the left-hander Dinkar Sakpal needlessly poked Ismail's delivery but Sudhir Naik dropped a sitter in the slips. Baroda was saved from being bundled for nineteen! Sakpal and Vikram Hazare took the score to forty-two before Sakapal got out to Shivalkar.

In the second innings, Bombay scored 354 for nine with a swashbuckling knock of 144 from Ramnath Parkar. He was severe on Anthony Fernandes and Narayan Satham, bisecting the field. Watching it, Vijay Hazare muttered, 'Little bit of Rohan Kanhai I see in this boy.' This was a big praise indeed.

Scoring 157 in the second innings, Baroda conceded a win to Bombay that ought to have been Baroda's. Ismail picked five wickets in the second innings. As we assembled that night at the Baroda station, Eknath Solkar with sandwiches in his hand began to sing 'ye kya hua, kaise hua' once again. The Bombay team had come by the rickety Indian train, but for Baroda, Bombay had come and gone like a storm, devastating everything in their path without courtesy. The song lingered in Bombay's mind for some days, but the impact that it would have had on Baroda can hardly be put in words. Perhaps 'kya hua, kaise hua' is indeed the only way to describe it.

Tamil Nadu vs Bombay, Ranji Trophy Final
Venue: Madras
18, 20, 21 April 1973

In his book, *Cardus on Cricket*, Neville Cardus says, 'Cricket is a capricious blend of elements, static and dynamic, sensational and somnolent. When cricket burns a dull slow fire it needs only a single swift wind of circumstance to set everything into a blaze that consumes nerves and senses. In no other game do events of import hang so bodefully on a single act. In no other game does one little mistake lead to mischief so irreparable.'

It seems these lines were written for this match. At Chepauk, at the end of the first day of the Ranji final, no one could foresee what was to come in the match. As early in the match as less than an hour on the second day, all hopes of the home team were dashed. Shivalkar bamboozled the batsmen beyond their senses.

The pitch was ideally suited for the two great spinners Venkataraghavan and Vaman Kumar, one offie and the other a leggie; both equally known to bowl an accurate and attacking line. Bombay won the toss and the openers Sunil Gavaskar and Ramnath Parkar went about picking ones and twos before the duo of Venkat and Kumar began to make their presence felt. In no time, Bombay lost their openers and later Ajit Wadekar.

Venkat and Kumar had hit the length. They were bowling a perfect line with tantalizing flight that was extracting enough turn to keep the close-in fielders busy. Sudhir Naik and Ashok Mankad were using pads to deliveries that had danger written all over them. Ball after ball was on perfect length, giving no respite to batsmen. However, both the batsmen were masters of concentration.

At lunch, Bombay was four down for 102. When the loose soil near the stumps was being swept, one could see that the pitch was getting too dusty for a five-day match. Ashok Mankad put his thinking cap on and began to place the ball to pick up quick runs. But Bombay eventually was folded up for 151. The score was excruciatingly low for Bombay standards. And it was a Ranji final, to top the embarrassment.

However, when Tamil Nadu lost both the openers for six, hopes were raised due to the presence of Shivalkar and Solkar and the dusty pitch. Young left-hander Abdul Jabbar who was playing his first season and both Michael John and Parsuram Dalvi, put their heads down and played each ball on its merit.

Jabbar said, 'This was my first season. I had not known the

meaning of spinning and seaming tracks. "Go and bat" was all I was taught. Dalvi too was batting without any problem and, frankly speaking, we didn't see a devil in the pitch. When at the end of the day's play we were two down for sixty-two, both Dalvi and I were batting very confidently and there was a talk in the party that evening that we should be able to take a good lead because batting in the fourth innings would be a difficult task.'

No two parties could have judged themselves differently! Here was a party where the Tamil Nadu team were discussing of the lead. At another corner of the field, Bombay players were busy cracking jokes. They knew something that Tamil Nadu didn't. They knew that it was they who were in a commanding position.

The next day was a state bandh and no play could ensue. When play resumed the day after, the second ball of Shivalkar's first over turned square. The number ten batsman Kalyanasundaram was sitting in colour trousers reading *The Hindu* in the pavilion. V.V. Kumar, the number eleven who was sitting next to him said, 'Kali, can you please be in flannels? Within an hour or before that both of us will be batting. Don't look at me. Do what I told you.'

At the MCC bar, Kali narrated the story in his impeccable style, 'As I began to change, I saw batsmen getting in and out of the dressing room with alarming frequency. Paddy Shivalkar was on a roll. Before one could realize what was happening, the entire team was back in the pavilion within forty-five minutes with eighty on the board. Within eighteen runs we had lost eight wickets.'

Shivalkar's bowling score read 17.5-10-16-8!

Gavaskar and Wadekar were sent back to the pavilion in a flash by Mukund. The score read six for two. Now, spin was introduced from both ends and the pitch became dicey. Says Kali, 'All my life we would get the new ball for a few overs; after that it was Venky and VV who performed their magic till our palms would get swollen for applauding them.'

Sudhir Naik was negotiating the spinners confidently and Tamil Nadu didn't know how to get rid of him. Naik, a typical Khaddoos Bombay batsman had put a big price on his wicket. By now the lead was of 183 runs and Bombay had four wickets still in hand. But Venkat smartly brought in Kalyanasundaram and in the next ten minutes Bombay were all out for 113 and Kalyanasundaram's bowling figures read 6.3-0-28-4.

The last innings was a haze. The gallant Abdul Jabbar scored twenty-eight out of the sixty-one runs that Tamil Nadu managed. Shivalkar and Solkar had demolished them, in every possible way. Together, in 25.1 overs they picked five wickets each giving only forty-one runs together.

The bright spot for the season for Tamil Nadu was Jabbar. He was the find of the season. As Bombay won, Dilip Sardesai headed for the Tamil Nadu dressing room. Jabbar remembers: 'He called me and said you are a terrific batsman. On a difficult pitch, I liked your approach. Keep up the good work. Later he wrote some good things about me in *Sportsweek*. I still have that piece.'

Unlike other matches where Bombay's supremacy surfaced too easily, this was one match which remained at the precipice throughout, giving ample time for members of each team to bite their nails. I am sure even Neville Cardus would have enjoyed the beauty of this see-saw battle.

Bombay vs Hyderabad, Ranji Trophy, Quarter-final
Venue: Wankhede Stadium
16 to 19 January 1976

The weather was pleasant that day, like it always is in the month of January in Bombay. But Hyderabad was keen to add some heat to the cold atmosphere. They arrived in full force with stars Jaisimha, Pataudi, Abbas Ali Baig, Abid Ali and Jayantilal, the offie Ramnarayan and the much talked about left-arm spinner Mumtaz Hussain who had bamboozled the Bombay University in late 1960s with his variations. The Bombay team, led by Ashok Mankad, didn't have the services of Sunil Gavaskar, Dilip Vengsarkar and Eknath Solkar who were away on national duty to New Zealand and West Indies.

The difference in the quality of the teams was evident before the match began. But another kind of difference could also be seen. While Ashok Mankad's boys were rigorously training in practice with a purpose, the Hyderabad stalwarts were doing 'social practice' as one former Bombay player said. Bombay won the toss and elected to bat on a pitch that had little moisture. Medium pacers Abid Ali and Jyoti Prasad stuck to their lengths very early and were handled carefully by the two stylish openers Sudhir Naik and Ramnath Parkar. Skipper Jaisimha assessed the situation and set a field that blocked on drives.

The match was not going in any certain direction. No one could guess the fate of the game after lunch. When offie Venkatraman Ramnarayan was introduced, he extracted bounce and turn with his peculiar action. Bombay's game plan was to build a good first-innings score but, they were stifled by

Ramnarayan and Mumtaz Hussain. Bombay had a long tail but when Ramnarayan consumed the bigwigs, confidence was shaken. Ramnarayan then ran through the side with seven for sixty-eight in thirty-five overs and Bombay was all out for 222.

Bombay had only four bowlers in Ismail, Shivalkar, Sandeep Patil and leggie Rakesh Tandon. Even the most wishful Bombay supporter would accept that the attack wasn't great to defend the 222 runs on the board.

But Ashok Mankad knew how to get the best out of nothing. Fielding at mid-off, Mankad shrewdly kept marshalling his resources and effected many bowling changes, having set the field with geometrical precision. Mankad wanted to use Sandeep Patil to curtail the run rate. Patil rose to the occasion by bowling a spell which read 49.4-16-79-4.

Indeed, when openers Abbas Ali Baig and Jayantilal started the innings, Hyderabad looked fit to get an innings lead. But just as the stage was set for the assault, Bombay bowlers rose to the challenge and broke the will of those who doubted them. Jayantilal was bowled at eighty-two by an away-swinger off Ismail. And then the combination of Shivalkar and Patil took over. Shivalkar made Pataudi struggle and finally surrender while Jaisimha was bowled by Sandeep Patil for a blob. Narsimha Rao was the only player to have batted sensibly to remain not out for sixty.

Hyderabad had taken a lead of eighty-nine runs. With a day and a half to go, the pitch was slowing down. All of a sudden it was Bombay pushing hard to get an outright win.

On the evening of the third day, Bombay was at 188 with three wickets down. On the crease were Ashok with eighty-nine and Rahul, his younger brother, not out on forty-nine. Bombay was only 100 runs ahead. That night must have been difficult for the father of the two men on the crease, the legendary Vinoo Mankad. He gave some strategic tips to son Ashok. 'Declare after batting for an hour.'

Remembers Ashok: 'I just couldn't understand what he was talking about! Here was a team of experienced players and Vinoobhai wanted me to give them only 150 runs? I didn't argue. Next day when I told my deputy Sudhir Naik about Vinoobhai's advice he too felt that 150 was too less a score. I wanted to give them a minimum of 225 but then there wouldn't have been time to bowl them out.'

Ashok continues, 'During the first drink interval when we were 160 plus, the twelfth man came with a message that Vinoobhai was near the dressing room and he wanted me to declare the innings. And there was Vinoobhai standing near the sight screen! His posture had anger written all over it. And I declared, with Hyderabad needing 186 runs in two-and-a-half sessions, a target which was easily achievable.'

As if this wasn't enough, to add to Ashok's misery, Baig and Jayantilal put on forty for the first wicket. Hyderabad looked like they were on their way to win the game comfortably. Mankad then introduced Shivalkar and Tandon, with close-in fielders hovering around the batsman. Mankad kept changing the ends and used Tandon in short spells of four overs. And all of a sudden, the loop, turn and the bounce of Tandon backed by alert fielding had Hyderabad struggling at eighty-six for six. Soon, except for Abid Ali, everyone was back in the pavilion: Pataudi with zero and Jaisimha four. Mumtaz Hussain kept blocking one end while Abid scored freely from the other end. They were settling into a partnership of forty-eight runs when Shivalkar struck followed by

Tandon, and there it was, Hyderabad was all out for 146! They lost by forty runs.

This match was really the rarest of matches! More than anything, it was because no one knew who the praise really belonged to! Jaisimha was all praise for Ashok Mankad. That evening he said, 'Unlike football or hockey, in cricket, captaincy makes a difference and Ashok was brilliant.' But Ashok had only Vinoobhai to thank for the miracle. 'This man was sitting at home and gave me inputs which worked.' But what if Ashok had listened to Vinoobhai and Bombay had lost the match?! But as Ashok said, 'Great cricketers visualize better and have a better sense of strategy'. This match is a rare incident of how the grand legacy, the gharana of Bombay cricket continues to win Bombay matches even without playing!

Bombay vs. Bengal, Ranji Trophy Semi-final
Venue: Eden Gardens
30 January to 2 February 1976

We have been talking about Bombay. But what was happening on the other side? Perhaps it's not possible to imagine what the opposition was thinking all these years while Bombay reigned as the undisputed champion of cricket in India. The only slight chance that they could hope for was when the stalwarts of Bombay went to play for the national side and the Bombay side was left looking terribly weak. In 1973 the scribes in Bengal had predicted a 90 per cent probability of Bengal's win. It was a semi-final and the stars of Bombay, Sunil Gavaskar, Dilip Vengsarkar and Eknath Solkar were all gone on the tour of New Zealand and West Indies. Bengal thought it as the one chance that they actually had to score a win over Bombay.

The Bengal team was balanced and knew the conditions well. Eden Gardens was known for conditions conducive to swing bowling. But after having watched the Bengal team in the nets, one wondered the logic behind the probability. Batsman Ambar Roy was worried. When the Bengal team found him, they felt that they had procured the one batsman who could effortlessly destroy any attack even on a tricky surface. Replete with class, Roy could embarrass selectors by making international bowlers look pedestrian.

The much awaited match began. Bengal was first. The breeze at the River Hoogly, hardly a few kilometres away, was in its full glory. It was ideal for the swing bowlers Abdul Ismail and Ajit Pai. But, for some reason, the bowlers seemed to be keen on bowling a line to contain the openers. At the same time, the batting side was also nervous. Gopal Bose (who was on the tour of England in 1974 with the Indian team) was the one expected to play shots, but now he seemed subdued. The batsmen had come with a firm plan. It was to see the new ball off without a mistake.

It was in fact the other opener, Palash Nandy who was constantly thinking of getting the scoreboard clicking. On one occasion Nandy almost got run-out by the fielding of Ramnath Parkar. The bespectacled Gopal Bose, being the senior of the two, told off Nandy for taking Parkar's reputation lightly. But, Nandy, underestimating the gravity of situation, soon called for a non-existent single that sent Bose back to the pavilion.

Seeing that Pai was not hitting the desired length, Mankad introduced Sandeep Patil to bowl cutters from one end. The plan was to stop Nandy from playing shots and test his patience. Further down, during the partnership of Raju Mukherjee and

Ambar Roy, things looked like the match will go Bengal's way. The two extremely stylish batsmen were playing Patil and Shivalkar without a sign of discomfort.

After lunch Mankad introduced Ismail and Pai back into the attack because of the presence of a cross breeze. Pai's inswingers were successful in beating left-hander Ambar Roy. Roy was generally elegant, but on that day he was in a hurry to play shots. He was defending gingerly as well while Raju Makherejee was sedate.

Ismail was using the breeze to its best, making his presence felt. Soon, balls were kissing edges and landing safe in keeper Sharad Hazare's 'safety vault'. Bengal was reduced to sixty-one for six in twenty-eight overs in that spell of play. Ismail's bowling had done wonders. In the morning of the second day, Bengal was all out for 310.

The Bombay openers, Sudhir Naik and Ramnath Parkar, made the conditions look batting-friendly. Barun Burman, with his long run-up was generating good pace but he was bowling too short, allowing the batsmen to play on the back foot. After Sudhir Naik was caught behind off a Burman delivery, Parkar and Mahesh Sampat handled Bengal's bowlers with confidence.

Bombay was at 161 for one and needed 142 runs to take the first-innings lead. Bengal's only hope was in left-arm spinner Dilip Doshi to strike. Because of Mankad's instruction, no batsman was willing to take any risk against Doshi. However, both Parkar and Sampat were struck at 161 and Bombay then collapsed like a pack of cards and slumped to 256 for eight.

But allow me to rewind the narrative for a moment. One incident that was to have a huge impact on the result of this game, had already happened on the first day of the match. Just after lunch on the first day, Nandy was bowled by Tandon by a topspinner which went on to hit keeper Hazare on the face and he began to spit blood. He lost his tooth as well. But skipper Mankad urged Hazare to keep wickets.

That evening Hazare's face was swollen and he couldn't eat solid food. He couldn't even eat fruits and he was getting quite weak. It was against this background that Hazare joined Tandon when Bombay needed seveny-four runs to win with one wicket in hand. That evening when play ended, Bombay was at 279 for eight, needing thirty runs to win. Hazare was struggling but Khaddoos that he was, he denied Bengal bowlers any chance of jubilation.

Thirty runs to go. The Bengal scribe who had predicted 90:10 in favour of Bengal was grinning from ear to ear and his beaming face seemed to say, 'I told you so.' Bengal, sensing a win, was naturally excited. When Parkar and Sampat were batting, their shoulders had dropped but that day one could see from their body language that they were all smelling victory.

Hazare was to face Burman. The first delivery was safely tucked to deep fine leg for a single. As the senior partner, Tandon had to play responsibly. He was great at mind games. He walked down, tapped the pitch and that angered Burman. Then, in a typical response of a fast bowler to any provocation, he bowled a short ball, which was pulled for four.

Bombay needed twenty-two runs to win. There was excitement in the stadium. But here was the sick Hazare, drained of energy. He was wobbly, but when he called for water, Tandon sent the water back. The next over when Tandon tried an ambitious shot, it was S.K. Hazare who showed him the lion (on the crest) on the shirt.

But from that moment, the Bengal players seemed to be wilting. Hazare had played bravely for three days and he had to ensure that the belligerent Rakesh Tandon does not leave it to the last wicket to take the lead. Hazare couldn't speak because of his swollen face but his eyes said everything to Tandon. And there it was – the winning shot. It was Tandon who scored it.

Mankad hugged Hazare, emotion overflowing. 'Bombay is Bombay', the players sighed. When the team assembled in the hotel room to celebrate, Hazare said, 'Now please don't give me beer with a straw' and the team cheered this unsung hero of Bombay cricket.

Bombay vs. Delhi, Ranji Trophy Semi-final
Venue: Wankhede Stadium
8 to 11 March, 1979

In 1971, when the Delhi team travelled by train to Bombay, the talk among the team members was about shopping and visiting various places. Eight years later in 1979, under the captaincy of Bishan Singh Bedi, the Delhi team, full of self-belief, arrived in Bombay two days before the semi-final and didn't waste time in hitting the net.

This team had a combination of skills. In the Chetan Chauhan–Venkat Sundaram duo they had a good, reliable opening pair followed by the Amarnath brothers, Surinder and Mohinder, in the middle order and a young Arun Lal. In bowling, the new ball was in the hands of Madan Lal and left-handed Sunil Valson who was known to bring the ball in at will. As a cover to himself, skipper Bedi had left-arm spinner Arun Khurana and the duo was backed by leggie Rakesh Shukla.

On paper, Bombay, with Sunil Gavaskar, Ashok Mankad and Dilip Vengsarkar looked very strong but there was a problem. Sandeep Patil who made a debut as a medium pacer was promoted to number six in the quarter-final against the wishes of Gavaskar who, it was learnt later, felt Patil played more with the cross bat, than with the straight bat but skipper Ashok Mankad who had an eye for talent stuck to his guns because he had seen Patil play some breathtaking shots in a local tournament.

Against UP in the quarter-final, Patil, after hitting a midwicket boundary off the offie Gopal Sharma, was bowled, attempting to repeat the same shot the very next ball. Gavaskar was proved right but Mankad would have none of it. Mankad said, 'There were quite a few in the selection committee who too felt that Patil should be demoted. Possibly they got carried away by Sunil's (Gavaskar) observations. I said as a captain I have faith in the stroke production ability of Sandeep and I will still send him at six and not lower down at nine.'

On the day of the match when I was having breakfast with some of the players near the dressing room, in walked Mankad and told Sandeep that he would bat at six and even if he got out for zero to a full toss, he would continue to bat at that number as long as he was captain. That statement was enough for Sandeep to feel confident.

Delhi batted first and scored 359. None of the batsmen played an impact innings though Surinder Khanna played sensibly for sixty-two and later Madan Lal, using the long handle, scored fifty.

The pitch had good carry and was good for playing strokes. But Delhi bowlers, taking advantage of the little morning moisture, were looking dangerous.

Valson brought a couple of balls in and when he pitched the

third ball on a length going away, Gavaskar hung his bat and was out for zero. When things seemed to be going well for Delhi, Bedi introduced Mohinder Amarnath who induced Vengsarkar into playing an on drive and was bowled.

Ashok Mankad looked under pressure against Valson. Both Mankad and Solkar were consumed by Arun Lal in the slips off Valson. Bombay was four down for seventy-two and didn't have any specialist batsmen left to follow. It was at that time Sandeep Patil walked in. With three slips, a gully, a forward short leg and a backward short leg, Bedi went on the attack.

But Patil was bisecting the field at will with perfectly timed shots. Suddenly the Delhi bowling looked innocuous. Drives flowed from Patil's bat. At the other end Rahul Mankad was working on singles and giving more strike to Patil.

There were no heaves from Patil's bat. He was out to prove his skipper was right in judging his batting talent. Fortunately, Bedi pulled a muscle and was off the field and though Arun Khurana was a left-arm spinner, he was no match for Bedi's guile.

Sandeep Patil knew that any irresponsible play on his part would affect Bombay's chances of making it to the final. Whenever he lofted, he cleared the field. What one liked about his batting was that he cut down his shots to the on side against Rakesh Shukla and Khurana. He played them on the merit of each ball because by third day noon the pitch was assisting the spinners.

Suru Nayak, Rajendra Jadeja, Zulfikar Parkar, Karsan Ghavri and Ranjan Baindoor had no pretensions to handle pressure and Patil was virtually playing from both sides when half the team was in the pavilion for 109.

At 292 for eight with sixty-six runs required to win the game,

Patil, facing the second new ball, was a bit too early on the delivery of Madan Lal and top-edged to Venkat Sundaram at covers. Then on, Bombay never recovered and lost the semifinal by conceding the lead of vital thirty runs to Delhi who then entered the final.

It was this match in which a new batting star was born in Sandeep Patil. There are many stories like this that have given birth to stars. Bombay keeps finding stars along the way to its victory. Also, while in the team Bombay players find their best. It is a circle that feeds itself in a delightful way.

Bombay vs Haryana, Ranji Trophy Final
Venue: Wankhede Stadium
3 to 7 May 1991

A day before the Ranji Trophy final I got a call from the chairman of the Bombay Ranji Trophy selection committee, Naren Tamhane, to come over and meet him immediately. Since I was the chief coordinator of the Bombay Cricket Association–Mafatlal Industries scheme for bowlers he asked me to get Balwinder Singh Sandhu with me. Both of us went to BCA to meet him. When we met him, he said he will be playing fast bowler Abey Kurvilla the next day.

We tried to reason out with him that Abey was picked for the BCA–Mafatlal scheme for bowlers barely two months back and had no clue about the intricacies of the game played at this level. Tamhane shot back, 'I am not seeking opinion. I am just informing you. Get him prepared mentally for tomorrow's game.'

Abey Kurvilla had a weird cricketing background. An

engineering student of the D.Y. Patil College, Abey was a tennis ball cricketer and played for fun. In the last week of December 1990, Abey attended selection trials of the Bombay University at the Wankhede stadium and was dropped from the trial for some atrocious bowling. Impressed with high arm action and the speed that he generated, I asked him to come over to the BCA–Mafatlal scheme nets. He looked totally raw in the nets but he was bowling at speeds of 140-plus km.

Soon the word went around that there is a fast-bowling sensation in the scheme and some selectors and senior players came to watch him. This was the background that convinced Tamhane of playing him so that Salil Ankola, who was quite quick, would get Abey to share the new ball from the other side.

Bombay team with two solid opening batsmen Shishir Hattangadi and Lalchand Rajput had a middle order consisting of the captain Sanjay Manjrekar, Dilip Vengsarkar, young Sachin Tendulkar and Vinod Kambli. The team had good pace attack in Raju Kulkarni, Salil Ankola and Abey Kurvilla.

Though Haryana had the great Kapil Dev leading the team with Ajay Jadeja and Chetan Sharma in their ranks, their team lacked experience. Haryana won the toss and elected to bat. The moisture ought to have helped the pace attack of Raju Kulkarni, Salil Ankola and debutant Abey Kurvilla.

When Abey's incoming delivery clipped the bails, Dhanraj Singh was out. One down for five, but Deepak Sharma and Ajay Jadeja gradually consolidated the position till the second wicket fell at the score of 181. Kurvilla got Jadeja to edge to the wicket keeper. The dada of domestic cricket, Amarjeet Kaypee, joined Sharma and very nicely kept the scoreboard moving.

Abey and Salil continued to bowl quickly but by noon the

wicket had slowed down. Haryana slumped from two down for 181 to seven down for 358. But number nine, Chetan Sharma, played a swashbuckling knock hitting some unorthodox shots which we get to watch only in T20s. Before anyone could realize, he had raced to ninety-eight and was the last man out.

Chasing 522 was a Herculean task because Haryana's new ball was shared by Kapil Dev and Chetan Sharma. Bombay's strength was batting. In the typical Bombay style, their batsmen began to work on ones and twos. But none of the batsmen was able to convert the good start into a big score.

When Bombay conceded a lead of 112 on the third day, the only option Bombay had was to get Haryana out quickly so that it could chase for an outright win. The pitch was getting increasingly slow and the turn was slow too.

Left-arm spinner Sanjay Patil bowled beautifully, varying line and length. From the other side the three medium pacers were bowling with 7–2 field, thereby curtailing the stroke production of Haryana batsmen. Haryana at the end of the fourth day's play were eight down for 159, a lead of 271. The wicket was playing well and when Polly Umrigar and Madhav Mantri returned after inspecting the pitch on that day, they felt that if Bombay batsmen put their head down they could chase a target of even 350.

Next day left-hander Banerjee along with Jain and Bhandari extended the lead to 354. Now the battle was on, but when Bombay lost Rajput, Hattangadi and Sanjay Manjrekar for thirty-four, it looked impossible to reach 354. But what a brilliant partnership between Dilip Vengsarkar and the young sensation Sachin Tendulkar! Of the 134 runs partnership, Tendulkar scored ninety-six. The best stroke of his innings was a lofted shot off Kapil Dev. Sachin was in a murderous mood hitting all the bowlers at will.

Vinod Kambli played a cameo knock of forty-five but other incoming batsmen struggled to support Vengsarkar who was in his elements. At this stage, the bowling figures for Bhandari, who took five wickets for 118 runs in the first innings, read: 17-0-124-2. Vengsarkar was targeting the roof of the stadium and in one over he hit Bhandari for twenty-six runs. Vengsarkar was unstoppable and though the heat was taking its toll on him, he was dealing with boundaries.

And when the number ten batsman, Sanjay Patil, ran himself out at the score of 305, Bombay needed forty-seven to win with rookie Abey Kurvilla being the last batsman. Kapil Dev, sensing victory exerted pressure. Along with him Chetan Sharma was bowling from the other end. Whether it was because of tiredness or any other reason, Vengsarkar, for five consecutive overs, took a single off the first ball of the over and Kurvilla was left to face Kapil Dev and Chetan Sharma.

Fatigued Vengsarkar complained of cramp and Lalchand Rajput came as a runner. Two runs were required when Sharma began his over. Vengsarkar took a single again. Kurvilla defended the next ball, but after that he played to the backward short leg and responded to the call of non-striker Rajput. Alert and experienced Amarjeet Kaypee swooped on the ball and threw to wicketkeeper Vijay Yadav and Kurvilla was stranded.

Bombay lost by two runs. Vengsarkar slumped to the ground and was seen weeping bitterly. Seeing him weep, even Kapil Dev comforted him and the scene brought tears to many in the stands. He had fought hard. His unbeaten 139 could count amongst the best of his first-class knocks.

Bombay vs Delhi, Ranji Trophy Final
Venue: Wankhede Stadium
1 to 3 and 4 to 5 April 1985

In the 1980s, the rivalry between Bombay and Delhi was always evident. Both the teams played cricket hard and it was an entertaining sight, thanks to Bishan Singh Bedi who inculcated in the northern players some anger against Bombay players. Says Bedi, 'When I started moving around the country for playing cricket, all that I would hear was only about Bombay. It was Bombay and Bombay and Bombay. I said to myself, "Here we are all working hard to win matches and just because Bombay has won the Ranji Trophy several times, everyone is following what the Bombay team is doing." When in 1980 we were to play against Bombay in the final at Delhi, I kept telling the boys every day, "hey, the enemy is approaching fast. Better be prepared." And it worked. We beat Bombay.'

The Delhi team became Bombay's toughest opponent, though Bombay raised the bar and combined well to win matches. The 1980 Ranji final too was fought, but one got the feeling Delhi had the upper hand after it took the lead of fifty-nine runs by the morning of the third day. With both teams well balanced, it was a matter of who got the first-innings lead. Once Delhi got the lead, all that was expected of them was to stay put in the second innings and bat out Bombay. In the second innings, Bombay had declared at 364 for seven, leaving Delhi to get 423 in a day and a half. Delhi had decided to play for a draw.

Bombay–Delhi matches were fought with mind games. They would be at each other's throat both on and off the field.

Both teams were trying hard to crack open the opposition. 'Ravi, polish the Ranji Trophy nicely. We will be taking it to Delhi tomorrow,' said Kirti Azad to Ravi Shastri after having called him to the Delhi dressing room. It was 1985, and it was the end of the fourth day of play for the Ranji Trophy final. Only the last day remained and Delhi having taken the lead was poised for a win. Azad might have said this in good humour or sheer pride, but he didn't know the effect this sentence was going to have on Shastri. Shastri's reply to Azad was quick and confident: 'No way will the trophy be yours'. Delhi manager Sunil Dev announced that DDCA would pay Rs 10,000 to each member of the team. Shastri took eight for ninety-one and one of those wickets was Azad's who was bowled for nought. Delhi was all out for 209, and Bombay won the trophy.

Had Azad not antagonized Shastri by his comment, perhaps Shastri wouldn't have put in the extra effort. Shastri recalls that day: 'There was nothing to lose and everything to gain. I certainly was motivated to put in that extra bit after what was said by Kirti in front of their team.' Azad not only humiliated Shastri but gave a false confidence to his mates that they just couldn't lose the game. This made the players too complacent. Kiran Mokashi, the other spinner in the match, makes for a great witness to the incident. He says: 'Since Delhi always ended losing to Bombay, the first-innings lead in that match went to their head. I think they picked the wrong player in Ravi who turned a different bowler the next day. Because of Kirti's caustic comment, Ravi was more focused and the fifth-day pitch helped him. That day, Ravi was brilliant in bowling long spells with a varying line, length and flight. Kirti himself was bowled for zero. I observed that the entire Delhi team seemed to be playing as if they had already won the match. Some played reckless shots. They learnt a bitter lesson to never ever take a win for granted against Bombay.'

In fact, when Azad came to bat, not only did the decibel level of the fielders increase but there was also sledging. Delhi had lost Chetan Chauhan, Manoj Prabhakar and Gursharan Singh before lunch. It was the responsibility of Azad, Bhaskar Pillai, Surinder Khanna, first-innings centurion Ajay Sharma and Madan Lal to ensure they didn't lose any more wickets, but Azad was bowled by Shastri first ball. The others just couldn't negotiate the spin, turn and bounce of the fifth-day pitch and Delhi were bundled out for a paltry 209. And Bombay won by ninety runs. Shastri, hurt by the remark of Azad, bowled with figures of 39.5-17-91-8. Azad's one remark cost Delhi the coveted Ranji Trophy.

With this we come to the end of the series of really fascinating matches. But these are hardly all the stories. There are too many of them, so many that it is impossible to take note of them. And that is because each day, in each street, a new and exciting match unravels. Each day interesting matches happen in Bombay, matches that go down to the wire, where the players wait with bated breath, where an injured player bats on to save his team from defeat. There are too many stories and they exist in the smallest corners of Bombay. The matches that we saw are not greater than these in any respect; it is just that more people happen to know of them.

Great stories are not made by perfect cricketers; they are made by cricketers who make mistakes. Cricketers who mess things up for themselves but make sure they revive their team at the end of it. Sometimes this does not happen. Often at the end of the day, the cricketer goes back home dejected, having been the principal cause of his team's loss. He has no option but to live through the night. He has to be alone; he has to remember every moment that he was the reason for his team's failure. He has no option but to suffer.

But the players become great by converting the suffering into an undying spirit that refuses to stay silent. There are humiliations, there are bad matches, but good players make sure they wake up the next day and try to make the day theirs. In every match that we read about, there is one winning side and a losing side. But it is not a battle where the good side has to win over the bad. There are no good sides, there are no bad sides. Everyone deserves to win as much as the other. In every fantastic story of an unexpected win is ingrained the pain of a loss from the clutches of victory. Anything can happen at the end of the day, and all said and done, the good team is the one that wins more often than it loses.

Bombay is one team which has won more matches than it has lost. And it is because of a variety of reasons. It is not as if the players of Bombay don't make mistakes, but they are always ready to correct their past mistakes. It is this culture of constantly trying to improve oneself that makes Bombay the greatest of the teams and a reservoir of the greatest stories. At the end of the day, watching a match can hardly give us anything. It does not fill our stomach, or pay our bills. All it does is that it gives us stories. And that is exactly why we should be obliged to the Bombay cricket team – for giving us stories to remember for a lifetime.

9

CONVERSATIONS ON CRICKET

PERSPECTIVES FROM PLAYERS
WHO PLAYED FOR BOMBAY

Ajit Wadekar

I was born in the Shivaji Park area which produced Test players like Subhash Gupte, Vijay Manjrekar and Hardikar at that time. I played a bit of gully cricket, but was more focused on studies. I took admission to Elphinstone College in the science faculty and used to travel with my neighbour Baloo Gupte, an arts student in the same college. Baloo Gupte offered me the role of twelfth man in their team for which I earned Rs 3 a day. So I started going to the nets after college, where Mr Madhav Mantri was the coach.

The inter-college cricket tournaments started and one of our bowlers was unable to play due to ill health and thus I got into the playing eleven. The opponents slammed 278 runs in the first session. Later, our captain Arvind Apte saw me having lunch in the dressing room and exchanged some heated words with me.

His frustrated words triggered me to play cricket. Next year, I shifted to Ruia College and played under the captaincy of Nandu Raje at college as well as Shivaji Park. Our coach Joe Kamath helped me improve my game a lot and thus I started playing serious cricket. I think the very next year I was in the Bombay Ranji team that won the trophy for fifteen consecutive years.

I played my first match against Madras at their home ground in the quarter-finals of the Ranji Trophy. At that time, I played with well-known players like Polly Umrigar and others. I was very young and new to the team, so seniors helped me with knowledge from their experience and helpful tips to improve my game at that level. Slowly I started scoring runs and then my relationships with the seniors became very strong. It was like achieving some goal in one's life.

During our days, the four-day game was the only format, so we believed in building the team innings by scoring runs and thus we all started to perform. Today, there is one-day and T20 cricket; so players try to play aggressive cricket and end up scoring forty or fifty-odd runs. That is why scoring runs by building a big innings in longer formats of the game is not happening and this is the result of players having an individualistic approach towards the game instead of a team approach.

The year I started playing the Ranji Trophy, some of our players went on national duty to the West Indies, so Ramchand was leading the team. The team was a formidable unit with a very balanced line-up. We had a good batting line-up and we were scoring runs regularly. A bunch of effective bowlers like Ramakant Desai, Ramchand, Polly Umrigar and Diwadkar were also in the team. We were combining well. And we were ruthless. 'Score runs and don't concede runs' was the team motto then.

Not surprisingly, we won the trophy for fifteen consecutive years.

The Bombay team always had high sporting spirit and played the game accordingly. Moreover, the 'khaddoos-ness' of Bombay players makes them different from other players. Bombay was also blessed with good all-rounders, making the team composition better. That is the special quality that Bombay possesses. No wonder Bombay has won the Ranji Trophy forty times.

During Bombay's golden years, the Indian team had five to six players from Bombay, and when I became the captain it was easy to manage with only six other players belonging to other states. There were some senior players who used to report late for the practice sessions while the Bombay players were punctual. But I used to shout at Bombay players for coming late so that the other senior players indirectly would get the hint to be punctual. It was still very challenging to make every player follow the rules, culture and discipline of the team.

Bombay has created many good batsmen at regular intervals and a few good bowlers too, but the latter at a rate of one in a decade. Most of the next-generation players have been following these batsmen as their role models and this has continued to be the case for over a few decades now. So the focus was always on batting. In Australia, you could have seen many players following Lillee and Thompson as their role models and this resulted in good-quality fast bowlers coming in to the Australian attack.

Bombay has won the Ranji Trophy so many times because of the performances of its players. So the players should also be given importance in terms of administration of cricket. It is these players who have a better idea regarding what exactly maidan cricket is and the good that can be produced from maidans for cricketers and consequently cricket. So the role of cricketers in administration will be very important to develop the quality of cricket.

I think the whole system has to be changed and the new system should give prominence to cricketers more than any other agenda. In our days, people contesting the elections would come together for improving cricket in Bombay. But today we can sense the existence of 'groupism' in Bombay, with the result that cricket in Bombay is suffering. People contesting the elections should come together irrespective of their win–loss record in elections and contribute in order to develop cricket in Bombay. The players must be the priority.

Previously, the BCA used to adjust matches in such a way that very rarely they clashed with Ranji Trophy. Thus many important players were able to represent their clubs as well as their state teams during the entire season. Now the number of teams has increased, so the association can have groups of four teams and give each team at least three matches.

Technical coaching and scientific methods emerged from England and other countries. County cricket was the one to adopt these methods. Similarly, other countries also followed technical and scientific methods. But today, we can see that England is struggling a bit in terms of implementing technical and scientific coaching methods and hence they are reverting back to natural talent. So I think even our coaching methods need to nurture the natural talent presently available in India.

Sunil Gavaskar

In maidan cricket, the pitches in my days were of quality and we enjoyed playing on them, but the outfield was not up to the mark. The lunch break used to be only for an hour, so everyone had to take a quick bite and return to the field before the innings resumed. The batsmen had to change their gear in front of everyone so there was no privacy, but still it was fun. Then, the maidan chai (Indian tea made with milk and sugar) with khara biscuits (spicy biscuits) were amazing. Maidan cricket was the one which helped us mould ourselves into professional cricketers.

College cricket was a bit different. There used to be a group of friends always coming to the ground to support and cheer us constantly, so we used to get that moral support even if we were playing against a strong team or if we were in a bad position. So we would always know that there was someone supporting and cheering us. My club Dadar Union taught me a good lesson – 'the game is bigger than an individual'. We had many former Test players and other seniors playing for our club. Every player was supposed to report thirty minutes before the toss, and the one who failed to do so would be dropped from the playing eleven even if he was a senior member of the team or a former Test player.

In my initial days, I played for Rajasthan Cricket Club and we won the C Division and were promoted to the B Division. That was when Dadar Union approached me. I was in the reserves for nearly half of the season, but it didn't matter to me because I wanted to be a part of that dressing room and listen to those senior players discussing about the game of cricket. It was like an apprenticeship for me to learn the nitty-gritty of the game. But today no one wants to be in the reserves, so, that is the reason players keep jumping from one club to another, which has affected the loyalty factor.

Bombay has made a great impact on Indian cricket. At the domestic level, Bombay has won the Ranji Trophy more often than any other state. There are many Bombay players who have represented India at the international level. And in their absence, there were other players who have come and performed well for Bombay. So the competitiveness at domestic-level cricket was always maintained by Bombay. Many teams judged themselves by the quality of their performances against Bombay, so the Bombay Ranji Trophy team had become a standard to which every team wanted to live up to.

Bombay had good new-ball bowlers, quality spinners, a good batting line-up and also many good fielders; so this made Bombay a strong unit. The dressing room atmosphere is always positive. There always used to be one or another player who would say something funny or positive to motivate the team even in bad conditions, so that was invaluable. The most important thing was the Bombay spirit of fighting till the last moment – that always helped us to be successful.

Today, cricket has changed a lot. Limited-overs cricket is what the players play more often than Test cricket. They know how to deal with that format, but they are not used to batting for long periods. So, that may be a reason which gives this feeling that Bombay's batsmanship standard has gone down, but I personally don't think so. A player like Rohit Sharma has got very good ability and he just has to start analysing his game in order to start performing well.

The pitches in Bombay are very good for batting. Also the pitches in the maidans were favourable for batsmen, so I guess it was a hopeless task for bowlers thereby hindering their development and eventually discouraging them. That's why Bombay has not produced bowlers of international quality.

Ideally, the tournaments should be played on a league basis.

But taking into consideration the limited availability of grounds on weekends with so many number of tournaments being played, it is more important to find an appropriate time slot in which the Ranji Trophy and the national team players can be available for most of the matches. Only then can club cricket become more competitive.

Bombay should continue to provide quality cricketers for the national side, and it should be the leader not only in playing the game but also in administering the game off the field.

I think any one should be able to stand for the MCA elections, but it is important that the ones who vote in these elections should have played cricket. It will be difficult to get 18,000 voters to come and cast their votes; so one possible solution could be letting the first-class umpires and players be the voters.

Dilip Vengsarkar

I think the overall infrastructure of Bombay cricket has helped me become a successful cricketer. It is amazing that the MCA has been conducting as many as eighty tournaments each year for so many years. Bombay has many turf wickets as compared to other states, and, of course, Bombay has great cricketing history. I feel the school and college cricket during my playing days were extremely competitive and well organized. My school, King George, produced as many as ten Test cricketers of repute. I guess that made a huge impact on my young mind when I started.

Besides, as a youngster, I lived in an area where great Test cricketers resided, which I feel was a motivating factor as well. I had a chance to watch the greats of the game at a very young age, and watching them from close quarters was a learning experience, which players from other states never get.

Dadar Union dominated Bombay's cricket for many years and it was one of the top teams in Bombay, for it won many titles consistently for many years. I learnt a great deal from players like Vasu Paranjpe, V.S. Patil and Sunil Gavaskar. It was a great honour for a fifteen-year-old to not only share the same dressing room but also the same taxi while going for matches. Not many had that privilege. The club instilled confidence in me, besides the virtues of discipline, commitment and focus.

The inter-club matches were certainly tough. Matches were of high standard, simply because not only first-class players played in these matches but also the Test cricketers. Bombay had many Test cricketers those days and others could learn from playing with them. It was always a great learning process for all the young players of Bombay.

It's a great experience playing on soft wickets and sometimes on drying wickets during Kanga League matches. One definitely develops back-foot play, to play with soft hands and play at deliveries as late as possible. Besides, one had to learn to hit over the top as well because of tall grass in the outfield. Basically one learns to adapt to varying conditions to be successful.

The fact is that many Bombay bowlers did get an extended run at the highest level. They were very good, good enough to play for the country for long. The likes of Karsan Ghavri or Ramakant Desai come to mind in this regard. Shivalkar didn't get chance at all. International cricket is so much these days; Test cricketers do not get time to play even first-class matches, not to mention club matches. I feel Bombay's club cricket, which produced many great players, is in serious trouble unless the BCCI makes it a point to reduce the number of international matches, but I guess it's wishful thinking. That's the reason the standard of cricket in Bombay has dropped drastically.

I thought I would not get the chance to play in the Irani Cup after my debut duck against Gujarat. Luckily for me, Solkar was still injured and I got in. I was in great form in all the inter-university, intercollegiate and inter-club tournaments in Bombay. I was confident and that showed during my innings in the Irani Cup. Playing for Bombay those days and for Dadar Union helped me immensely as I was playing with Test players in almost every match. As a result my development as a cricketer was much faster. Later I realized that to be a consistent performer at international level, one has to have patience as very rarely a batsman gets loose deliveries. I had to adapt in those matches.

Take, for instance, the knock against Michael Holding in the Jamaica Test in 1976. After the West Indians lost the third Test match at Trinidad, Lloyd was on the verge of losing his captaincy had they lost the last Test at Jamaica. There was a ridge in the middle of the wicket and sometimes the ball took off awkwardly. Holding bowling at great speed had all the batsmen ducking. A few batsmen got injured too as the bowler was bowling around the wicket aiming particularly at the head of the batsmen. He not only bowled bouncers repeatedly but also hurled beamers. Unfortunately, the umpires preferred to be mute spectators to all this. It was a desperate attempt by the West Indies captain to save himself. It was sad but very true indeed. I enjoyed my knock as I kept hitting him straight. Perhaps his bowling suited my style of play. Besides, the best way to get rid of pressure is to be consistent. One has to be focused and disciplined all the time. After all, pressure builds up when you struggle to perform.

Coaches play a crucial role in all this. It's important for coaches who are well versed in the art of cricket coaching to apply it judiciously. They must know the individual needs, mental strength, maturity of the players, etc. A coach's main job is to guide the players and motivate them and inculcate strong values.

Bapu Nadkarni

I come from Nasik, which was almost a village those days and we were playing on the matting. Nari Contractor was in a boarding school and we regularly played against each other. When I came down to Poona, I played better cricket but that was no comparison to the cricket that was played in Bombay. Awesome is the only word one can describe cricket in Bombay.

I joined the Associated Cement Companies in 1955 and they told me that being a Bombay company they would give special leave only if I played for Bombay. Hence my decision to play for Bombay. Another reason was that Bombay being a strong team, there would be many opportunities for me to perform.

I was playing for a company which had a strong team with Madhav Mantri and Polly Umrigar in it. What I observed was that to cricketers in Bombay cricket was a religion. They were extremely disciplined on and off the field and even a club cricketer was focused. Every day, you were learning. In Bombay they played to win and when you play with that sort of a mindset, you win most of the time.

I am not exaggerating but I would bowl for not less than three hours on one stump with India wicketkeeper Nana Joshi keeping wickets. I was a competent middle-order batsman but I knew my limitations as a bowler. I didn't spin the ball much, nor did I turn the ball. So I had to rely on accuracy. If you keep bowling three hours on one stump every day, you will be accurate.

Pataudi never had any confidence in me. Possibly he wanted a bowler with variety. But you can't say that I was a defensive bowler. In the 1963-64 series against England I bowled 212 overs in five Tests out of which 120 were maidens and I never used to bowl outside the stump. I used to be all the time on the stump. Why didn't batsmen try to hit me? It's not easy when you are landing on a length all the time.

During the Bombay Test against Australia in 1959, batsmen like Neil Harvey and Norman O'Neill were trying to step out and hit me. But I bowled fifty-one overs for taking six wickets and out of which five batsmen were bowled. What I am saying is that you try and be accurate and even attacking batsmen will get frustrated. In the Barbados Test in the 1961-62 series I bowled 67-22-92-2 to attacking batsmen like Sobers and Kanhai.

A cricketer has to believe in his ability. It's because of the ability and performance in the domestic matches that you are playing for the country. If you have a strong self-belief, you can face the challenge of bowling to any attacking batsmen. During the time I played for India, batsmen of Australia and West Indies were always attacking, whatever may have been the situation. I never changed my style of bowling. When attacking batsmen were trying to get at me, I was still bowling a tight line. A bowler must consistently bowl on the stumps to get the batsman out. Most of my dismissals were either bowled or lbw. In a nutshell, a bowler must practise hard to master his style of bowling.

Not getting enough wickets could be called being out of form, but in my case it hardly happened. I was in and out of the Indian team and I never ever thought about it. If you love the game, these things shouldn't bother you. Keep spending time in the middle. The principle is simple: you must bat or bowl as much as possible in a match when you are not happy with your form.

I enjoyed being the coach of the Indian team and the chairman of the national selection committee. But I felt hurt when, for no fault of mine, I was unceremoniously removed from the national selection committee. I had some plans for the country. The team that we selected played for four years. There was this stupid controversy over Mohinder Amarnath landing at Chandigarh when the selection committee was to meet to pick the team against the West Indies in 1988. Vengsarkar was invited to join us. I know why Amarnath landed there, how it happened. I was a witness to that but there is no point washing dirty linen in public.

We had quite a few seniors on that tour of Australia in 1980. A coach of an international team must realize that no player, whether senior or junior, goes out there in the middle to fail. And when they do fail, they must be given some breathing space for them to know what went wrong and how. I had good interaction with the players and when you command respect, you get it.

Ravi Shastri

My cricket started basically by chance. Like every Bombay boy, I used to play on the streets or at home in the backyard. I studied in Don Bosco School which encouraged football, volleyball, hockey and even billiards but not cricket. It was during the last two years of my school that they started cricket, and I was part of the team. I was leading the team in Giles Shield and in the second year we won the Shield. Now that's what sparked my interest in cricket and then I joined a college that was very good in cricket – Podar College. In collage, my game was groomed under the coaching of Mr Vitthal Patil and with his guidance I started playing club cricket for clubs like Karnataka Sporting, CCI and Islam Gymkhana in various tournaments, and started scoring runs and taking wickets. From there, I didn't turn back.

The selection for the under-twenty-two team was at Wankhede stadium. And I still remember that the wicket was damp, so no one wanted to bat. And I went out there in nets and smashed everyone. I was also bowling well, but even after that I wasn't selected as an all-rounder. I was crestfallen. I think I was the best player on view. Then after performing consistently for the next three months, I was selected for the Bombay Ranji Trophy for the quarter-finals, but then that was because there was a big Purshottam or Talim Shield final and I had scored a half-century in each innings and also picked wickets against Dadar Union, which was a very strong side.

It was a great feeling to be in the dressing room with players like Sunil Gavaskar, Dilip Vengsarkar and Sandeep Patil who were already playing for India, and a few more players from the same Bombay team were on the verge of getting selected for the national side. I was trying to listen to and latch on to every word and learn things by watching them. At that age I needed to pick up everything about cricket – how they planned their innings, the special things they did in the dressing room, everything.

I still remember the Ranji Trophy match in my last year of playing Ranji Trophy. It was a very young Bombay side playing against Karnataka. Karnataka had scored 400-plus runs and we were 160 or 170 for the loss of six wickets and were playing for a draw. There was no way we could have won. We managed to draw the game. It is one of the most memorable matches for me.

Of late, Bombay has failed to produce world-class bowlers and all-rounders. I think it has a lot to do with the one-day cricket that is played. In our time, we used to play one-and-a-half-day or two-day games. That helped to develop the ability to build an innings or bowl longer spells. Now, that is missing. The bowling spell of nine or ten overs in one-day and of four overs in T20 formats do not allow a bowler to develop. Youngsters should bowl for hours in order to develop their game and reach a certain level. Same is the case with batting. One-day cricket doesn't develop the technique in a batsman and emphasizes more on stroke play.

During my days, I used to play at least three to four Ranji Trophy matches in a year, and all other Indian players used to do the same. My first Irani Cup match included players like Kapil Dev, Shivlal Yadav, Madan Lal, Dilip Doshi and Chetan Chauhan in the opposing team – I got nine wickets. So if one scores runs and takes wickets against such opponents, it will surely help.

Today we cannot find any of the national players representing their respective states in Ranji Trophy matches because the number of international matches have increased to such an extent that none of these players are available to play domestic cricket. For example, if Sachin Tendulkar had played at least three to four matches in the Ranji Trophy every year, just imagine how much the youngsters could learn from him just while being with him in the dressing room. So what we used to call as 'Talking Cricket' doesn't happen much these days.

In previous years, Ranji Trophy players and national players used to play club cricket, but now we do not see any of them playing club matches. To improve the quality of cricket, I would say, 'Cut down the number of tournaments and emphasize on quality.' What is the use of having quantity? League format will allow Ranji Trophy players to represent their respective clubs in a few league matches as per their availability.

It is really a good idea to give voting rights to the over 25,000 registered cricketers. If there is something that can improve the infrastructure and quality of cricket, there would be nothing like it. If players are given voting rights, they can be encouraged to get into the real stream of administration. Ultimately a cricket association is for cricketers. The more cricketers you have in the association the better it is for the game.

Sometime back I was invited to talk to MCA academy boys. I only tried to explain to them that they are playing for a great state. All of them just need to emphasize on the work ethic rather than anything else. A player should always treat a practice session as if it's a real match and should have a plan in his mind before going to the nets. For example, a player can decide to bat like in a Test match and lay emphasis on his defence for the first ten minutes and then play shots or try to play some different shots in the last ten minutes of his nets session. So, I think this kind of planning, organization and attitude can really help the players to develop themselves for the next level.

Farokh Engineer

I studied in Don Bosco School where football was the main sport, so I found goalkeeping quite fascinating. But my first love was always cricket and I was extremely fortunate that my parents and my brother Darius encouraged me immensely to play cricket.

My impression of Bombay, my most favourite city in the world, was and has always been extremely good, and the standard of cricket extremely high. People played the game with a lot of passion. This, despite the travelling hours involved in order to reach the grounds; that too in crowded public transport.

Playing in the Kanga League was immensely beneficial for me both in batting and wicketkeeping as the wickets were uncovered. Playing in the tournament during the off season prepared me for the season, as the ball would jump from a spot thus making wicketkeeping very difficult. Obviously when I began to play for Lancashire, playing in the Kanga League helped me immensely.

Tatas were the first and the only company to have encouraged me to improve my cricketing career, and I shall always be most grateful to them. Besides my dear dad, there was also a doctor in Tatas who helped me all his life. The inter-company matches were very good for cricketers who took pride in turning out for their employers, who ensured that we had security in life as a cricketer would hardly get any money while playing either for a state or for the country.

I enjoyed opening the innings as the gaps in the outfield were much wider, and that helped my aggressive approach to batting as I loved blasting the new ball all over the place. I had all the shots and thought that if I could give a good start to my team, a strong total could put the opposition in trouble. I enjoyed opening with Sunil Gavaskar for several years both for Bombay and India. Sunny had tremendous concentration and talent, so little wonder he was one of the finest ever. His tremendous record speaks for itself.

My message to all Bombay cricketers is that you guys are following some very illustrious predecessors who have made a mark not only for Bombay cricket but internationally, so you must keep up the winning habit and endeavour to emulate the great tradition of past Bombay cricketers.

Sandeep Patil

I feel very lucky that I was born in Bombay, but more importantly that I was born in Shivaji Park which is a nursery of cricket. My cricketing career was all thanks to the Patil family in which I was born, as my entire family was sports-oriented. My great-grandfather, grandmother and parents not only loved all sports but also played sports. So the atmosphere in our home was healthy, right from the initial days. Subhash Gupte and Baloo Gupte were my next-door neighbours and used to play tennis-ball cricket along with Ramakant Desai and Ajit Wadekar. I used to watch these stalwarts playing, while sitting in my window, so the atmosphere was always very sporty. My school Balmohan Vidyamandir, and my college, Ruia College, supported me in my academics and helped me to develop as a cricketer.

Playing in the Ranji Trophy was like a dream come true for me. I remember once Vijay Manjrekar and Ajit Wadekar invited me to play for Shivaji Park Gymkhana against Islam Gymkhana in the Police Shield. I always used to watch these players playing in the nets, and then to share the same dressing room with them was something fantastic. My mother used to say, 'If you are good first get selected for Shivaji Park Gymkhana; if you do well, you may get selected for Bombay, and then we will see how it goes.' So when I got selected for Bombay, I was really thrilled because playing for Bombay was like playing for India in those days. All thanks to Ashok Mankad who was instrumental in shaping my career.

I think the Bombay players and Bombay cricket were certainly different from the players and cricket in other states. One should never compare in cricket, but I continue to think that the Bombay team of those days was like the Australian team in terms of attitude. Regardless of whether the chips were down or if it were dominating a match, the team never used to get affected. And when you have captains like Ashok Mankad, Gavaskar, Vengsarkar and Ravi Shastri, it is bound to make an impact on the games of other players.

If you look at the history of Indian Cricket, it's different for each state. While Karnataka has given us spinners, Bombay has contributed in producing batsmen. Players like Kapil Dev, Sunil Gavaskar and Sachin Tendulkar are exceptions. The history of Bombay cricket has always been about producing batsmen because in Bombay, school cricket has contributed immensely to produce batsmen as you get to play on different surfaces in different atmospheres and under different pressures.

Though more than a third of India's runs were scored by Bombay batsmen, Bombay has not produced many good batsmen for India in the past decade. In earlier days, when we used to discuss cricket, we used to talk about our clubs and our performances first, so the loyalty factor was good. Today's players think about themselves and about the clubs which can provide them with better facilities. When players start thinking about something other than cricket, their performances are bound to get affected. The other reason is that now the Bombay players don't get a chance to test their mettle and their skills against quality players and that has brought down the standard of Bombay cricket.

It is obviously a good idea to give voting rights to the over 25,000 registered cricketers, but it is up to the MCA to give thought to this because I have always stayed away from the administrative part of the sport and its politics. The current Bombay management seems to be concerned about cricket, so if they feel it is good, they will surely implement it. The current system is one which has been used for many years; so changing the existing system and implementing a new system is a process which will take some time.

Milind Rege

In school, I was part of the India Schools team. The experience of playing a foreign team was enormous. How else would one explain the joy of playing a 'Test' and that too at all Test centres? Crowds of over 30,000 watching kids aged fifteen, sixteen and seventeen. Travelling by first class in trains, staying in hotels you would never dream of seeing, eating food one has never seen in one's life – all this was an exhilarating experience. On the morning of the match, being awarded an 'India' cap was something that made us feel we were ahead of all other cricketers. Imagine being selected to represent India Schools!

Out of that lot were born cricketers, the likes of Gavaskar, Amarnath, Solkar and Kirmani who were India's legends. Till this series started, we were confined to Rajkot and Baroda, but even that gave us a high. Travelling together, staying in hotels, playing in different conditions – it was truly an experience beyond words for those like Gavaskar and me, who were products of St Xavier's

High School, having never seen what a cricket pitch looks like.

We had practised in school on a wicket which was half-matted following the advice of our director of sports, Father Fritz, whose mantra was 'Good ball block, bad ball lagaao'. Also, we played on pitches at Liberty School ground opposite the theatre on a pitch which was ready. We were playing with leather balls which were generally possible only when one got older. The balls were meant to be new balls but were quite worn out. Fritz decided they needed to have a shine, so the balls would be polished by the good priest all night with cherry blossom shoe polish.

Sunil and I played for the senior team in the Harris Shield when we were twelve years old in class seven. Facing huge hulks who were distinctly overage, we played against Anjuman Islam School when Gavaskar batted at ten and I at eleven. That was our introduction to real cricket. The school depended on the two of us. We did not have to buy any clothing as our school uniform was almost the colour of flannels. But we belonged to a pedigree and Madhav Mantri, our teacher, decked us up in whites.

College was different. The likes of Ashok Mankad, Kishore Rao, Kailash Gattani, Mahesh Sampat and Jayendra Lal, whom we had seen from the boundary lines, had turned into our heroes after their performances; they gave us a different idea of what was in store for us. Beautiful girls watching us used to make us feel very elated. If you performed at St Xavier's College, as you walked through the corridors of the college, you got the feeling that everyone was watching you. Overnight you became famous.

The matches that we played versus Siddharth College in the first year were memorable. It was real tough competition, who's who of Bombay, the selectors, India cricketers all came to watch those matches. It was tension at its peak. In the first two years, we won one and lost one. I remember at Shivaji Park Gym, where we played Siddharth, it was one of the more frightening moments of my life. The crowds grew restless as Siddharth College had to score ten runs with their last pair in and the crowd was on the plot almost at the batsman's throat. Some with knives, others with long iron sticks. We lost and the next thing, we found ourselves in the mayor's bungalow hiding from these hooligans. But forty-two years on, these memories are still fresh. Intercollegiate cricket made you into tough Bombay cricketers. Success at that level was the path to higher levels of cricket.

The biggest advantage that a Bombay cricketer enjoyed was that he rubbed shoulders with players who played for Bombay and India. Complacency was tossed out of the window as you got only one opportunity to perform. One had to hang on to that one chance! One was lucky that someone noticed you, that you played for the right club. I honestly feel there were so many who were far more talented than me but my strength was that I hung on to that one chance. That gave an impression to the selectors that the attitude I had was good. And mind you, the selectors were Merchant, Mantri, Umrigar, Hardikar, Manjrekar and Diwadkar ... all great visionaries. In the ultimate analysis playing Rohinton Baria was the cornerstone to one's future. One got educated to be someone in life and also rub shoulders with players you admired in school.

I was told on the morning of the Ranji Trophy match by Mr Manohar Hardikar, our captain, that I would get an opportunity to play in the eleven. He also told me that this opportunity came because the selectors saw a spark in me at the age of eighteen having done well at the college and university level. I entered the ground amidst greats whom I had seen only from the North Stand. Greats such as Hardikar, Baloo Gupte, Ramakant Desai and Madhav Apte were all playing. However, I was also a part of the team of fifteen in 1966 when I saw Bapu Nadkarni, Farokh Engineer, Wadekar, Sardesai, Desai, Gupte and so many others very closely. The important issue was that these greats took us under their wings and mollycoddled us, especially Sunil and me.

Coming back to the debut game, these greats were very kind to me and encouraged me which made me trash the feeling of fright just after the first hour or so. Brabourne stadium was also a great venue and having played there many times before, it was like a stage I was used to. In those days, like even today, playing for Bombay was the ultimate ambition. Just being in the fifteen was a dream come true ... thinking of playing for India was an idea that was very distant for us.

Bombay was a formidable Ranji team during our times, because Bombay had never lost. One had never experienced any result other than a win; or that there could be any other option. And to crown it all, the names that adorned the portals were the greats of Indian cricket. Other teams were weak; the moment they played us their body language spoke volumes of their incompetency. We hardly ever got to bat; in my time Gavaskar, Mankad, Parkar, Naik, Wadekar, Sardesai, Bhosle were really huge run getters. Someone or the other managed the show and to be honest, my friend and mentor, Dilip Sardesai, really dented the opponent's confidence by asking if they had booked their return ticket!

Bombay's dressing room atmosphere was something else. No one touched Wadekar's, Sardesai's or Ashok Mankad's seats. It was an unwritten rule that each dumped his kit at the same seat. And on the field, all positions were fixed. The skipper never told us where to field. The dressing room was fun with Sardesai and Ashok Mankad making things pretty easy. And then there was that laughing assassin, Abdul Ismail, who had the loudest laugh and those who were left out of the reasons for the laugh were told why Abdul laughed, for Abdul to again laugh louder.

I was known as the perpetual complaint maker. But even today they all agree that had it not been for me we would not have got that eventual sandwich or the coke. I must admit that Wadekar was a huge influence on all of us. As a captain he never ever indicated that there was any tension. Sardesai was the torch-bearer even in tense moments, though they were very few; he relieved us of all the tension by his sense of humour. Nobody ever was upset with the other; such was the belief and camaraderie. Ashok Mankad and Sudhir Naik were an influence on all of us juniors. I have to pay a special tribute to two of the greatest bowlers that Bombay produced – Paddy Shivalkar and Abdul Ismail.

Paddy bowled like a batsman. The reason for the analogy is very simple. A batsman goes out to bat wanting to get a century. Shivalkar had the same attitude: 'I am going out there to win the game for Bombay; I will be satisfied only if I captured six for fifty or even lesser.' Give him a pitch that turned an inch and he would spin it a yard. Ismail at the other end was different. With an action that defied all logic, he would bowl these huge outswingers. They hunted in pairs. The others were only a part of that drama.

The other man one has to pay tribute to will have to be my old schoolmate Eknath Solkar. A delightful cricketer, he brimmed with the confidence and that enthused the team. Never afraid of any consequences on the field, he was easily a captain's delight. The most stylish fielder I have seen in the past fifty years.

We wined and dined together and those six days spent together were days to remember. On my first trip outside, the great Sardesai took me aside as his room partner; I had only seen him from the North Stand. I was on the moon. I kept my wallet on the bed at Sholapur and he said, 'Never do this, it could get stolen.' And Sardi being Sardi, the ultimate prankster, wanted to know if I had my girlfriend's picture in my wallet. He opened it only to find that the picture there was of *him* with that classical off drive. *For the first and last time I saw Sardesai blush.* He was very fond of me. I miss him.

I consider myself to be lucky to be a part of the Dadar Union (DU) team. I owe this to three gentlemen – Mantri, Tamhane and Vasu Paranjpe. Can you imagine playing for DU when I was in class ten? Being a product of St Xavier's, I had hardly any clue on the vagaries of the game. Mantri and Tamhane took me under their wings, took me to lunch on match days. I sat next to them all day, did not speak a word, only heard what they said and at DU only cricket was of priority.

All of us were petrified of Mantri but were also sure that he had our cricket interests at heart. To my mind, the man who turned the ethos of DU will have to be Vasu Paranjpe. An outstanding thinker on the game, he thought all of us were 'Supermen'. He made us laugh, made us think, told us stories of Sir Don. We believed in our captain. I for one benefited from his cricketing skills. Positivity was the word at DU. We lost once or twice and Vasu never took it well. He would say, 'How could you let yourselves down?' We were the happiest team on the maidans of Bombay.

After Sachin Tendulkar we haven't produced anyone to be a real star. The MCA gives so much to the players in terms opportunity. Can't fathom why the players are not rising. You have Tendulkar as a role model just as he had Gavaskar. It's the socio-economic scene that is the major cause. Everyone wants to reach the top without climbing the steps. Money, I guess, is the root cause and it's OK to make money. By all means make it but don't reach for it.

Shivalkar was someone who should have played, Ismail was way ahead of Mohol and Govindraj, Raju Kulkarni was treated shabbily. Weren't Gupte and Diwadkar great bowlers? Even an opportunity was denied to them. Nilesh Kulkarni was a force to reckon with and so was Bahutule. But Ramesh Powar, to me he is the best one has seen. But where are the opportunities? Too much quota systems at the end; remember not many teams scored 350 against Bombay. Nobody has played at number four for India for twenty-one years! So, maybe there were no places then. I also feel it's idol worship too.

Registered cricketers should be allowed to vote for three to four seats. I had suggested it when I was a co-opted member of the managing committee. My suggestion was thrown in the dust-bin as those concerned were not forward-looking. The mindset now is only garnering votes and my fears are coming true that the MCA will soon be a vast political body and less and less cricketers will want to come forward. Also, the modern-day cricketer has no interest in the affairs of administration. Take the case of cricketers of the mid-1990s. No one seems to be bothered; they do not want a sense of belonging. And those in the administration want to have a tight control so that cricketers are not encouraged to participate in such affairs.

The idea of playing tournaments in league format is excellent but we are inundated with ninety-odd tournaments. The calendar is overcrowded. But this can certainly help cricketers who are idle when their clubs have lost. This has been discussed several times in the Cricket Improvement Committee (CIC). The willingness to implement the decision is completely lacking.

10

HOW THE REST SAW THEM

OPPONENTS AND NATIONAL TEAMMATES ON BOMBAY CRICKETERS

Mansur Ali Khan (Tiger) Pataudi

I think Bombay cricketers in those days were, and continue to be to date, highly professional; much more professional than we were. Some of them were playing as professionals for money, so we got a pretty good idea of what Bombay cricketers would teach us. They knew how to play the game as professionally as possible. Vijay Manjrekar was a player that excited one the most, although later on he turned out to be quite a bit slow on the field. But in his younger days before his knee injury, I think he was probably the best of them. I played for South Zone against West Zone, played for Hyderabad when Ashok Mankad was the captain of Bombay in 1976. I remember Hyderabad taking fifty-odd-runs lead, and those days matches were of three days. Yet Bombay won outright. What I observed was that their second string too was playing tough cricket. They seem to give you the impression that they love hard cricket. They might know you, but out there in the middle they mean business.

At the time of Independence, cricket was being played only in Bombay, Indore, Baroda and Patiala and a bit in the south. No cricket at all in Bengal, Haryana, Punjab. The principalities were merged into the Union. They couldn't afford to keep these places, so the whole emphasis shifted to Bombay. In the 1950s there was no other cricket except for Bombay. A stage was reached where a player played for India, but could not find a regular place in the Bombay team – I think his name was Manohar Hardikar – so good they were. Gradually, the focus shifted a bit to the south and the north but central remained out; Calcutta was out apart from one or two players.

Bombay cricket relied mainly on school, college and club cricket. The inter-corporate tournaments were taken very seriously because that is where the cricketer got his security. He got a job even if he didn't have a qualification and he even became an officer out of turn, so the security angle was taken care of by corporates. And mind you, that cricket was tougher than some of the Ranji Trophy games. Now you find there are no cricketers from Bombay. That is strange; one should look at that also.

Subhash Gupte was probably the best leg-spinner I have seen, apart from Shane Warne. There was Ramakant Desai. There was Padmakar Shivalkar. I thought he was a very good bowler, but then Bedi was there and Shivalkar couldn't get in. It was very difficult for Shivalkar to get in as long as Bedi was there. But I agree Bombay should have produced many more, but that is only because of the wickets. The wickets in Bombay were superlative both at Ranji level and club level. It was a bit disheartening for bowlers. That's why I think most of them stuck to batting. Probably bowlers found it tough to bowl to high-quality batsmen on good batting tracks. And Bombay produced some top-quality batsmen from Merchant to Tendulkar.

When I became India captain, I was the baby of the team. Everybody was senior to me. It was possible due to special help from people like Polly Umrigar, Vijay Manjrekar. Contractor, of course, was injured, so he was in no position to travel. They helped me so much that I didn't feel uncomfortable. They didn't let me feel that I was the juniormost, and that gave me confidence.

A player could play for India but couldn't for the Bombay side, that just showed the sort of standards we are talking about. They had the batting certainly, and they would out-bat anybody. The bowling may not be there, but if you are chasing 600 it wasn't that easy against Bombay. It is not at all surprising then that Bombay won the Ranji Trophy in forty out of eighty finals. Gradually, other teams came up – Tamil Nadu, Karnataka ... despite that Bombay still continued to win.... I think for that you go back to the strength of Bombay cricket. The strength was its clubs and the system. They are more professional than even the southern cricketers.

I think the Bombay batsmen were very English in their outlook, in the sense that they would bat out a situation, unlike the Australians or West Indians who would hit out to get over a bad situation. A Bombay cricketer would never ever do that. They handled the pressure situation much better. I think they would all handle it in their own separate ways – someone would keep quiet, someone would talk too much, and someone would not be able to sleep.

As far as the structured method of coaching in Bombay goes, it depends on what level of cricket one is referring to. If you are coaching a ten-year-old, fine, because you have to teach basics to a kid. You have to learn basic techniques and if you don't get them right, you will never succeed. But when you reach international cricket, where you have already done what needs to be done, the coach has to look at your individual capacity to do things in a situation. He has to bring out the best in you. He has to look at the individual more. At a young age, everyone must conform and must play front-foot and back-foot strokes in the particular, prescribed manner. But if someone is good at sweeping, don't stop him. At a young age, you may say 'take it easy' but don't stop him from using it.

Who are these coaches who oppose qualified coaching methods? I have seen the quality of coaching in this country. I wish them good luck. I don't think the kind of coaching that they give will help at international level. Our Indian coaches failed at the international level because they began to treat international cricketers like kids. They never looked at them from the individual angle. That sort of coaching might be of use at lower level but international cricket is way beyond most of our coaches. That is why we have to get our coaches from abroad. Whether it's Test cricket, football or hockey, we cannot do without outside coaches because we don't have coaches who are good enough.

Chandu Borde

The Bombay team during my time was an India team. Practically all those who were playing for Bombay were in the India team. Many players failed against Bombay because they had not played enough against them, but I was lucky to play against them when the Bombay club teams would tour Poona to play practice matches, and sometimes we would tour Bombay. So I never faced problems playing Bombay players in the Ranji Trophy. I was used to them playing tough cricket.

Bombay players were like Australians. They gave the impression that they never liked losing, and they were sledging when you were playing well. I won't forget the Baroda–Bombay game of 1955. I tried to play a sweep shot to Subhash Gupte and missed. There was a loud appeal for lbw which was turned down by the umpire. We had lost five wickets and if I had got out Gupte and Vinoo Mankad would have run through the side. Then the sledging started. Madhav Mantri was the wicketkeeper, and I asked him what my fault was in me being declared not out by the umpire? He said, 'You concentrate on your game if you have to play higher class of cricket.' I scored an unbeaten 110 in that match after Baroda lost five wickets quickly.

Obviously Bombay players handled pressure better than anyone else in the team because they were playing tough cricket throughout the year. I saw matches between two top clubs, Dadar Union and Shivaji Park. You could see the determination. Vijay Manjrekar, who was a great batsman, would never play forward blindly. He would watch the ball closely and that helped him play under pressure. Once when England spinner Tony Lock was turning the ball with fielders surrounding Manjrekar, he played him confidently. And when Lock indulged in sledging, Manjrekar returned the compliment.

Though we had a strong side, the second-string Bombay team, which was full of collegians in the Ranji Trophy final in 1971, knew how to handle the pressure. Milind Rege took my brilliant catch, and the Bombay team exerted so much pressure that our batsmen found it difficult to handle. I have seen Bombay trailing on the first innings and yet winning the game outright. Unless you know how to handle pressure, you can't do that.

Why has Bombay not produced bowlers of international class? My observation is Bombay bowlers were bowling in too many matches. Apart from Ramakant Desai who was a medium pacer, the Gupte brothers, Shivalkar and Diwadkar were very good spinners. You can say that bowling continuously on the maidans of Bombay may have affected the bowlers. But let me tell you that though Bombay batsmen stuck to their style, some of the Bombay bowlers were trying to be too technical. The moment they would stop getting wickets, they would get into technicalities and that would not work.

E.A.S. Prasanna

When I saw Bombay batsmen play a typical waiting game, frustrating bowlers, and bowlers bowling a containing line, I really admired their proficiency and competence. Not to give up was their motto. Whatever may be the pitch, they just would not give up. For batting, that worked but, for bowlers, I am afraid it doesn't work. Apart from Paddy Shivalkar who was an attacking bowler, the rest would bowl to 7–2 off-side field and kept bowling outside the off stump. They were testing the patience of batsmen. It worked in domestic cricket, but in international cricket, unless you attack the batsman you can't succeed.

The first time I bowled to Vijay Manjrekar in the nets when I was in the Indian reserves, I became his fan. He too took a liking for me. He was technically so correct that beating him was difficult. Once he scored a big hundred against me and

Chandra on a rank bad turner. I don't remember Manjrekar struggling against top-class spinners on turners. It is not an exaggeration when I say that Gavaskar plus Vishwanath equals Vijay Manjrekar.

Sunil Gavaskar was one of the greatest batsmen in the world and a brilliant captain. As a batsman he had all the shots, but he had to play the role of a sheet anchor. Being a good student of the game, he could handle the situation superbly. He was the captain of the Indian team on the tour of Australia in 1985 when I was the manager. I found him extremely analytical and logical. Once he was convinced that we had to do a particular thing, he would go ahead and do it on the field.

Wadekar was a typical batsman who rarely allowed a bowler to bowl a maiden over to him. He would pounce on a loose ball, but would steal a single and observe a bowler from the non-striker end. Once he assessed a bowler, he would attack him. He scored 323 runs against me and Chandra at the Brabourne stadium in a Ranji Trophy match.

Sardesai, I thought, was the most intelligent batsman against spinners, but he didn't have the heart of, say, Manjrekar or Gavaskar. When things were not going in his favour, he would not stay there. And Dilip Vengsarkar was one of the natural strikers of the ball. In the Irani Cup, once he hit me and Bedi for seven sixes, and he was a teenager playing his second first-class game. He was one batsman who played in front of the pads, and that posed a problem to bowlers.

Wadekar was a defensive captain. Once in the India–England Test at Chepauk in 1972, I had not bowled in the first session of the England second innings. Mike Denness and Keith Fletcher were having a partnership, and things were not going our way.

We knew that chasing 150 on the turning pitch would be very difficult. Wadekar threw the ball to me and told me to bowl tight. I refused. We needed wickets, and by bowling tight we wouldn't have got wickets. One good thing was he listened to me, and I picked four for sixteen and we won the game.

Bombay was the champion team in Ranji Trophy for fifteen years in a row, but Karnataka under my captaincy broke that record. After that, though Bombay has been winning the Ranji Trophy, they haven't been able to dominate. The bowlers have not been able to get wickets the way they were getting earlier. Bombay produced some great batsmen, but now that is also not happening.

But Bombay cricketers were very good because they played better and tough cricket in Bombay. Unless you handle the situations, you will not know how to handle the pressure. Bombay batsmen knew that.

B.S. Chandrasekhar

I saw some of the Bombay players in my first Test. They were really skilful, but again I hadn't seen much quality cricket. Having been brought up on matting wickets, I had seen stroke players but these Bombay players were real grafters. That's the way to play five-day cricket. One thing was common in all the Bombay batsmen: they wouldn't just throw their wickets away. Their approach was absolutely professional. Occupying the crease for longer period was their main aim and I was impressed with their approach.

I saw very little of Vijay Manjrekar as he retired in 1965 from international cricket and that was my first year of cricket, but he was a class player on any pitch. He was technically sound against any bowling and gave the impression that he knew what he was doing. To him, the condition of a wicket didn't matter at all.

Gavaskar was a world-class batsman. He knew where his off stump was. Imagine facing world-class fast bowlers and scoring consistently. Like a typical Bombay batsman, he believed in staying at the wicket. To him, that meant opportunity to keep the scoreboard ticking.

In my opinion, Wadekar ought to have played Test earlier. He was a bit attacking but never took risks. Sardesai used to be nervous initially, but once he gauged the pace of the wicket he played intelligently. He was a good player of spin bowling.

Frankly speaking, Wadekar, like other captains, didn't tell me anything. He gave me the field I wanted. I needed a slip, leg slip, forward short leg and a fielder on the left of the square-leg umpire for pull shot. I didn't bother about placing of other fielders. A captain must have confidence in the ability of a bowler and Wadekar had that in me. Whenever batsmen would attack me, he never changed my bowling. He knew I would strike. In the series against England in 1972-73 in India, I got more than thirty wickets in five Tests.

During my time, except Bombay no other place had three-day matches. Playing three-day games, a player learns to develop skills and learns to handle situations. That's possibly the reason Bombay players could handle pressure better, but now every team is competing with Bombay's skill levels. Players from the other teams too have learnt the art of handling pressure.

Till the 1980s, Bombay dominated because of the quality tournaments they played in Bombay. Even the monsoon league (Kanga League) would test their skill levels. The Bombay players just wouldn't give up. Their formula was not to throw their wickets away and not to let the opposition batsmen score freely.

But slowly, players from the other states copied their approach, and you can see the change.

S. Venkataraghavan

I had heard a lot about the Bombay batsmanship. Vijay Merchant, Polly Umrigar, Ramchand and Vijay Manjrekar were the batsmen who kept scoring consistently. I remember having watched the quarter-final between Madras and Bombay at Madras as a schoolboy and I distinctly remember Bombay beating Madras by ten wickets. Umrigar didn't play as he was injured, but Hoshi Amroliwala scored an unbeaten half-century. They played tough cricket, which I was to watch from close quarters when I played against them.

Watching the batsmen in that team and later playing against most of them, I observed that they were thorough professionals. To tell you frankly, we were in awe of Bombay cricketers. All of them had one special quality – they would get stuck and not give anything away. Possibly because they were not only playing a lot of cricket in Bombay but on a turf which most Indian cricketers were not lucky to get. To them, winning was a habit.

The Ranji final in 1968 was quite interesting. We were eight down for 109 on the first day, but the partnership between Bhaskar and Prabhakar of ninety-seven runs for the ninth wicket helped us get a decent score. When Bombay batted, these two players gave us quick breakthroughs by getting three Bombay wickets. Then there was one incident which I think was the turning point of the match.

After Bombay lost three wickets, Ashok Mankad and captain Manohar Hardikar came together. Ashok hadn't scored much when he played a ball by me straight into the hands of Satvinder Singh at short extra cover. It was a simple catch and Satvinder Singh didn't appeal. But to our dismay, not only did Mankad not walk but began to tap on the pitch. For not appealing for the catch, the umpire ruled Mankad not out. Mankad went on to score a century and Bombay took the lead. This was the first lesson we learnt – stick to the rules. Even for a simple catch, a player must appeal. It was a usual Brabourne stadium wicket which had consistent bounce. Both Hardikar and Solkar started playing with pads. In between, we dropped a couple of sharp chances, but like typical Bombay batsmen these two just didn't give up and played two sessions after lunch and won the game.

Again, during the final match in 1973, the Bombay batsmen, even after getting beaten, kept taking singles. After getting them out for 151, we were two down for sixty-two and I thought if we could get a good lead in the first innings, we would win the game as we wouldn't have to chase more than 50–60 runs. But as the thought was going through my mind, we started to lose wickets and were bundled out for eighty. From two down for sixty-two to eighty all out was terrible. We lost the game.

Kapil Dev

When I was a schoolboy, people would only talk about Bombay cricket. Today, though, things have changed. We used to hear that it was more difficult to play for Bombay than to play for India. But I didn't know much about it till I started playing domestic cricket. Bombay players were always more professional than other players. Professionalism was in terms of how to build the innings, how to play at the right time. Since they had dominated domestic cricket for almost 30–40 years, they knew how to finish the game. They had more talent and confidence, which is why they produced so many great cricketers. Bombay cricketers were always ready to grab an opportunity, unlike players from other parts of India. They had class and ability. They also had the advantage of former players who encouraged younger players.

Dilip Vengsarkar should give credit for a lot of things to Sunil Gavaskar. Maybe because they played for the same club and state, Dilip was influenced by Gavaskar's style of play. Dilip arrived on the domestic scene hitting sixes and fours, but later he too batted like a typical Bombaikar. I must say he was a professional who always played for the team. Never did he throw away his wicket.

Sandeep Patil was totally different from the usual Bombay cricketers. He was probably the most ruthless striker of the ball Bombay ever produced. Though he didn't have the finesse of Gavaskar, he played shots.

The Bombay batsmen could handle pressure better than anybody else because they played with a free mind. When you have depth in your team, you can always play better. They played tough cricket, and that made them handle pressure better.

It is very sad we don't have more cricketers coming from Bombay. The Bombay team is not what it was in our time. I think Bombay needs to go back and look at its cricket. It has to learn something from other states. They had the ability and they produced players who could deliver.

Dilip Doshi

I first heard about the tenacity and the obvious skill of the then Bombay players in the cricketing circles of Calcutta maidan during my college days in the mid-1960s. I do not recall any particular names except the obvious Test players. I heard that Bombay cricketers were very tough mentally and that the batsmen would never throw away their wickets and the bowlers would make you earn every run. I also saw Bapu Nadkarni wheel away maiden overs to Colin Cowdrey at Eden Gardens in 1964 with superb control on length and line.

Bombay was able to play cricket round the year and the intercollegiate cricket and local club rivalry was fought with intensity and tremendous loyalty. My late friend, Mr Adi Rabadi, was a close friend of Farokh Engineer and used to tell us captivating stories about Bombay cricket. It tickled me as a collegian to picture thousands of Bombay students supporting Podar and Ruia College in the finals. This I guess was the great romantic side of Indian cricket then.

We had no cricket in Calcutta from May to September due to the monsoon, football season and, of course, the nature of sticky soil as opposed to Bombay's red and hard soil. I would visit Bombay during these months to practise at the CCI and play friendly matches as an outstation player. This was my first brush with Bombay players starting from the CCI nets and hard-fought matches at the Brabourne stadium. My access to the CCI was solely through the courtesy of the Mankad brothers, Ashok and Atul. The great Vinoobhai was always in the background behind the nets, and I can assure you I did everything possible to impress this great cricketer. Bombay players like Ashok Mankad and Sardesai would play in the nets with astounding seriousness, as opposed to the light-heartedness which I was used to seeing in my fellow Bengal players. This suited me to the hilt as I always took my bowling extremely seriously.

Bombay had another huge advantage – the likes of Hanumant Singh and Wadekar also came to the nets for State Bank of India, making my whole experience much richer. Bowlers had to tell the batsmen to imagine the field placing and the battle began in the nets. To Bombay's credit, this attitude I did not observe even in my county cricket days. I thoroughly enjoyed my stint at CCI in those years and can only thank everyone involved.

All Bombay batsmen that I played with gave their wickets dearly. The technique was adaptable to any kind of pitch and state of the match as I observed often in my playing days. Gavaskar was my college contemporary and a prodigy from the very outset. He had a hunger for scoring runs that I have not seen very often. On the other hand, Ajit Wadekar was a fluent stroke player. Sardesai was a solid batsman in typical Bombay mould and a superb all-round player. Wadekar was a left-hander's dream. Vengsarkar was the most elegant Bombay batsman and an underrated player. He had the uncanny ability to lift the ball cleanly against all kinds of bowling. Both Sandeep Patil and Ravi Shastri merit mention here as they became tremendous cricketers.

When you are a part of a winning team or you have been watching their winning ways, you learn the art of winning. With the Bombay team, winning was a habit. They were not prepared to lose. So they would be under pressure if they were losing but funnily, not having got into a situation in pushing Bombay, many teams like my Bengal team would not press for a win. On many occasions Bengal let them off the hook when Bombay was losing because the Bengal team, not having won many matches, was under pressure. To Bengal, winning was a pressure, and to Bombay, losing was a pressure. They play inter-club and inter-company matches very hard. No player takes these matches lightly. Let's face it, winning the national championship forty times is a very big thing.

I have known Gavaskar from college days. He was a great batsman and good captain, and he would have been a great captain had he not indulged in personal likes and dislikes, which I have written in my autobiography. I may have taken 100 wickets in three years under his captaincy, but you will observe that I have not had many five-wicket hauls. After I would get three or four wickets, I would be sent to the boundary line and medium pacer Karsan Ghavri would be asked to bowl left-arm spin. We certainly had a difference of opinion, but to get medium pacer Ghavri to bowl left-arm spin was a bit too much.

Rahul Dravid

I must say that the memories of the 1993-94 Ranji Trophy match against Bombay are not very pleasant. We were a young and upcoming Karnataka side playing against Bombay. At that time, Ravi Shastri was leading the Bombay team consisting of a few young players which later performed well to win the match against Karnataka on first-innings lead. Karnataka scored 400-plus in the first innings, and in reply to that Bombay had lost five wickets with not much of runs on the scoreboard. It was Ravi Shastri and Sairaj Bahutule who forged a good partnership and took the game away from us. So what I have always seen is that Bombay is a team which has players who can come and win the game any time for them.

Bombay has good local cricket, so the players play a lot of matches. So the Bombay players are sort of match-ready. They know how to play the game of cricket; they know how to win a game. We hear that they are khaddoos, they are tough. But other than that, I will say they have a very, very professional approach towards the game and they know how to perform in crunch situations and win the game. They play many local cricket matches and this has helped them to develop to that level. They are cricket-smart.

The Irani Cup match was expected to be a big game because it had the full-strength Bombay squad led by Sachin Tendulkar pitted against the Rest of India. The Rest of India had V.V.S. Laxman, Sourav Ganguly, Harbhajan Singh and me playing for them. The ball was turning and Ramesh Powar bowled really well in the first innings which really surprised us. Bombay did very well in that game, but the Rest of India consisted of that quality of players who batted well in the second innings to win the game.

I have been following Ranji Trophy for a long time, and other than Karnataka, it was Bombay which I always supported because Sunil Gavaskar is my hero and he used to play for Bombay. So I always wanted Bombay to win matches, provided they are not playing against Karnataka. I still remember the game which I watched in 1981 at Bangalore, in which Karnataka took the first-innings lead against Bombay and Sunil Gavaskar batted left-handed in that match. So as a youngster, I followed cricket and the West Zone or Duleep Trophy matches played at Bangalore.

One thing we must agree on is that Bombay is a big city and had a good cricketing culture. They had good cricketing facilities which were better than in any other city in India at that time. I remember I played my first match on turf at the age of seventeen, whereas in Bombay a player plays on turf from his childhood days. So they had more advantages than anyone else. Today, things have changed because the cricket infrastructure and facilities in other states have improved, the number of matches played in other states has increased and the quality of pitches has improved. This gives an advantage to other players as well. Hence it is difficult for a particular city to continue its tradition of providing the maximum number of quality players for the national team. But irrespective of all these things, I think Bombay will always be a competitive Ranji Trophy team and will continue to dominate in domestic cricket because of their well-developed local cricket structure.

Sachin Tendulkar himself is an example of a Bombay player being developed in the maidans of Shivaji Park. He told me that sometimes he used to play two matches in a day. So he batted for nearly five to six hours a day, whereas a boy in any other city would bat for forty-five to sixty minutes in a week. So there is lot more difference. He enjoys the game and one can almost feel that he is still playing for Achrekar XI, the way he feels the joy while playing.

The preparation for every tournament varies and it completely depends on how comfortable Sachin is with it. Sometimes you can find him batting for hours in the nets, sometimes he bats for just a few overs or sometimes he just does the knocking with throwdowns. But you can easily make out that every day he mentally readies himself for a big match.

Considering that there are eighty tournaments, 25,000-plus registered cricketers, 100 grounds and 329 affiliated clubs in Bombay, it surprises me why Bombay couldn't produce international-quality players in the past ten years. But one thing we have to accept is that talent is now going to come from small towns and cities because they have all the necessary facilities and time in order to develop themselves in cricket. Someone also told me that even in Bombay the talent is coming from Thane and the suburbs and the outskirts of Bombay. The reason is that facilities have grown all over India, and it will be difficult for any one city to dominate the Indian team as Bombay did in the 1960s and '70s.

Sometimes I feel that Bombay's philosophy and tradition has been in batting, so Bombay tends to bat positively and score heavily, and then bowl defensively. But you can't do that in Test cricket as you have to bowl attackingly in Test cricket. The tendency to bowl defensive can become a hindrance in Test cricket because it doesn't allow you to learn how to attack a good batsman with bowling and take wickets. But I really like the attitude and professionalism of Bombay players towards the game of cricket, their desire to win constantly, their desire to play tough cricket. One can sense all these things when one plays against Bombay.

To be honest, Bombay has made an impact on Indian cricket due to their performance. They have won the Ranji Trophy forty times which is more than anyone else. They have produced great cricketers – absolutely the legends of the game. Indian cricket owes a lot to Bombay as it was the place where cricket flourished and they kept the banner flying for a long time.

Nari Contractor

Frankly speaking, I was curious to watch Vijay Merchant because he was scoring big hundreds all the time. And when I was five years old, my uncle took me to Bombay to watch the Bombay–Baroda Ranji Trophy match in which Merchant scored 141 and an elegant left-hander Khandu Rangnekar scored ninety-eight. I think both of them got out to full tosses. I was impressed with the way both played.

Those days, cricket that was played in Bombay was top class and much better organized than what it is today. We were playing from July till end of March. Kanga League, which is played in the monsoon, attracted and involved everyone connected with the game. It was started with the intention of getting to play on wet pitches, because Indians while touring England didn't know how to play on wet pitches. But later, this sort of cricket prepared you mentally for the season. To survive on those sorts of pitches, a batsman had to adjust all the time. Getting twenty-five runs was compared to scoring a century. You had to play with soft hands. Since there was tall grass, we had to run quick singles because you just couldn't hit a boundary. For a game to be played on Sunday, the teams would meet on Friday to discuss strategy. When a match would be called off because of heavy rains, we would get disappointed.

Great batsmen like Merchant and Hazare, with some others, were playing in the Pentagulars. Bombay cricketers grew up watching them score runs rather than the bowlers dominating. This aspect influenced young cricketers to such an extent that they were inclined to bat rather than bowl. Not to throw away their wicket and not to let the opposition score heavily was the simple strategy.

There were thirteen Test cricketers in Bombay at that time. For any youngster to get into the Bombay team was impossible. But when the Indian team was to tour West Indies in 1953, the BCA decided to have some trial matches to watch talented youngsters. Though I top-scored in two out of three matches, the selectors didn't pick me. They still picked some players who were past thirty. Watching one of the matches was the Gujarat captain Pheroz Khambata. He invited me to play for Gujarat because I was born in Gujarat. Initially I declined, but when I was not selected for Bombay, I sent a telegram to him that I was available for selection. I received a telegram from the Gujarat Cricket Association that I should report to Baroda because Gujarat was playing against Baroda. When I went over there, they made me play in the nets but didn't assure me that I would play as they had already selected the final eleven. But on the day, captain Khambata reported unfit and I got a chance to play. Batting in the middle order, I scored a century in each innings on debut, and that's a world record.

Mohinder Amarnath

B ombay players always played like professionals. Not to throw away the wicket and not to let the opposing batsmen score freely has been the philosophy of Bombay players. Since Bombay has many tournaments, the players know how to plan an innings. Bowl a good consistent line. I have not seen Bombay batsmen trying to get out of a situation by hitting out. They would wait for their chance to pounce on you, and I really enjoyed that sort of competition.

I had heard a lot about Bombay from my father, who scored a Test century on debut in Bombay. Those days, all the players would come to Bombay to play because you would get good opposition. My father would always say that by playing in Bombay, you would learn cricket in a better way. Look, in the north, there is no cricket culture. You have to have a proper cricket culture to learn good things, and Bombay had that cricket culture.

I played for one company in Bombay when I was staging a comeback. It was tough cricket. Firstly, there were hardly any tournaments in the north. These corporate tournaments, which are played in a competitive spirit, have helped many outstation players because that sort of competition was not available elsewhere in the country.

Chetan Chauhan

Before playing for the India team, I had met the Bombay cricketers in Ranji Trophy when I played for Maharashtra against Bombay and also when they played for West Zone in Duleep Trophy. I found the Bombay players to be very professional in their approach, when they were on the cricket ground. Their focus was always on cricket, whether they were batting, bowling or fielding. They used to give 100 per cent, especially when they were playing for Bombay. The good thing I liked about them was that they used to support and praise one another and it left a very good impression amongst the players from other states.

I played with Ajit Wadekar in the Indian team and West Zone and also against him, while playing for Maharashtra. Ajit was a very nice person, though an introvert. I received a lot of encouragement and motivation from him. He was a brilliant fielder and I enjoyed fielding in the slips with him. During the overs he would tell jokes to keep the pressure down.

I opened the innings with Dilip Sardesai for West Zone. He was a very good player and always played with authority. He would never go into a shell. He enjoyed his cricket. He was absolutely an extrovert and was a great company after the match. People enjoyed his company, but at times he was very sarcastic about other players. He was very proud to play for Bombay and that is what I appreciated most. His only problem was that he loved good food and had sometimes even a running stomach the next day. He played like a champion in the West Indies series in 1971, but for some reason, he could not repeat that performance again. He was a fierce competitor on the ground and he used to play very hard.

I first saw Sunil Gavaskar when he played for Bombay University and I played for Poona University. Subsequently, we both played for West Zone in the Vizzy Trophy and became very good friends. He was absolutely a professional and worked on his technique and his game. He would think a lot about his cricket. One thing I learnt from him was never to throw away my wicket. He was very mean as far as his batting was concerned and always made bowlers slog to earn his wicket. His entire focus used to be on cricket when he was on the ground. I was amazed at his appetite and hunger for runs right from the university days. He would take time to become friendly and would not easily open out his thoughts and views to many people, but once he was sure that the person was harmless he was a great company after the game.

I opened with him for India in thirty-five Test matches and had excellent understanding with him on the ground and outside, when the game was over. I think I was one of the very few people in whom he confided regarding the cricket team and about the players. He too was a typical Bombaywalla and would go out of his way to support a player from Bombay.

On the ground, when we were batting, he gave great support

and advice and would even caution me if I was playing loose shots. I was one of the very few cricketers he would ask between the overs if he had committed any mistake while playing. We would encourage and motivate each other because we knew that since we were opening, the team depended on us. We would always stay on at the wicket as long as possible so that it became easier for the batsmen who would follow. Needless to say, because of our understanding we helped and motivated each other. We had nearly ten century partnership for India.

Dilip Vengsarkar and I went together on the tour of Australia in 1977 and became very good friends, and this friendship has lasted all these years. We speak to each other at least once a month. I always admire him for his batting, especially his cover drives and on drives. He was absolutely an introvert and had very few friends in the Indian team. He confided in very few people and was mostly aloof. He would have been a superstar, but unfortunately, because of Sunil Gavaskar, Vishwanath and Kapil Dev he did not receive enough publicity and recognition. His three centuries in a row at Lords demonstrated what a great player he was. He was a bit lazy off the field, but on the ground he always gave 100 per cent, whether he was batting or fielding. I got along with him very well and he used to call me 'Master' out of affection. Because he used to speak less, people always used to misunderstand him, but the good thing about him is that he was not scared and would give his views in the team meetings or whenever asked for.

Sandeep Patil loved and enjoyed his cricket. He was a very useful cricketer and a very attractive batsman. He was an aggressive batsman and loved to play his shots, whatever be the situation. In 1981, he was hit on the head by a short ball from

Len Pascoe. I still remember the chat with him when he was playing for India against Queensland in a four-day game. It was a green wicket and I was watching the game, as I was resting. When told that he was slightly late in leaving shot deliveries and he should start wearing helmet, he joked that he would wear a helmet only after he was hit on the head. Unfortunately, in the first Test match in Sydney, he was hit by a fierce delivery from Pascoe. He was a very gutsy player and in the next Test match itself he scored brilliant 174 runs and hit the fast bowlers all around. It was a great knock which I will remember and so will others who saw that knock at Adelaide. In fact, we had a partnership of nearly 140 runs and managed to draw the match. He was a great company and had tremendous sense of humour. One could pass many hours in his company and would not get bored. He is a very sweet person and would never speak ill about anybody. He is an absolute gentleman.

I met Karsan Ghavri for the first time when I played for Maharashtra and he played for Saurashtra. He then moved to Bombay and became a regular member of the Bombay cricket team.

Karsan was an extrovert but a very useful player to any side. He would bowl fast or medium, and if required, he used to bowl left-arm spin. He would give his 100 per cent on the ground and relaxed once the game was over. He would always speak well about his fellow cricketers, when he was playing for India. Since he used to give 100 per cent to the game, he was liked and admired by every captain, whether he was playing for Bombay or India.

Because of the attitude and professionalism of the Bombay players, especially their batsmen, Bombay has contributed substantially to Indian cricket. All the players we have spoken about focused on cricket and would never throw away their wickets while batting. Because of this, each of them scored heavily in domestic cricket as well as in international cricket. The great thing about Bombay batsmen was that whatever be the situation, they would never throw away the game. Even if there was no interest in the game and it was heading towards a tame draw, the Bombay batsmen would hang on and score runs and would not throw away their wickets.

Bombay has also produced spinners of international class, but barring Ramakant Desai, they have not been able to produce fast bowlers. Because of the approach of Bombay batsmen towards batting, they would always produce cricketers like Gavaskar, Tendulkar and Vengsarkar. I do not see any reason why they are not able to produce good fast bowlers. They did have a very good spinner in Padmakar Shivalkar but unfortunately because of the presence of Bishan Bedi, he could not play Test cricket. Had he played Test cricket, he would have made a mark in international cricket. I do not see any reason why Bombay has not been able to produce outstanding bowlers, compared to batsmen who have contributed immensely to Indian cricket. One reason I can think of is the weather which is hot and humid throughout the year. But considering the humidity and movement which the new-ball bowlers get in Bombay, I think Bombay should have produced quality fast bowlers of international class.

I cannot think of any reason why only few players like Wadekar, Desai, Gavaskar, Vengsarkar and Sandeep Patil have contributed to the total runs in Indian cricket. Some others may have been overshadowed by the above players and maybe they developed some kind of a complex and so could not contribute runs in big numbers. The other players who could have scored more runs were Eknath Solkar, Vinod Kambli and Ashok Mankad. All the three had good temperament and actually should have scored more runs than what they actually did. Vinod Kambli and Ashok Mankad were slightly susceptible against genuine pace bowling and that is the reason they failed.

The most impressive captains of Bombay, if put in order, would be Ashok Mankad, Sunil Gavaskar and Ajit Wadekar. Ashok was a very shrewd captain and would play only according to the rules. He showed no mercy towards the opposition and would go to the extent of a denying a runner to an injured batsman. He was absolutely a rule maniac and played very hard. He was a thinking captain and would always plan to defeat the opposition.

Sunil Gavaskar was a bit of an introvert and was not an aggressive captain. Though he was also a thinking captain, he was not as shrewd as Ashok. He used to concentrate on the game and depended on only a few bowlers, whereas Ashok would get the best out of each member of the team.

Bombay has won the Ranji Trophy forty times, which is an outstanding feat for a team. Initially, the facilities at Bombay were the best in the country and that is the reason players from a lot of other cities moved to Bombay. The cricket played there was very competitive and very well organized. They played one-day matches, three-day matches. Besides, club cricket was very professional. A lot of private as well as government companies gave jobs to upcoming and talented players and that is another reason why good players moved to Bombay and started living there and playing for Bombay. There was a time when barring one or two players, the rest of the players in the Indian team were from Bombay.

The great thing about the Bombay team was that they used

to gel together very well. They received tremendous support from their associations as well. Bombay players were thorough professionals and they all knew what their job was and there was no need to tell them. Even the players from outside Bombay who moved to Bombay would play like the Bombaywallas for their states. Their approach was shrewd and mean and would not give any room to the opposition. They played fiercely and from their heart. The great thing I liked about them was the attitude of 'never say die'. Even in bad situations they would bounce back and win the games. They would fight till the end and would never give up, and maybe this spirit came from senior players.

The match I remember most was the one that I played for Maharashtra against Bombay at Kolhapur in 1972. Bombay had a full team led by Ajit Wadekar which included Gavaskar, Sardesai, Ashok Mankad, Solkar and others. They scored 340 runs in the first innings but Maharashtra chased these runs and won on the first innings. I scored 186 and remained not out till the end.

Bombay cricket has had a great impact on Indian cricket and will always have in future too because they will always produce Gavaskars, Tendulkars and Vengsarkars. They have taught Indian players how to be professionals. During my playing days, the word around was that 'if you want to improve your cricket, especially batting, you must go and play cricket in Bombay'. Moreover, the facilities at Brabourne stadium were excellent and the playing conditions were superb, including the wicket.

The whole ethos/culture at Brabourne stadium/CCI was of cricket and people simply waited eagerly to play a match at CCI. The saying that players learnt to be shrewd and competitive and play hard from the Bombay cricket team still holds good. Of course, now other associations have also developed international facilities due to commercialization of cricket and the support received from BCCI (the Board of Control for Cricket in India).

The ethos/culture of Bombay cricket is 150 years old, which is very heartening and, as I stated earlier, the best facilities for cricket are located in Bombay. It has created history in Indian cricket. It is only in the last 15–20 years that other states have developed and improved teams and started giving a tough time to Bombay.

Bombay cricketers are very proud and have produced brilliant players and that is why they have won Ranji Trophy forty times. In fact, Bombay was considered to be the Mecca of Indian cricket. The kind of culture which was there at CCI was unbelievable. At the CCI where the older cricketers used to assemble for the match or after the game or for social functions would only talk about cricket and the cricket news of Bombay. I am sure the present coaches of Bombay and administrators of Mumbai Cricket Association must be reminding constantly the present players about the performance of great players produced by Bombay and the history and culture of Bombay.

Since the facilities are now developed in other states, which are as good as that of Bombay, the earlier practice of players rushing to Bombay for jobs and cricket has reduced. Because of this, the supply of quality players from other states to Bombay has stopped and this can also be one of the reasons why the general standard of Bombay cricket has come down. At one stage, Bombay had players like Salim Durrani, Hanumant Singh, Rusi Surti, Nari Contractor and Vijay Manjrekar living and playing in Bombay but played cricket for other states.

It will be a good idea to have a museum on the history of

Bombay cricket located in Bombay. Many youngsters who would visit the museum would get inspiration and motivation from watching the great cricketers produced by Bombay.

Bombay has eighty cricket tournaments. I think they are too many and the number should be reduced. I would always go for quality instead of quantity.

I gather that most tournaments are on knockout basis wherein a team can miss in the first round and be out of the tournament. This reduces the opportunity for the good players in the tournament, as they would have to wait for the next tournament if their team lost in the first round. It will be better if the tournaments are played on league-cum-knockout basis so that they get to play more games and more opportunities to perform.

As regards giving voting rights to the young players of above twenty-one years in the running of the association, I am not really inclined towards this. I think it is better that the players concentrate on their game and improve their cricket instead of getting involved in the politics of the cricket association. I think voting should be left to the clubs or institutions. More the members with voting rights more are the groups and complications in the running of the association. For running the association, I would suggest the involvement of retired cricket players in the various clubs for which they have played. Once they come on the management of the clubs, automatically they can contribute their expertise/experience to the club as well as to the association. I am happy to see that players like Vengsarkar, Hemant Waingankar and Lalchand Rajput are elected members of the association. I am sure they must be contributing immensely towards Bombay cricket.

I would be happy if Mumbai Cricket Association continues

its culture and history and contribution of the past to Indian cricket and produce quality players from Bombay, who would contribute to Indian cricket.

Yajuvendra Singh

Club cricket in Bombay was very competitive and the players were very eager to perform for their clubs. Dadar Union, Hindu Gymkhana and Shivaji Park Gymkhana had Bombay players and other state-level players playing for them. It was unheard of that any player ever opted out of a match. As a person from outside, my first impression was the pride and commitment that each player had playing for his side.

Playing for Mahindra's was the best cricketing decision of my life. It not only made you play against the present and past cricketers of India, but also along with some of them. Ramnath Kenny, my colleague at Mahindra's, was one of the best players I have seen against spin. Even at the age of fifty, he was there smothering and playing shots against Shivalkar, Uday Joshi, Prasanna and so on. Just partnering him and talking to him in the middle taught me how to handle spin. His advice was to play the ball with the bat rather than the pad and play it at the pitch as much as you can. This was only possible by stretching one's legs or using one's feet. Just watching Wadekar, Hanumant, Sardesai, Bhosle, Gavaskar, etc., and playing the likes of Ramakant, Nadkarni, Diwadkar, V.S. Patil even in their later days was the best education that one could ever have received.

Bombay was unquestionably the best side in India. They made sure during my time that they remained there by getting the talent from other states. This they could do with very little effort as corporate jobs and cricket were in Bombay. They had the fighting spirit and the confidence of a winner. Even at times when they were down, the most unexpected player would deliver either runs or wickets for them. They just churned out cricketers who valued their existence in the middle. We were happy with a century or an attractive half-century. A Bombay player was always there for a big score. This was because a place in the Bombay side was very hard to get and could not be taken for granted.

Playing for other sides was much easier as one was quite sure of playing the season even through a few failures. What made Bombay a formidable side was their mental strength and their desire to win. This was so amply shown by Gavaskar at Nasik against us (Maharashtra) when, with a broken finger, he stuck on in the middle to ensure that new batsmen did not come out to play Salgaonkar before the close of the day's play. It is this sort of commitment that made Bombay a winning side.

In knockout, if the players are not available because of their company commitments and their team loses in the first round, players miss that tournament and there is no opportunity for them to perform in that tournament. During our time, most of the cricket that we played was club cricket. Most of the times we only played four first-class matches and at least three of them on matting. With today's schedule, a league format is always welcome as more the matches that one plays, better the chances are of finding talented young cricketers. Cricket can sometimes be harsh to some very gifted players. And so the more they play, the easier it would get to decide the calibre of each player.

Bombay cricket was the backbone of Indian cricket. The reason was that the team won the Ranji Trophy even with their B team when their stalwarts were on duty for India. Bombay churned out mentally tough and fighting cricketers and the game at the highest level is not about ability only but also mental toughness, and that was the DNA of Bombay cricket. Although one wishes Bombay cricket would grow through the corporate set-up, the present situation calls for specialization. Therefore, cricket now has become a serious occupation and so has to be looked at professionally. Creating an opportunity to unearth raw talent, nurturing it and preparing it for playing at higher levels is of prime importance. So Bombay cricket should have talent search initiatives, more academies and cricket centres with trained coaches, trainers and career advisors.

I do not think the standard of batting of Bombay cricketers today is in any way inferior. The problem is the lack of application and mature thinking. The modern analysis of runs per ball, exciting stroke play, playing for the spectators, instant results have all led to lack of patience and application. Therefore, when the wicket is lively, the understanding of defence with calculated aggression becomes a problem for today's players.

I enjoyed playing Kanga League for Jolly. I think it is an important DNA for Bombay cricket as it teaches one to play in a difficult condition. It teaches one to innovate and learn the most important aspect of batsmanship – to alter the feel, tightening and loosening of the grip according to the situation, which is normally after the ball pitches. Today more matches are cancelled because of the unsuitable outfield conditions and wetness of the wicket. As regards the wicket, the wet one should not be a deterrent but the outfield should be the responsibility of MCA. Today there are several solutions to ensure that water absorption is possible.

APPENDIX

BOMBAY CRICKET TRIVIA

Bombay has a unique place in Indian cricket. The following statistics and records make this amply clear.

- 464 matches played by Bombay are the highest number of matches played by any team in the Ranji Trophy championship.

- 222 victories earned by Bombay are the highest number of victories earned by any team in the Ranji Trophy championship.

- Bombay's percentage of outright victories is 47.84: 222 victories out of their 464 matches.

- 164 matches were won by Bombay on first-innings lead.

- Bombay's percentage of victories coupled with victories on first-innings lead, amount to 83.19 (222 outright wins + 164 wins on first-innings lead = 386 out of their 464 matches = 83.19 %).

➤ Only twenty matches were lost by Bombay in their seventy-nine seasons since 1934-35.

➤ Fifty-one matches were lost on first-innings deficit by Bombay.

➤ Four matches ended as incomplete.

➤ On two occasions the matches were decided on the toss of a coin.

➤ One match was decided on better quotient.

➤ Bombay missed just one season of the tournament – in 1942-43.

➤ **Ranji Trophy match venues in the city of Bombay are the most in one single city of India**

Grounds in the city	Matches played
Bombay Gymkhana	6
Brabourne Stadium	84
Wankhede Stadium	119
RCF Ground	2
MIG Club Ground	2
Bandra Kurla Complex Ground	7
Dr D.Y. Patil Sports Academy	1
Total	221

Note: Six matches played in Thane were in fact hosted by Bombay, but are not counted in this table,Thane having been shown as a separate venue.

- 296 players have been played by Bombay in their 464 Ranji Trophy matches.

- Bombay enforced the follow-on upon their oppoents sixty-eight times, out of which Bombay won fifty-one times and on seventeen occasions the matches were drawn.

- Ninety-eight times Bombay raised totals of over 500.

- Nineteen times Bombay's opponents raised totals of over 500.

- On four occasions Bombay dismissed their opponents for less than 100 runs in both innings.

- On five occasions, Bombay dismissed their opponents for a total of less than 100 runs:
  - 42 by Gujarat
  - 45 by Nawanagar
  - 79 by Saurashtra
  - 94 by Uttar Pradesh
  - 98 by Hyderabad

- **Bombay enforced the follow-on upon their opponents on sixty-eight occasions – maximum by any team in the tournament.**

- **Highest team aggregate – a world record**
  Bombay is involved in the world record aggregate of both the sides – the first two highest aggregates.

Year	Venue	Teams	Scores in innings		Remarks
			First	Second	
1948-49	Poona	Bombay	651	714 for eight declared	The match was played over seven days. One batsman was retired hurt. So a total of thirty-seven wicket fell.
		Maharashtra	407	604	
		Total runs	1,058	1,318	
		Grand total	2,376 runs for 37 wickets		

Highest team aggregate — second highest world record

Year	Venue	Teams	Scores in innings		Remarks
			First	Second	
1944-45	Bombay	Bombay	462	764	The Ranji Trophy Final match lasted six days from 4 to 9 March 1945
		Holkar	360	492	
		Total runs	822	1256	
		Grand total	2,078 runs for 40 wickets		

➤ **Longest match**
Bombay vs Maharashtra match at Poona in 1948-49 was played from 5 to 11 March 1949, lasting for seven days.

➤ **Toss of a coin for result**
For the first time the toss of a coin was resorted to for deciding the winners, when even after four days, the first innings of Bombay and Baroda were not completed at Bombay in 1945-46. Baroda was favoured by the coin.

Bombay scored 133 for two and Uttar Pradesh replied with 133 for no loss at Kanpur in 1992-93. Toss of a coin decided the match in favour of Uttar Pradesh.

➤ **All six balls hit for six**
R.J. Shastri hit sixes off all the six balls of the over from Tilak Raj, left-arm slow spinner from Baroda, in the match against Baroda at Wankhede stadium, Bombay, in 1984-85 and shared the world record with Nottinghamshire's Garfield Sobers who hit six sixes in the over from Glamorgan's Malcolm Nash at Swansea in 1968. Tilak Raj bowled his tenth over from Garware End and Shastri hit the

first ball	to long on
second ball	straight drive
third ball	straight drive
fourth ball	to square leg
fifth ball	to long on
sixth ball	straight drive

➤ **Fastest century**
Shastri's unbeaten knock of 200 included one of the fastest centuries in first-class cricket – seventy-one minutes, off eighty balls with nine fours and four sixes – vs Baroda at the Wankhede stadium in Bombay in 1984-85.

➤ **Fastest double century – a world record**
Shastri's double century was the fastest century in world first-class cricket – 200 runs in 113 minutes, off 123 balls with thirteen fours and thirteen sixes – vs Baroda at the Wankhede stadium in Bombay in 1984-85.

> **Most sixes in an innings – a record for Bombay**
> Shastri's thirteen sixes in the knock of 200 not out is the highest for Bombay batsmen – vs Baroda at the Wankhede stadium in Bombay in 1984-85.

> **Centuries by Bombay batsmen – most by one team in the Ranji Trophy tournament**
>
> | | |
> |---|---|
> | 100s | 461 |
> | 200s | 58 |
> | 300s | 7 |
> | **Total** | **526** |

> Twenty or more centuries by Bombay batsmen:
>   thirty-five by Wasim Jaffer
>   twenty-eight by A.A. Muzumdar
>   twenty-three by V.G. Kambli
>   twenty-two by Ashok Mankad
>   twenty by S.M. Gavaskar

> Sanjay Manjrekar's knock of 377 vs Hyderabad at Wankhede stadium, Bombay, in 1990-91 comprised fifty-one hits to the fence, which is the highest number of boundaries in an innings by a Bombay batsman.

> Wasim Jaffer's career aggregate of 9,737 runs scored at the average of 60.48 in 118 matches during the period from 1996-97 to 2013-14 is the highest for any batsman in the Ranji Trophy tournament.

> Amol Muzumdar's 131 Ranji Trophy matches for Bombay (100 from 1993-94 to 2007-08), Assam and Andhra are the

highest number of Ranji Trophy matches ever played by an individual player.

➤ Amol Muzumdar's debut in the Ranji Trophy in 1993-94 was sensational when he created a world record for a debutant cricketer by making the highest score of 260 against Haryana at Faridabad.

➤ Wasim Jaffer holds yet another record of 153 catches in his 118 Ranji Trophy appearances during the period from 1996-97 to 2013-14, which is the highest for any fielder in Ranji Trophy.

➤ Wasim Jaffer also holds a record of most catches in a season of Ranji Trophy – 23 catches in nine matches of the season 2003-04 for Bombay.

➤ Vinayak Samant, wicketkeeper from Assam, Bombay (sixty-five matches) and Tripura during the period from 1995-96 to 2011-12, holds the record of most dismissals behind the stumps – 333 comprising 296 catches and thirty-seven stumpings in his ninety-five Ranji Trophy appearances.

➤ Wasim Jaffer captained Bombay in most number of matches, forty, winning fifteen and drawing twenty-four, and losing just one match, vs Karnataka at Bangalore in 2013-14.

➤ Likewise, Sunil Gavaskar captained Bombay in thirty-nine matches, winning ninteen and drawing ninteen, losing just one match – the final vs Delhi in Delhi in 1979-80.

> **First triple century**
> The first triple century was scored by V.M. Merchant (as a captain) – 359 not out vs Maharashtra at Bombay in 1943-44, scored in 640 minutes with thirty-one fours.

> Out of 32 triple centuries recorded in Ranji Trophy, Bombay batsmen have recorded the maximum – seven triple centuries – a record in Ranji Trophy.

> **Best batting average in a career**
> Vijay Merchant scored 3,639 runs in thirty-two matches at the average of 98.35.

> Sachin Tendulkar scored 4,281 runs with eighteen centuries in thirty-eight matches at an average of 87.37 in thirteen seasons from 1988-89 to 2013-14. (He did not participate in the tournament in twelve out of twenty-five seasons.)

> **Gavaskar bats left-handed**
> Sunil Gavaskar batted left-handed for about half an hour in Bombay's semi-final against Karnataka at Bangalore in the season 1981-82, when Karnataka's slow left-arm spinner Raghuram Bhat was simply unplayable. Gavaskar, entering at number seven in the second innings, batted right-handed and then left-handed and scored an unbeaten eighteen, in the drawn encounter. It is reported that he played as a genuine left-handed batsman in the innings. The ball was turning at right angles on that day and was beating the bat continuously. The only way to play the wickedly turning deliveries from Raghuram Bhat on that day was to play left-handed. He played

left-handed to Bhat for some 12–13 overs and went back to batting right-handed against the bowler from the other end, which was mostly a fellow left-arm spinner B. Vijayakrishna, who would give more air to the ball.

➤ **Highest fourth-innings total**
  • 604 by Maharashtra at Poona in 1948-49 (Bombay won the match by 354 runs)
  • 352 by Bombay vs Haryana at Bombay in 1990-91 (Bombay lost the match by two runs)

➤ **Centuries in consecutive matches – record in Ranji Trophy**

	Score	Opponent
In seven consecutive matches by Rusi Modi (spread over two seasons)	168	Maharashtra
	128	Western India
	160	Sind
	210	Western India
	245*	Baroda
	113	Northern India
	151	Holkar

➤ **Centuries in consecutive innings**

	Score	Opponent
In five consecutive matches by Rusi Modi	168	Maharashtra
	128	Western India
	160	Sind
	210	Western India
	245*	Baroda

➤ **Most centuries in an innings**

	Score	Name
Four by Bombay batsmen	132	K.C. Ibrahjim
	171	V.M. Merchant
	136	U.M. Merchant
	113	K.M. Rangnekar

➤ **Most centuries in a match**

	Score	Name
Five by Bombay	200	M.K. Mantri
	143 and 156	U.M. Merchant
	131 and 160	D.G. Phadkar
Four by Maharashtra	143	M.C. Datar
	133 and 100	M.R. Rege
	146	S.D. Deodhar

➤ **First five-wicket haul**
Eight for forty by H.J. Vajifdar vs Northern India at Bombay

➤ **First five-wicket haul against Bombay**
six for 101 by D.R. Puri of Northern India vs Bombay at Bombay

➤ **Hat-tricks against Bombay**
- B. Kalyansundaram of Tamil Nadu performed the first hat-trick against Bombay at Madras in the final of 1972-73, capturing the wickets of Rakesh Tandon, Padmakar Shivalkar and Sharad Hazare.
- Raghuram Bhat of Karnataka also performed a hat-trick against Bombay by dismissing Ghulam Parkar, Ashok Mankad and Suru Nayak at Bangalore in 1981-82.

➢ **Only two bowlers used in an innings**
Against Mysore at Bangalore in 1951-52 (D.G. Phadkar and V. Mankad)

➢ **Only two bowlers used in an innings against Bombay**
By Baroda at Baroda in 1971-72 in Bombay's first innings of 129 on the first day (A.L. Fernandes and N.Y. Satham).

➢ **Most wickets in a day's play**

Bombay's total of 129	10 wickets	on the first day of the match at Baroda in 1971-72
Baroda's total of 42	10 wickets	

➢ **Century and five wickets in the same match**

M.N. Raiji	130 and 5 wkts for 95	vs Maharashtra
D.G. Phadkar	134* and 6 wkts for 71	vs Madras
V. Mankad	111 and 5 wkts for 124	vs Madras
P.R. Umrigar	102 and 5 wkts for 38	vs Maharashtra
R.J. Shastri	158 and 5 wkts for 61	vs Madhya Pradesh

➢ **Bombay at their lowest ebb – five wickets for zero.**
Bombay's first five batsmen – Sahil Kukreja, Wasim Jaffer, Hiken Shah, skipper Amol Muzumdar and Rohit Sharma – were back in the pavilion with no score on the board in their total of 145 in the second innings on the second day, in the semi-final of the Ranji Trophy match against Baroda at the Motibaug Palace stadium in Baroda in 2006-07. Even after such a debacle, Bombay finally won the match by sixty-three runs.

Sahil Kukreja	c R.V. Pawar	b I.K. Pathan
Wasim Jaffer	c P. Shah	b R.B. Patel
Hiken Shah	c S.S. Parab	b I.K. Pathan
Amol Muzumdar		b R.B. Patel
Rohit Sharma	lbw	b I.K. Pathan

Fall of wickets :   1 for 0 (Sahil Kukreja – 0.4 over)
2 for 0 (Wasim Jaffer – 1.6 overs)
3 for 0 (Hiken Shah – 2.4 overs)
4 for 0 (Rohit Sharma – 2.5 overs)
5 for 0 (Amol Muzumdar – 3.2 overs)

Earlier Kerala also had lost five wickets without score in the Ranji Trophy match against Mysore at Bangalore in 1963-64 in their total of twenty-seven.

India holds the world record of this nature in Test cricket, when four of their batsmen (Pankaj Roy, Dattaji Gaekwad, Madhav Mantri, who was promoted to number three in the second innings from number eight in the first innings, and Vijay Manjrekar) lost their wickets without a run on the board in the second innings of the first Test against England at Leeds in 1952.

➤ Out of eighty Ranji Trophy finals, Bombay hosted as many as twenty-nine finals in the city of Bombay – a record in the Ranji Trophy.

➤ Out of six instances of batsmen scoring a century in each innings of the Ranji Trophy finals, two Bombay batsmen have figured in this record:

- Sachin Tendulkar – vs Tamil Nadu at Bombay in 1994-95 – 140 and 139
- Rohit Sharma – vs Uttar Pradesh at Hyderabad in 2008-09 – 141 and 108.

> **Shortest final**

The five-day final between Tamil Nadu and Bombay in Madras in 1972-73, ended on the third day with just one ball bowled on the third morning, which brought victory to Bombay by 123 runs. The match was virtually over on the second day itself. Tamil Nadu in their second innings were sixty-one for nine at the end of the second day's play and Bombay had to bowl just one more ball on the third morning to wrap up the match.

Scores: Bombay 151 and 113. Tamil Nadu eighty and sixty-one.

Bombay in Tests

> A total of 280 cricketers represented India in their 478 Tests. Seventy cricketers from Bombay out of 280 India Test cricketers played in these 478 Tests.

> Bombay's contribution to India's Tests is 25.00 per cent in terms of Test cricketers from Bombay.

> Bombay players scored 74,246 runs out of India's total of 2,39,763 runs in 480 Tests, i.e., Bombay's contribution to India's total runs is 30.97 per cent.

➤ In short, Bombay's contribution in terms of Test cricketers is 25.00% and in terms of runs it is 30.97%.

➤ Cricketers who played a major part of their first-class cricket for Bombay or in Bombay, like Phadkar, Ramchand, Nadkarni, Ghavri, Vinoo Mankad, Sairaj Bahutule and Zaheer Khan are treated as Bombay players.

➤ Those who played for Bombay for a short while and a major part of their career for their own state teams are also counted as Bombay cricketers, such as E.S. Maka, Ghulam Guarad, Anwar Hussain, Chandu Sarwate, Shrirang Sononi, Sadu Shinde, P.E. Palia, G.R. Sundaram, M.M. Patel, etc.

➤ The three grounds of Bombay Gymkhana, Brabourne stadium and Wankhede stadium have hosted a maximum of forty-three Tests in the country. Bombay thus holds a record of staging most Tests in India.

➤ Bombay and India's Vijay Merchant stands next to Bradman's best average, with 71.22 for his 13,248 runs in first-class cricket matches during the period from 1929 to 1951.

➤ Sunil Gavaskar held the honour of being the first batsman to score over 10,000 runs in Tests – in the 212th innings of his 124th Test – vs Pakistan at Ahmedabad on 7 March 1987.

➤ Sachin Tendulkar is the only sportsperson to be bestowed with the highest civilian honour of Bharat Ratna.

➢ Sachin Tendulkar has monopolized all batting records in Tests – a world record of all sorts:

    200 Tests (ninety-four on home grounds and 106 abroad)
    329 Innings
    15,921 Runs
    fifty-one centuries
    sixty-eight half centuries
    eighty-five century stands

➢ India produced thirty-one captains in their 478 Tests since 1932. Bombay's contribution to India captaincy is eight out of thirty-one:

    Vinoo Mankad
    Polly Umrigar
    S. Ramchand
    Ajit Wadekar
    Sunil Gavaskar
    Dilip Vengsarkar
    Ravi Shastri
    Sachin Tendulkar

➢ **Most Bombay players in India Test teams (eight)**
First Test vs Pakistan at Dacca, 1954-55

1 M.K. Mantri
2 V.L. Manjrekar
3 P.R. Umrigar
4 D.G. Phadkar
5 G.S. Ramchand
6 V. Mankad
7 N.S. Tamhane
8 S.P. Gupte

> ## Most Bombay players in India Test teams (seven)
Fourth Test vs Pakistan at Madras, 1952-53
1 V. Mankad
2 M.L. Apte
3 P.R. Umrigar
4 D.G. Phadkar
5 G.S. Ramchand
6 R.V. Divecha
7 S.P. Gupte

Second Test vs West Indies at Bridgetown, 1952-53
1 V. Mankad
2 M.L. Apte
3 P.R. Umrigar
4 V.L. Manjrekar
5 D.G. Phadkar
6 G.S. Ramchand
7 S..P Gupte

Third Test vs West Indies at Port-of-Spain, 1952-53
1 V. Mankad
2 M.L. Apte
3 P.R. Umrigar
4 V.L. Manjrekar
5 D.G. Phadkar
6 G.S. Ramchand
7 S.P. Gupte

Fourth Test vs West Indies at Georgetown, 1952-53
1 V. Mankad

2 M.L. Apte
3 P.R. Umrigar
4 V.L. Manjrekar
5 D.G. Phadkar
6 G.S. Ramchand
7 S.P. Gupte

Fourth Test vs Pakistan at Peshawar, 1954-55
1 P.R. Umrigar
2 V.L. Manjrekar
3 G.S. Ramchand
4 V. Mankad
5 N.S. Tamhane
6 D.G. Phadkar
7 S.P. Gupte

Fifth Test v Pakistan at Karachi, 1954-55
1 P.R. Umrigar
2 V.L. Manjrekar
3 G.S. Ramchand
4 V. Mankad
5 N.S. Tamhane
6 D.G. Phadkar
7 S.P. Gupte

First Test vs New Zealand at Hyderabad, 1955-56
1 V. Mankad
2 P.R. Umrigar
3 V.L. Manjrekar
4 G.S. Ramchand

5   D.G. Phadkar
6   N.S. Tamhane
7   S.P. Gupte

Second Test vs New Zealand at Bombay, 1955-56
1   V. Mankad
2   P.R. Umrigar
3   V.L. Manjrekar
4   G.S. Ramchand
5   D.G. Phadkar
6   N.S. Tamhane
7   S.P. Gupte

Fourth Test vs New Zealand at Calcutta, 1955-56
1   V. Manakd
2   V.L. Manjrekar
3   P.R. Umrigar
4   G.S. Ramchand
5   D.G. Phadkar
6   C.T. Patankar
7   S.P. Gupte

Fifth Test vs New Zealand at Chennai, 1955-56
1   V. Manakd
2   V.L. Manjrekar
3   P.R. Umrigar
4   G.S. Ramchand
5   D.G. Phadkar
6   N.S. Tamhane
7   S.P. Gupte

Second Test vs Australia at Bombay, 1956-57
1 V. Mankad
2 P.R. Umrigar
3 V.L. Manjrekar
4 G.S. Ramchand
5 D.G. Phadkar
6 N.S. Tamhane
7 S.P. Gupte

First Test vs West Indies at Bombay, 1958-59
1 P.R. Umrigar
2 V.L. Manjrekar
3 G.S. Ramchand
4 M.S. Hardikar
5 N.S. Tamhane
6 Ghulam Guard
7 S.P. Gupte

➢ **Bombay players not figuring in India teams for a Test**

1. Only Test vs England	Lord's	1932
2. Second Test vs West Indies	Calcutta	1966-67
3. First Test vs Australia	Bangalore	2004-05
4. Second Test vs Australia	Chennai	2004-05
5. First Test vs Zimbabwe	Bulawayo	2005-06
6. Second Test vs Zimbabwe	Harare	2005-06
7. All three Tests vs West Indies	West Indies	2011

➢ **Bombay players not figuring in touring India teams for Tests**

India on their tour of West Indies in 2011 for a three-Test series – no cricketer from Bombay was on the tour.

> **Bombay players not figuring in the Rest of India teams in Irani Cup tournament**
> Irani Cup tournament is played since 1959-60 between the Ranji Trophy champions of the previous year and the Rest of India. Out of the forty-two contests since then, Bombay has figured in the tournament on fifteen occasions. However, when Bombay were not the champions of the Ranji Trophy, Bombay players represented Rest of India. Tamil Nadu won the Ranji Trophy title in 1987-88 and hence they played the Irani Cup match against the Rest of India at Madras in 1988-89. The Rest of India was not represented by any of the Bombay cricketers in the fixture. The Rest of India team comprised

I.B. Roy	Bengal
N.S. Sidhu	Punjab
Arun Lal (C)	Bengal
S.J. Kalyani	Maharashtra
N.K. Churi	Railways
S. Viswanath	Karnataka
K. Jeshwanth	Karnataka
Sanjeeva Sharma	Delhi
Gopal Sharma	Uttar Pradesh
Rashid Patel	Baroda
N.D. Hirwani	Madhya Pradesh

None from Bombay.
On all other occasions the Rest of India was represented by at least one Bombay cricketer.

➤ **President of India presents the Ranji Trophy to Bombay captain**
The first and the only occasion in the history of Indian cricket when the presentation of the Ranji Trophy was held at the Rashtrapati Bhavan in Delhi was in the season 1956-57. The president of India, Dr Rajendra Prasad, presented the Ranji Trophy and its replica to Madhav Mantri, skipper of the Ranji Trophy champions Bombay after their final against Services at Delhi.

➤ **Cricket in three generations**
Vinit Indulkar has been playing for Bombay in the Ranji Trophy since 2004-05. His father Ajit Mahipat Indulkar represented Maharashtra in the Ranji Trophy in 1981-82. Ajit Indulkar's father Mahipat Shankar Indulkar played for Baroda/ Maharashtra in the Ranji Trophy from 1941-42 to 1951-52. Three generations of Indulkars represented in the Ranji Trophy championship of India.

Mahipat Shankar Indulkar		Baroda/Maharashtra
Ajit Mahipat Indulkar	Son	Maharashtra
Vinit Ajit Indulkar	Grandson	Bombay

➤ **Youngest player to make a debut**
Sachin Tendulkar was fifteen years and 230 days old, when he played for Bombay in their match vs Gujarat at the Wankhede stadium in Bombay in 1988-89 (10, 11 and 12 December 1988).

➤ Tendulkar was also the youngest to hit a century, at the age of fifteen years and 230 days, in the aforesaid match.

➤ **Oldest players to make a debut**
  - R.J.D. Jamshedji made his debut in the Ranji Trophy – vs Northern India at Delhi in 1935-36 (20–22 March 1936) at the age of forty-three years and 123 days.
  - F.E. Kapadia (b. 1892) made his debut in the Ranji Trophy for Bombay in their match vs Maharashtra at the Deccan Gymkhana in Poona in 1934-35 when he was over forty-three years old.
  - B.K. Kalapesi (b. 1895) was over forty years old when he first played for Bombay in their match vs Maharashtra at Poona (during 10–12 December 1935).
  - H.J. Vajifdar (b. 1894) was forty years and ninety-seven days old at the time when he first played for Bombay in their match vs Northern India at the Bombay Gymkhana in Bombay in 1934-35 (during 9–11 March 1935).

➤ **Bombay along with Delhi have recorded six or more consecutive victories in Ranji Trophy tournament.**
  - Bombay recorded their victories over Baroda, Saurashtra, Gujarat, Madhya Pradesh, Hyderabad and Tamil Nadu after the first drawn game against Maharashtra of the season 1972-73.
  - Delhi emulated the feat by winning the first seven fixtures against Jammu & Kashmir, Punjab, Haryana, Services, and Railways in the North Zone League and knockout matches against Gujarat and Rajasthan in the season 1974-75.

> **Bombay produced most Test umpires for India**

Sl. No.	Umpires	No. of Tests	Season
1	D.K. Naik	1	1948-49
2	J.R. Patel	9	1948-49 to 1958-59
3	H.R.E. Chowdhary	4	1959-60 to 1964-65
4	A.M. Mamsa	6	1963-64 to 1972-73
5	J. Reuben	10	1969-70 to 1976-77
6	M.V. Gothoskar	14	1972-73 to 1983-84
7	P.R. Panjabi	7	1978-79 to 1981-82
8	D.N. Dotiwala	6	1981-82 to 1987-88
9	P.D. Reporter	12+2 in Pakistan	1984-85 to 1986-87
10	M.Y. Gupte	1	1984-85
11	Suresh Shastri	2 in Sri Lanka	2006-07

- Bombay's late D.K. Naik is the first Indian to umpire a Test in India. Earlier, foreigners umpired in three Tests in India in 1933-34.
- P.D. Reporter, along with V.K. Ramaswamy of Hyderabad, has earned the unique honour of being the first ever umpire to be invited to umpire a Test in a foreign country. In addition to his twelve Tests on Indian soil, he has also umpired two Tests in Pakistan – the second and third Tests vs West Indies at Lahore and Karachi respectively, in the season 1986-87.

> **Unparallelled and unprecedented record of the Ranji Trophy**
> Out of the forty-four occasions of figuring in the finals, Bombay has won the coveted Trophy forty times – thirty-three times outright and seven times on first-innings lead – and only on four occasions were they the runners-up in the finals to

1. Holkar	in 1947-48	Bombay lost by nine wickets
2. Delhi	in 1979-80	Bombay lost by 240 runs
3. Karnataka	in 1982-83	Bombay lost on first-innings deficit
4. Haryana	in 1990-91	Bombay lost by two runs

> From 1958-59 to 1972-73, Bombay were the champions of the tournament for fifteen years in succession

> Headquarters of the Board of Control for Cricket in India are situated in the city of Bombay at 'Cricket Centre' at the Wankhede stadium in Churchgate, Bombay, where the offices of the president and chief administrative officer of the BCCI form part of the premises.

> Dr H.D. Kanga Memorial Library – the only library in the world for books exclusively on sports – also forms part of the Wankhede stadium in Bombay.

> Bombay and India Test cricketers are immortalized by Bombay Cricket Association at the Wankhede stadium.

Vijay Merchant Pavilion – West Stand
Sunil Gavaskar Pavilion – East Stand
Sachin Tendulkar Stand – North Stand
Vinoo Mankad Gate – at the Southern Gate near the sea
Polly Umrigar Gate – at the Southern Gate near railway line
Vijay Manjrekar Dressing Room

➤ All the three greats of Bombay – Vijay Merchant, Sunil Gavaskar and Sachin Tendulkar – laid their bat to rest when they were at their peak of form, by announcing their retirement from Test cricket well in advance.

Compiled by Sudhir Vaidya